SECURITY IN THE 21ST CENTURY

Security in the 21st Century
The United Nations, Afghanistan and Iraq

ALEX CONTE
University of Canterbury, New Zealand

ASHGATE

Published by
Ashgate Publishing Limited
Gower House
Croft Road
Aldershot
Hants GU11 3HR
England

Ashgate Publishing Company
Suite 420
101 Cherry Street
Burlington, VT 05401-4405
USA

Ashgate website: http://www.ashgate.com

British Library Cataloguing in Publication Data
Conte, Alex, 1971 -
    Security in the 21st century : the United Nations,
    Afghanistan and Iraq
    1.United Nations - Afghanistan 2.United Nations - Iraq
    3.Intervention (International law) 4.Security,
    International 5.Afghanistan - History - 1989-2001
    6.Afghanistan - History - 2001- 7.Iraq - History -
    1991-2003
    I.Title
    341.5'84

Library of Congress Cataloging-in-Publication Data
Conte, Alex, 1971-
    Security in the 21st century : the United Nations, Afghanistan, and Iraq / Alex
Conte.
        p. cm.
    ISBN 0-7546-2442-0
    1. Security, International. 2. Intervention (International law) 3. United Nations.
4. Afghan War, 2001- 5. Iraq War, 2003. I. Title: Security in the twenty first
century. II. Title.

    JZ5588.C67 2005
    958.104'7--dc22

                                                                2004062696

ISBN 10: 0 7546 2442 0
ISBN 13: 978 0 7546 2442 4

Reprinted 2006

Printed and bound in Great Britain by MPG Books Ltd, Bodmin, Cornwall

Contents

Author

Alex Conte   LLB (Cant), LLM (Hons)(VUW)
                        Barrister of the High Court of New Zealand
                        Lecturer in Law, University of Canterbury,
                        New Zealand
                        General Editor, *New Zealand Yearbook of
                        International Law*

Preface

The prime objective of this work is to provide an examination and commentary on the legality of the interventions in Afghanistan and Iraq and to consider, within the context of those interventions, the role of the United Nations and the functioning of the Charter of the United Nations. The text undertakes this through what is essentially a case study of each conflict, although the scope of the analysis is limited to issues concerning the legitimacy of the decisions to use force, rather than the manner in which force was used, and to the role of the United Nations as the institution through which international peace and security is to be maintained.

This work is aimed at international lawyers, historians and political scientists. Because of the nature of the issues involved in the conflicts, and by undertaking case-specific approaches to the discussion of those issues, the text should also serve as a useful teaching tool. Graduate and undergraduate students in these disciplines should find it useful to see how the international framework for security and the non-use of force is applied in the context of actual events and, likewise, come to appreciate the limitations and failings of that system. Extensive use of primary materials is made throughout the work and a selection of documents appended.

I have drawn this work from numerous papers, presentations and discussion forums I have prepared or participated in over the past three years, including conferences and workshops of the United Kingdom Society for Legal Scholars, the Australian and New Zealand Society for International Law, the International Law Group at the University of Canterbury, New Zealand and specialized events such as the *Challenge of Conflict: International Law Responds* conference in Adelaide, Australia and the workshop in Suva, Fiji, *How Should Fiji Respond to the Threat of Terrorism?*

I am grateful for the help and courtesy of the staff at Ashgate Publishing. Neither the work for nor the publication price of the present book has been subsidized by any official source of private foundation.

Alex Conte
School of Law, University of Canterbury, New Zealand
August 2004

Chapter 1

Introduction

The twenty-first century has seen two major international conflicts thus far, through the interventions in Afghanistan and Iraq. Despite such a brief encounter into the 2000s, the international community and the United Nations have already been challenged with many significant issues concerning the use of force between States and the role of the UN, the Security Council in particular, in the maintenance of peace and security.

This text gives consideration to the lawfulness of the interventions, from a *jus ad bellum* rather than a *jus in bello* perspective, and to the various issues that arise from such a reflection.[1] By undertaking an approach akin to a case study of each conflict, and by making dominant reference to primary materials, it is hoped that this work can stand as one that is of value to international lawyers and academics, diplomatic and political scientists, and historians alike. By way of confession, it should be acknowledged that the author takes a reasonably normative approach to the subject matter. That is, an approach that, while legalistic and also realistic, is grounded in the conviction that the prohibition against the use of force between States is one that should not be done away with lightly and in the belief that the United Nations framework for international peace and security, whilst not perfect, is to be supported and improved upon.

This chapter will provide a very basic overview of the international law governing the use of force between States, to establish a backdrop for consideration of specific issues within the following chapters. Also by way of introduction, Chapter 2 undertakes a review of international law and UN responses to international terrorism, this being of significant relevance to the intervention in Afghanistan under *Operation Enduring Freedom*, considered in the succeeding chapter. Chapter 4, while still considering Afghanistan, turns to an evolving role, adopted by the Security Council and the United Nations in general, in the political and economic reconstruction of States that are or have been subject to conflict. Next, Chapter 5 returns

---

[1] In simple terms, *jus ad bellum* governs the lawfulness of miliary intervention, whereas *jus in bello* dictates the rules of war during the conduct of an intervention.

to the issue of international terrorism but in the context of the Bush doctrine on pre-emptive strikes in the "war on terror".

The attention of the book then shifts from Afghanistan to Iraq, examining the legality of the recent coalition intervention in Chapter 7, but first looking at the involved decade prior to that intervention (and upon which the 2003 intervention so greatly depends as its basis of validity) through Chapter 6. Having thus considered the major *jus ad bellum* issues arising from this century's large-scale wars, Chapter 8 looks at the difficult question of United Nations reform, having regard to the preceding chapters and the role of the UN in the maintenance of international peace and security.

To assist, various documents are appended. Notably, Appendix 1 sets out the Charter of the United Nations, Appendix 2 contains selected resolutions of the Security Council, General Assembly and Commission on Human Rights concerning international terrorism and Afghanistan, and Appendix 3 contains selected Security Council resolutions pertaining to Iraq.

An Introduction to the Use of Force Between States

A Historical Overview[2]

The use of force between States has only relatively recently been prohibited as a means of diplomatic relations and acquisition of territory. Prior to that, the Roman Empire's concept of just and unjust wars prevailed, holding that so long as the use of force complied with the divine will, then it was just and could be used against another. In the early 17th century, Hugh Grotius redefined just war in terms of defence. If the use of force was required to protect property or to punish wrongs suffered by a State's citizens, then this – according to Grotius – was deemed to be a just war. The concept of just and unjust war was done away with under the Treaty of Westphalia in 1648, with the *European Club* agreeing to conduct themselves in accordance with certain principles and treaties.[3]

Due to the atrocities experienced during the First World War, and vowing to guarantee that such devastation would not occur again, the

---

[2] Based primarily on Brownlie, I., *International Law and the Use of Force by States* (1963), and Dale, J., *International Law / Use of Force*, Law Courseware Consortium (1995).

[3] The European Club comprised the most powerful States in the world at that time (Spain, Britain, Greece and France).

Allied Forces established the League of Nations.[4] The Covenant of the League of Nations provided that, where any States found themselves in a conflict situation, their dispute had to be referred to arbitration and only following a three-month "cooling-off" period, could resort to war be had.[5] The Covenant did not, however, entirely prohibit recourse to the use of force as a solution to international conflicts. The later *General Treaty for the Renunciation of War* of 1928, commonly referred to as the Kellogg-Briand Pact (which remains in force), provided as follows:[6]

> Article I. The High Contracting Parties solemnly declare in the names of their respective peoples that they condemn recourse to war for the solution of international controversies, and renounce it as an instrument of national policy in their relations with one another.

> Article II. The High Contracting Parties agree that the settlement or solution of all disputes or conflicts whatever nature or whatever origin they may be, which may arise among them, shall never be sought except by pacific means.

While a positive step, the General Treaty was restricted to the technically defined concept of "war" and States claimed exemption from the prohibition on the basis that they were involved in a conflict and not a war. The advent of the Second World War, however, provided the impetus for a comprehensive prohibition against the use of "force", using that term instead of the less successful concept of "war".

The Legal Framework under the United Nations Charter

On 26 June 1946, fifty States (representing the vast majority of the international community at that time) joined to form the United Nations with the following aims:[7]

> to save succeeding generations from the scourge of war, which twice in our lifetime has brought untold sorrow to mankind, and

> to reaffirm faith in fundamental human rights, in the dignity and worth of the human person, in the equal rights of men and women and of nations large and small, and

---

[4] Under the League of Nations Covenant of 1919.

[5] Article 12 of the Covenant.

[6] Almost all States in the entire international community were, at the commencement of the Second World War, party to the General Treaty. The General Treaty was referred to by the Nuremberg Tribunal as reflecting customary international law.

[7] As set out in the first part of the preamble to the Charter of the United Nations.

to establish conditions under which justice and respect for the obligations arising from treaties and other sources of international law can be maintained, and

to promote social progress and better standards of life in larger freedom,

It is the first-stated principle of the United Nations to maintain peace and security, suppress acts of aggression and achieve the peaceful settlement of disputes.[8]   Article 2(1) of the United Nations Charter expresses the foundation of the United Nations as being based upon the principle of the sovereign equality of all members. Member States are directed to settle disputes by peaceful means in such a manner that international peace and security is not endangered.[9] The United Nations itself is prohibited from intervening in the domestic affairs of any member without their consent and unless otherwise permitted under the Charter.[10] Most significantly, under article 2(4), members of the United Nations are directed that they must refrain from the use or threat of use of force in international relations. The latter provision is regarded by most international lawyers as a norm of *jus cogens*, a peremptory norm of customary international law from which no derogation is permitted:[11]

> Article 2
> The Organization and its Members, in pursuit of the Purposes stated in Article 1, shall act in accordance with the following Principles.
> ...
> 4.   All Members shall refrain in their international relations from the threat or use of force against the territorial integrity or political independence of any state, or in any other manner inconsistent with the Purposes of the United Nations.

Under the Charter of the United Nations, there are two situations in which States are permitted to use force against another State: when either acting in self-defence or when authorized by the UN Security Council. As to the first authorization, article 51 of the Charter retains the inherent right of a State to act in defence of itself, and extends the principle to one of "collective self-defence", whereby members of the United Nations are also

---

[8] Article 1(1) of the Charter of the United Nations.
[9] Article 2(3) of the Charter of the United Nations.
[10] Article 2(7) of the Charter.
[11] See, for example, the judgment of Sir Ivor Jennings in *Case Concerning Military and Paramilitary Activities in and Against Nicaragua (Nicaragua v United States)*, Merits Phase [1986] ICJ Reports 4, 518–524; and Henkin, Pugh, Schachter and Smit, *International Law Cases and Materials*, 1980, 910.

permitted to use force in the defence of a State seeking the assistance of others to defend itself:[12]

> Article 51
> Nothing in the present Charter shall impair the inherent right of individual or collective self-defence if an armed attack occurs against a Member of the United Nations, until the Security Council has taken measures necessary to maintain international peace and security. Measures taken by Members in the exercise of this right of self-defence shall be immediately reported to the Security Council and shall not in any way affect the authority and responsibility of the Security Council under the present Charter to take at any time such action as it deems necessary in order to maintain or restore international peace and security.

The Security Council, composed of five permanent members[13] and ten non-permanent members,[14] is charged under article 24 of the Charter with the primary role of maintaining international peace and security. All United Nations members are bound to accept and carry out the decisions of the Security Council.[15] The Council has two means of achieving that objective under the Charter: the provisions within Chapter VI, pertaining to the pacific settlement of disputes; and the well-known Chapter VII enforcement action provisions. Decisions of the Council are made by the affirmative vote of at least nine members, with the proviso that the permanent members may, without needing to justify their position, exercise a veto under article 27(3).[16] In exercising enforcement action under Chapter VII, the Security Council is required to first determine whether there is a threat to or breach of peace entitling it to take such measures:

> Article 39
> The Security Council shall determine the existence of any threat to the peace, breach of the peace, or act of aggression and shall make recommendations, or

---

[12] *Nicaragua v United States*, ibid, 534–536.

[13] The permanent members being China, France, Russia, the United Kingdom and the United States: article 23(1).

[14] Elected to sit on the Council for two years: article 23(2).

[15] Article 25.

[16] Quaere: should there be a power of veto in the hands of the permanent members? It can be argued that the power of veto is a safety feature aimed at preventing irrational decisions, albeit by a majority of at least nine out of 15 members. It was a criticism of the United States in the Iraqi crisis that the veto acted as an encumbrance upon the ability of the Security Council to make decisions, although the subsequent lack of evidence of weapons of mass destruction might in fact support the "safety" aspect of the power of veto. This is discussed in further detail within Chapter 8.

decide what measures shall be taken in accordance with Articles 41 and 42, to
maintain or restore international peace and security.

If so determined, the Council then has the provisions of articles 40 to 42 at
its disposal: it may impose provisional measures aimed at preventing an
escalation of any threat to or breach of peace (article 40); non-military,
normally trade, sanctions (article 41);[17] or it may authorize the use of
military force under article 42. Mention should also be made of article 43
which is also, at least technically, a provision affecting the Security
Council's ability to discharge its role. Article 43 makes provision for the
establishment of a standing army of the United Nations, by special
agreement with member States for the provision by members to the United
Nations of personnel and equipment. No such agreement has ever been
established, resulting in the Security Council needing to delegate the
authority to use force not to its own standing army, but to multinational
forces established by its members.[18]

It should be acknowledged that there are arguments in favour, and
against, further grounds upon which a State may use force against another.
Two such (controversial) positions may be taken with respect to
"humanitarian intervention" (the idea that States may intervene by use of
force against another State where the latter state is committing gross human
rights violations and where immediate action is necessary to prevent further
loss of life); and "anticipatory self-defence" (permitting an act in the
defence of the State where an armed attack against that State is imminent,
rather than waiting for such an attack to occur before being able to
respond). The latter concept of anticipatory self-defence, or "pre-emptive
strikes", is given specific consideration within Chapter 5. Humanitarian
intervention is not considered, however, since it is beyond the scope of the
relied upon or even arguable grounds of intervention in Afghanistan and
Iraq.

In crude terms then, the international law on the use of force can be
summarized as follows. The use of force between States, or threat of such,
is prohibited by the United Nations Charter and by way of what most see as
a peremptory norm of customary international law. Intervention is
permitted only where a State is acting by way of "individual or collective
self-defence", within the narrow terms of article 51, or where authorized by
a decision of the Security Council, acting under Chapter VII of the Charter.

---

[17] As it has done in various situations, including South Africa (e.g., United Nations Security
Council Resolution 418 of 4 November 1977, S/RES/418 (1977)) and Iraq (e.g., United
Nations Security Council Resolution 661 of 6 August 1990, S/RES/661 (1990)).

[18] This is considered further within the context of the intervention in Afghanistan: Chapter 4.

The United Nations Human Rights Committee

In the context of inter-state conflicts throughout the 20th century, and the use of force against Afghanistan and Iraq during these first few years of the 21st century, it is interesting to note the General Comments of the UN Human Rights Committee (established under the International Covenant on Civil and Political Rights)[19] pertaining to the use of force between states. The Committee described war and other acts of mass violence as a scourge of humanity that takes the lives of thousands of innocent human beings every year. It emphasized the fact that, under the Charter of the United Nations, the threat or use of force by any state against another, except in exercise of the inherent right of self-defence, is prohibited. The Committee considered that States therefore have a "supreme duty" to prevent wars, acts of genocide and other acts of mass violence causing arbitrary loss of life.[20] Every effort they make to avert the danger of war, especially thermonuclear war, and to strengthen international peace and security would constitute the most important condition and guarantee for the safeguarding of the right to life, the Committee said in its General Comment 6.

---

[19] Adopted 16 December 1966, 999 UNTS 171 (entered into force 23 March 1976).
[20] Human Rights Committee, *General Comment 6, Article 6*, para 2: HRI/GEN/1/Rev.1 (1994) 6.

Chapter 2

International Terrorism

Introduction

International terrorism is not a new phenomenon. Indeed, the origin of the word *terrorism* dates back to the French Revolution of 1788 as the label used by the establishment to describe the conduct of revolutionaries.[1] Likewise, terrorism has been a subject of concern with the United Nations since the 1960s, following a series of aircraft hijackings.[2] Notwithstanding the long-held attention of the international community upon terrorism, the subject deserves special attention within this book for several reasons. Terrorism has, some would argue, entered a new phase since September 11, 2001: an age where trans-national activity has intensified and been made easier, and where technology and the media can be taken advantage of by terrorist entities to further the impact of terrorist conduct and the delivery of messages or fear-inducing images.[3]

Perhaps more importantly, the issue of terrorism and the "war on terror" is one that is intimately linked with the intervention in Afghanistan[4] under *Operation Enduring Freedom* (discussed within Chapter 3) and with the controversial Bush doctrine on pre-emptive strikes against terrorist entities and facilities (discussed within Chapter 5). The aim of this chapter, then, is to provide an introduction to the concept of terrorism and how this links with the role of the United Nations to maintain peace and security. In doing so, consideration is also given to another principle and purpose of the United Nations, the promotion and maintenance of human rights, and how these two objectives interrelate.

---

[1] French Ambassador to Fiji, His Excellency Berg, "Terrorism: The New International Challenge", presentation at the public workshop, *How Should Fiji Respond to the Threat of Terrorism?*, hosted by the Citizens' Constitutional Forum and the Fiji Human Rights Commission, 17 July 2004, Suva, Fiji.
[2] Discussed further below.
[3] Berg, above, n 1.
[4] And, some would argue, to a lesser extent with the intervention in Iraq.

International Law on Terrorism

The starting point in looking at the international law on terrorism is to acknowledge the problems with defining terrorism. The United Nations Terrorism Prevention Branch describes terrorism as a unique form of crime. Terrorist acts, it says, often contain elements of warfare, politics and propaganda.[5] It continues, stating that "[f]or security reasons and due to lack of popular support, terrorist organisations are usually small, making detection and infiltration difficult. Although the goals of terrorists are sometimes shared by wider constituencies, their methods are generally abhorred".

One of the major obstacles facing the fight against terrorism is the inability of the international community to achieve consensus on a global definition of terrorism. The Executive Director of the International Policy Institute for Counter-Terrorism, Boaz Ganor, has emphasized the point, saying that UN Security Council Resolutions can only have an effective impact once all States agree upon what type of acts constitute terrorism.[6] Despite this, there is still no definition of the term to which all States subscribe.

Generally speaking, the twelve international treaties on counter-terrorism[7] deal with specific forms of terrorist conduct and are thereby precise in nature and not of general application. Furthermore, they are not a solution in themselves, since treaties are only binding upon states parties to treaties.[8] Nor does the United Nations Charter contain a definition of the term. Likewise, the Rome Statute of the International Criminal Court does not include terrorism as one of the international crimes within the Court's jurisdiction.[9] Perhaps most surprising is the fact that Security Council

---

[5] United Nations Office for Drug Control and Crime Prevention, "UN Action Against Terrorism", web site <www.odccp.org/terrorism.html>, 19/06/02.

[6] Ganor B, "Security Council Resolution 1269: What it Leaves Out", 25 October 1999, website of the International Policy Institute for Counter-Terrorism, <www.ict.org.il/articles/articledet.cfm?articleid=93>, 01/06/02.

[7] To be discussed further in this chapter.

[8] *Pacta tertii nec nocent nec prosunt.*

[9] Rome Statute of the International Criminal Court, opened for signature 17 July 1998, 2187 UNTS 90 (entered into force 1 July 2002). The Court has within its jurisdiction the "most serious international crimes", according to its preamble. It was proposed, within the draft Statute, to include terrorism within the Court's jurisdiction, but the failure of States to agree upon a definition of the term resulted in the crime being removed from the scope of the Court's jurisdiction and subject matter of the constitutive treaty. There are arguments, however, that terrorist acts fall within the jurisdiction of the Court as constituting crimes against humanity, as crimes under article 7 of the Rome Statute.

Resolution 1373, which imposes the various obligations concerning counter-terrorism, does not define the term.[10]

Attempts to Define Terrorism

Attempts to define the term have been made since before the establishment of the United Nations. The Draft League of Nations Convention had provided that terrorism comprised of:[11]

> All criminal acts directed against a State and intended or calculated to create a state of terror in the minds of particular persons or a group of persons or the general public.

This provision was never adopted due to dissent over the definition.

There have been suggestions that terrorism be defined as the peacetime equivalent of war crimes. In a Report to the UN Crime Branch, Schmidt proposed taking the already agreed-upon definition of war crimes (comprising deliberate attacks on civilians, hostage taking and the killing of prisoners) and extending it to peacetime.[12] Terrorism would then simply be defined as the "peacetime equivalents of war crimes". Again, however, this did not gain acceptance. Schmidt appears to have been more successful in gaining acceptance of a more complex definition of terrorism, as identified by the UN Office for Drug Control and Crime Prevention (ODCCP):[13]

> An anxiety-inspiring method of repeated violent action, employed by a (semi-) clandestine individual, group or state actors, for idiosyncratic, criminal or political reasons, whereby – in contrast to assassination – the direct targets of violence are not the main targets. The immediate human victims of violence are generally chosen randomly (targets of opportunity) or selectively (representative or symbolic targets) from a target population, and serve as

---

[10] Having said this, the lack of definition was most likely due to the fact (as will be seen through subsequent discussions) that there is a lack of consensus on just what amounts to terrorism. In a desire to issue a forceful, and at the same time early, resolution in the wake of September 11 it is likely that the Council saw use of the term, without definition, as the only viable option in the short term. The problem with this approach is that it has left the question of defining the term with individual member States, leading to inconsistent definitions and, arguably, a weak rather than forceful resolution.

[11] Draft League of Nations Convention. See discussion on this point within the website of the United Nations Office for Drug Control and Crime Prevention, "Definitions of Terrorism", <www.odccp.org/terrorism_definitions.html>, 19/06/02.

[12] This definition was put to the United Nations Crime Branch by A.P. Schmidt in 1992: ibid.

[13] Ibid.

message generators. Threat and violence-based communication processes between terrorist (organisation), (imperilled) victims, and main targets are used to manipulate the main target (audience(s)), turning it into a target of terror, a target of demands, or a target of attention, depending on what the intimidation, coercion, or propaganda is primarily sought.

What might be observed is that the common threads throughout this, and various other, definitions are as follows: firstly, that the *physical* targets of a terrorist act are not the *intended* targets (the target against whom a message is being sent, usually a Government or International Organisation); next, that the purpose of the threat or violence is to intimidate and create a situation of fear or terror (hence the term *terror*ism); and, finally, that this is intended to persuade or dissuade the primary target to do or abstain from doing something.

Why a lack of consensus? The sticking point, it seems, is not so much with the technical wording of what physical conduct amounts to a terrorist act. The problem appears to lie with the purpose of the conduct. For instance, does a bombing carried out by a rebel group, which is directed towards the destabilization of fascist authorities (the Pol Pot Regime, for example), amount to a terrorist act or an act of "freedom fighters"? The point to make is that this is not just a cliché. To give two very striking examples, the United States keeps a list of the most wanted terrorists.[14] That list featured, at one time, Yassir Arafat and Nelson Mandela – both of whom were subsequently awarded the Nobel Peace Prize: clearly evidence that this is a highly political and controversial issue. An observation made by a journalist on this point encapsulates the issue very nicely:[15]

Terrorists are those who use violence against the side that is using the word.

A number of States argue that a subjective analysis and definition of such conduct (by examining the purpose of the conduct) should therefore be made. The United Nations ODCCP reports that Arab States such as Libya, Syria and Iran have all campaigned for a definition that excludes acts of "freedom fighters" from the international definition of terrorism by

---

[14] This is maintained by the United States Federal Bureau of Investigation and may be accessed by internet: <www.fbi.gov/mostwant/terrorists/fugitives.htm>.

[15] *The Observer*, 30 September 2001, quote contained within *Submissions of the Indonesian Human Rights Committee to the Foreign Affairs, Defence and Trade Committee on the Terrorism (Bombings and Finance) Suppression Bill*, TERRO/88, Parliamentary Library, Wellington.

employing the argument that a justified goal may be pursued by any available means.[16]

While it must be acknowledged that these positions are firmly held by a small number of States, it should also be pointed out that the majority of States adhere to an objective definition of terrorism (one which does not take into account the motives of the conduct). In 1994, the UN General Assembly adopted the Declaration on Measures to Eliminate International Terrorism.[17] The Declaration was based on the notion of peace and security and the principle of refraining from the threat or use of force in international relations.[18] It pronounced that terrorism constitutes a grave violation of the purpose and principles of the United Nations.[19] While it did not purport to define "terrorism", it did say that criminal acts intended or calculated to provoke a state of terror in the general public for political purposes are in any circumstances unjustifiable:[20]

The States Members of the United Nations solemnly reaffirm their unequivocal condemnation of *all* acts, methods and practices of terrorism, as criminal and unjustifiable, *wherever and by whomever committed*, including those which jeopardize the friendly relations among States and peoples and threaten the territorial integrity and security of States. [emphasis added]

Of even greater value in this respect, according to the Executive Director of the International Policy Institute for Counter-Terrorism, is the Security Council's Resolution 1269.[21] While the Resolution also fails to define terrorism, it does clearly take an objective approach to the question of terrorist conduct, stating that the Security Council:[22]

1. *Unequivocally condemns* all acts, methods and practices of terrorism as criminal and unjustifiable, *regardless of their motivation*, in all their forms and manifestations, wherever and by whomever committed, in particular those which would threaten international peace and security; [emphasis added]

---

[16] Above, n 11.

[17] United Nations General Assembly Resolution 49/60, *Measures to Eliminate International Terrorism*, A/RES/49/60, 9 December 1994 (Appendix 2I herein).

[18] Ibid, as is evident through its preamble.

[19] Ibid, paragraph 2.

[20] Ibid, paragraph 1.

[21] Above, n 6.

[22] United Nations Security Council Resolution 1269 of 19 October 1999, S/RES/1269 (1999) – Appendix 2B herein.

International Conventions on Counter-Terrorism

Following the September 11 attacks, the United Nations was quick to defend its position, stating that it has long been active in the fight against international terrorism.[23]   This is correct in substance, since the organization has, from as early as 1963, been a catalyst for the creation of a number of agreements providing the basic legal means to counter international terrorism, from the seizure of the aircraft to the financing of terrorism.

The phenomenon of terrorism became an international concern in the 1960s when a series of aircraft hijackings hit the headlines. When the 1972 Munich Olympic Games were disrupted by a Palestinian group's attempt to take Israeli athletes hostage, the then Secretary-General of the UN, Kurt Waldheim, asked that the issue be placed on the General Assembly's agenda. In the heated debate that followed, the Assembly assigned the issue to its Legal Committee, which subsequently proposed several conventions on terrorism. There are now 12 conventions and protocols on terrorism, all of which have now entered into force.[24]

In chronological order, one starts with the *Convention on Offences and Certain Other Acts Committed on Board Aircraft 1963*.[25] The Convention applies to acts affecting in-flight safety. It authorizes the aircraft commander to impose reasonable measures, including restraint, on any person he or she believes has committed or is about to commit an act affecting in-flight safety, when necessary to protect the safety of the aircraft. It also requires contracting States to take custody of offenders and to return control of the aircraft to the lawful commander. The second and third conventions are also concerned with air safety. The *Convention for the Suppression of Unlawful Seizure of Aircraft 1970*[26] makes it an offence for any person on board an aircraft in flight to "unlawfully, by force or threat thereof, or any other form of intimidation, seize or exercise control of that aircraft" or to attempt to do so. It requires parties to the Convention to make hijackings punishable by severe penalties. It requires parties that have custody of offenders to either extradite the offender or submit the case

---

[23] UN Press Release, 19 September 2001.

[24] A situation that had not existed at the time of the September 11 terrorist attacks, as discussed below in the context of United Nations Security Council Resolution 1373 of 28 September 2001, S/RES/1373 (2001) – Appendix 2D herein.

[25] Opened for signature 14 September 1963, 704 UNTS 219 (entered into force 4 December 1969).

[26] Opened for signature 16 December 1970, 860 UNTS 105 (entered into force 14 October 1971).

for prosecution and also requires parties to assist each other in connection with criminal proceedings brought under the convention. The *Convention for the Suppression of Unlawful Acts Against the Safety of Civil Aviation 1971*[27] makes it an offence for any person unlawfully and intentionally to perform an act of violence against a person on board an aircraft in flight, if that act is likely to endangėr the safety of that aircraft; to place an explosive device on an aircraft; and to attempt such acts or be an accomplice of a person who performs or attempts to perform such acts. As for the Seizure of Aircraft Convention just mentioned, it requires parties to make offences punishable by severe penalties and again requires parties that have custody of offenders to either extradite the offender or submit the case for prosecution.

In 1973, the *Convention on the Prevention and Punishment of Crimes against International Protected Persons, including Diplomatic Agents* was adopted.[28] Internationally protected persons are defined as a Head of State, a Minister for Foreign Affairs, a representative or official of a State or of an international organization who is entitled to special protection from attack under international law (these people being popular terrorist targets). The convention requires each State party to criminalize and make punishable by appropriate penalties which take into account their grave nature, the intentional murder, kidnapping, or other attack upon the person or liberty of an internationally protected person, a violent attack upon the official premises, the private accommodations, or the means of transport of such person; a threat or attempt to commit such an attack; and an act constituting participation as an accomplice. Also within the theme of protecting persons, the *International Convention against the Taking of Hostages 1979*[29] states that "any person who seizes or detains and threatens to kill, to injure, or to continue to detain another person in order to compel a ... State, an international intergovernmental organisation, a natural or juridical person, or a group of persons, to do or abstain from doing any act as an explicit or implicit condition for the release of the hostage" commits the offence of taking of hostage within the meaning of this Convention.

---

[27] Opened for signature 23 September 1971, 974 UNTS 177 (entered into force 26 January 1973).

[28] Opened for signature 14 December 1973, 1035 UNTS 167 (entered into force 20 February 1977).

[29] Opened for signature 18 December 1979, 1316 UNTS 205 (entered into force 3 June 1983).

Next in time is the *Convention on the Physical Protection of Nuclear Material 1980*.[30] This criminalizes the unlawful possession, use, transfer, etc., of nuclear material, the theft of nuclear material, and threats to use nuclear material (to cause death or serious injury to any person or substantial property damage).

The *Protocol on the Suppression of Unlawful Acts of Violence at Airports Serving International Civil Aviation 1988* was a further addition to air-safety-related counter-terrorist conventions.[31] The Protocol extends the provisions of the Montreal Convention of 1971 to encompass terrorist acts at airports servicing international civil aviation.

The *Convention for the Suppression of Unlawful Acts against the Safety of Maritime Navigation* was adopted in 1988.[32] Here, the treaty establishes a legal regime applicable to international maritime navigation that is similar to the regimes established concerning international aviation. More specifically, it makes it an offence for a person unlawfully and intentionally to seize or exercise control over a ship by force, threat, or intimidation; to perform an act of violence against a person on board a ship if that act is likely to endanger the safe navigation of the ship; to place a destructive device or substance aboard a ship; and other acts against the safety of ships. As an optional protocol to the latter convention, the *Protocol for the Suppression of Unlawful Acts against the Safety of Fixed Platforms Located on the Continental Shelf* was also adopted in 1988,[33] at the same time as its parent convention. Again by way of extension, the Protocol establishes a legal regime applicable to fixed platforms on the continental shelf (similar to the regimes established against international aviation).

Last in the list of conventions relating to air safety, and within the jurisdiction of the Secretary-General of the International Civil Aviation Organization, is the *Convention on the Marking of Plastic Explosives for the Purpose of Identification 1991*.[34] This is designed to control and limit the used of unmarked and undetectable plastic explosives (negotiated in the aftermath of the 1988 Pan Am 103 bombing). Parties are obligated in their respective territories to ensure effective control over "unmarked" plastic explosive, i.e., those that do not contain one of the detection agents described in the Technical Annex to the treaty. Each party must, among

---

[30] Opened for signature 3 March 1980, 1456 UNTS 124 (entered into force 8 February 1987).

[31] Opened for signature 24 February 1988, ICAO Doc 9518 (entered into force 6 August 1989).

[32] Opened for signature 10 March 1988, 1678 UNTS 221 (entered into force 1 March 1992).

[33] Opened for signature 10 March 1988, 1678 UNTS 304 (entered into force 1 March 1992).

[34] Opened for signature 1 March 1991, ICAO Doc 9571 (entered into force 21 June 1998).

other things: take necessary and effective measures to prohibit and prevent the manufacture of unmarked plastic explosives; prevent the movement of unmarked plastic explosives into or out of its territory; ensure that all stocks of such unmarked explosives not held by the military or police are destroyed or consumed, marked, or rendered permanently ineffective within three years; take necessary measures to ensure that unmarked plastic explosives held by the military or police are destroyed or consumed, marked, or rendered permanently ineffective within fifteen years; and ensure the destruction, as soon as possible, of any unmarked explosives manufactured after the date of entry into force of the convention for that State.

More recent in time is the *International Convention for the Suppression of Terrorist Bombing 1997*.[35] As the name suggests, this creates a regime of universal jurisdiction over the unlawful and intentional use of explosives and other lethal devices in, into, or against various public places with intent to kill or cause serious bodily injury, or with intent to cause extensive destruction of the public place. Finally, there is the *International Convention for the Suppression of the Financing of Terrorism 1999*.[36] Of the 12 conventions, this is possibly the most controversial. It requires parties to take steps to prevent and counteract the financing of terrorists, whether direct or indirect, though groups claiming to have charitable, social or cultural goals or which also engage in such illicit activities as drug trafficking or gun running. It commits States to hold those who finance terrorism criminally, civilly or administratively liable for such acts and provides for the identification, freezing and seizure of funds allocated for terrorist activities, as well as for the sharing of the forfeited funds with other States on a case-by-case basis. Bank secrecy will no longer be justification for refusing to cooperate under the treaty.

Utility of the international conventions. The number and scope of these conventions might, at first instance, seem impressive and comprehensive. They have, however, various limitations. To begin with, they only apply to States parties to the conventions. Even then, the conventions themselves are of limited application because of the very precise subject matter of each treaty. The conventions are not of general application but, rather, relate to specific situations in which terrorist acts might have effect, whether on board aircraft, in airports or on maritime platforms.

---

[35] Opened for signature 12 January 1998, 2149 UNTS 286 (entered into force 23 May 2001).
[36] Opened for signature 10 January 2000, 2179 UNTS 232 (entered into force 10 April 1992).

The only potentially wide-impacting treaty is the International Convention for the Suppression of the Financing of Terrorism 1999. This is said for two reasons. Firstly, the Convention mirrors most of the suppression of financing obligations contained in Resolution 1373. As a resolution binding upon all members of the United Nations,[37] this has had a significant impact upon the status of the Convention. Prior to September 11, 2001, there were just four states parties to the Convention and, accordingly, the convention was not in force. Since then, and largely in response to UN Security Council Resolution 1373 and the work of the Counter-Terrorism Committee, almost 120 States have becomes parties to the convention, which has now come into force.[38]

The other reason the Suppression of Financing Convention is of greater relevance is the fact that, in prohibiting the financing of terrorist entities or operations, it defines (for those purposes) what type of acts one may not finance:

> Any other act intended to cause death or serious bodily injury to a civilian, or to any other person not taking an active part in the hostilities in a situation of armed conflict, when the purpose of such act, by its nature or context, is to intimidate a population, or to compel a government or an international organization to do or to abstain from doing any act.

The Convention does therefore have some potentially wider application and is useful for States in determining the type of conduct they are to prohibit.

Draft Comprehensive Convention on International Terrorism

Almost one year prior to the September 11 attacks, India had proposed that there be a comprehensive convention against terrorism, and there is much merit in this. Likewise, Kofi Annan had called for an extensive coalition to combat terrorism and has predicted that such a campaign will be a long one and must involve all countries. Shortly after September 11, he followed in the steps of the Indian proposal and indicated that the General Assembly would take steps to complete a comprehensive anti-terrorism treaty encompassing all current conventions.[39]

---

[37] By application of article 25 of the Charter of the United Nations.

[38] The convention came into force on 10 April 2002. There are now 132 signatories and 117 parties: see <http://untreaty.un.org/ENGLISH/Status/Chapter_xviii/treaty11.asp> at 12 July 2004.

[39] United Nations Secretary-General's Report to the United Nations General Assembly, 56th General Assembly Meeting, GA/9914, 24 September 2001.

It has already been mentioned that the UN General Assembly adopted the Declaration on Measures to Eliminate International Terrorism in 1994.[40] At the end of 1996, it established an Ad Hoc Committee, known as the Ad Hoc Committee Established by General Assembly Resolution 51/210.[41] The Committee was primarily tasked with work on conventions for the suppression of terrorist bombings and financing of terrorist operations and, thereafter, to address means of developing a comprehensive legal framework dealing with international terrorism.[42]

India's Draft Comprehensive Convention on International Terrorism (2000) was subsequently referred to the Ad Hoc Committee. As yet, the Convention has not been finalized and is likely to be some time away, if ever. Due to the lack of unanimity on various issues, and the range of issues involved, the Committee has concluded that finalizing a comprehensive international treaty on terrorism will depend primarily on agreement as to whom would be entitled to exclusion from the treaty's scope, and on what grounds.[43] Otherwise, the majority of the 27 articles of the Draft Convention have been preliminarily agreed upon by the Committee.

One of the sticking points, as expected, has been definitions, not just in terms of defining what amounts to a terrorist act (draft article 2), but also with regard to the wording of draft article 18, which concerns exemptions. In particular, problems have been encountered in the definition and/or inclusion of acts of "armed forces" or "parties" to a conflict (this being relevant to the proposed limited exemptions from jurisdiction and/or liability under the Convention); whether "foreign occupation" should be included within that category of exemptions; and whether the activities of military forces should be "governed" or "in conformity" with international law. Draft article 18 was described by the Chairman of the Committee as the crux of the convention.[44] Hinging on those definitions was a lack of consensus on a preamble.

The draft Convention definition of terrorist acts is as follows:

Article 2
1. Any person commits an offence within the meaning of this Convention if that person, by any means, unlawfully and intentionally, causes:

---

[40] Above, page 13.
[41] Established under General Assembly Resolution 51/210 (1996) – Appendix 2J herein.
[42] Ibid, paragraph 9.
[43] Article 18 of the Draft Comprehensive Convention.
[44] Ad Hoc Committee Established by General Assembly Resolution 51/210, UN Press Release L/2993.

(a) Death or serious bodily injury to any person; or
(b) Serious damage to public or private property, including a place of public use, a State or government facility, a public transportation system, an infrastructure facility or the environment; or
(c) Damage to property, places, facilities, or systems referred to in paragraph 1 (b) of this article, resulting or likely to result in major economic loss, when the purpose of the conduct, by its nature or context, is to intimidate a population, or to compel a Government or an international organization to do or abstain from doing any act.

2.   Any person also commits an offence if that person makes a credible and serious threat to commit an offence as set forth in paragraph 1 of this article.

3.   Any person also commits an offence if that person attempts to commit an offence as set forth in paragraph 1 of this article.

4.   Any person also commits an offence if that person:

(a) Participates as an accomplice in an offence as set forth in paragraph 1, 2 or 3 of this article;
(b) Organizes or directs others to commit an offence as set forth in paragraph 1, 2 or 3 of this article; or
(c) Contributes to the commission of one or more offences as set forth in paragraph 1, 2 or 3 of this article by a group of persons acting with a common purpose. Such contribution shall be intentional and shall either:
    (i) Be made with the aim of furthering the criminal activity or criminal purpose of the group, where such activity or purpose involves the commission of an offence as set forth in paragraph 1 of this article; or
    (ii) Be made in the knowledge of the intention of the group to commit an offence as set forth in paragraph 1 of this article.

Customary International Law Norms

It should finally be noted that international law on terrorism is not restricted to the twelve Conventions listed. For example, the Geneva Convention of 1949 (which is widely accepted as representing customary international law norms, and is therefore binding upon all States) prohibits violence to life, in particular murder, mutilation, cruel treatment and torture, and the taking of hostages. Being customary international law, it automatically has force of law within domestic jurisdictions.

By way of specific example, Article 13(2) of the Optional Protocol states that:

> The civilian population as such, as well as individual civilians, shall not be the object of attack. Acts or threats of violence the primary purpose of which is to spread terror among the civilian population are prohibited.

United Nations Action

Beyond the work of the Committee of the Sixth (Legal) Committee of the UN General Assembly in working towards the various counter-terrorism conventions discussed, both the General Assembly and Security Council have been working in concert on the issue of counter-terrorism. The extant resolutions and declarations of the UN will now be discussed.

United Nations General Assembly

In December 1994, the UN General Assembly adopted the Declaration on Measures to Eliminate International Terrorism.[45] The Declaration was based on the notion of peace and security and the principle of refraining from the threat or use of force in international relations.[46] It pronounced that terrorism constitutes a grave violation of the purpose and principles of the United Nations.[47] While it did not purport to define "terrorism", it did say that criminal acts intended or calculated to provoke a state of terror in the general public for political purposes are in any circumstances unjustifiable.[48] The Declaration urged all States to consider, as a matter of priority, becoming party to the conventions on terrorism adopted up to that time.[49] It called on States to refrain from organizing, instigating, assisting or participating in terrorist acts, and from acquiescing in or encouraging activities within their territories directed towards the commission of such acts.[50]

In particular, States were directed that, in order to fulfil this obligation, they must refrain from facilitating terrorist activities. Paragraph 5(a) of the 1994 Declaration appears to indicate that a State must be proactive in doing so, obliging States to take appropriate practical measures to ensure that their territory is not used for terrorist installations or training camps, or for the preparation or organization of terrorist acts. Paragraph 5(b) then refers

---

[45] Above, n 17. The Declaration has been restated and adopted in subsequent resolutions of the General Assembly, with the contents being much the same: see UNGA Resolutions A/RES/50/53 of 11 December 1995; A/RES/51/210 of 17 December 1996; A/RES/52/165 of 19 January 1998; A/RES/54/110 of 2 February 2000; A/RES/55/158 of 30 January 2001; A/RES/56/88 of 24 January 2002; A/RES/57/27 OF 15 January 2003; and A/RES/58/81 of 8 January 2004.

[46] Ibid, as is evident through its Preamble.

[47] Ibid, paragraph 2.

[48] Ibid, paragraph 1.

[49] Ibid, paragraph 6.

[50] Ibid, paragraph 4.

to the obligation to apprehend and prosecute or extradite perpetrators of terrorist acts.

The practical observation to make is that, although compelling and strongly worded, this is a declaration of the General Assembly and therefore does not have the same weight as a convention, nor does it have signatories that are bound by its content. Indeed, article 10 of the UN Charter specifically provides that resolutions and declarations of the United Nations General Assembly are recommendatory only:

> Article 10
> The General Assembly may discuss any questions or any matters within the scope of the present Charter or relating to the powers and functions of any organs provided for in the present Charter, and, except as provided in Article 12, may make recommendations to the Members of the United Nations or to the Security Council or to both on any such questions or matters.

It is clear through reading minutes of General Assembly meetings immediately following September 11 that there were calls for the United Nations to engage its full potential to identify and attempt to eradicate the roots of terrorism.[51] India's representative pointed out that integral to the efforts to end terrorism and prevent armed conflict is the need to deny to the perpetrators of such conduct access to arms and ammunition.[52] A first step towards this has been the adoption of a *Programme of Action by the United Nations Conference on the Illicit Trade in Small Arms*. Likewise, the General Assembly has given specific consideration to the issue of counter-terrorism within its very lengthy Resolution on *General and Complete Disarmament*.[53] The General Assembly has also urged all States to become parties to the International Convention for the Suppression of the Financing of Terrorism.[54] It recently issued a resolution concerned with strengthening international cooperation and technical assistance in

---

[51] See, for example, Ad Hoc Committee Established by General Assembly Resolution 51/210, *Report of the Ad Hoc Committee Established by General Assembly Resolution 51/210 on a Draft Comprehensive Convention on International Terrorism*, A/AC.252/2002/CPR.1 and Add.1, 1 February 2002.

[52] United Nations Press Release, "Poverty Reduction, Terrorism, Disarmament, Humanitarian Relief Discussed as General Assembly Continues Review of Secretary-General Report", from the 56th General Assembly Plenary Meeting, 25 September 2001, statement of Kamalesh Sharma, United Nations General Assembly representative for India.

[53] United Nations General Assembly Resolution 56/24 of 29 November 2001, *General and Complete Disarmament*, A/RES/56/24, see Part T "Multilateral Cooperation in the Area of Disarmament and Non-Proliferation and Global Efforts Against Terrorism".

[54] See United Nations General Assembly Resolution 54/109 of 9 December 1999, *International Convention for the Suppression of the Financing of Terrorism*, A/RES/54/109.

promoting the implementation of the terrorism conventions and protocols within the framework of the activities of the ODCCP Centre for International Crime Prevention.[55]

United Nations Security Council

On the day after the September 11 attacks, the United Nations Security Council adopted Resolution 1368, through which it unequivocally condemned the terrorist attacks and expressed that it regarded them as a threat to international peace and security.[56] It called on all States to urgently work together to bring justice to the perpetrators, organizers and sponsors of the terrorist attacks.[57] Security Council Resolution 1373 was later adopted, through which the UNSC determined that all States were to prevent and suppress the financing of terrorist acts, including the criminalization of such financing and the freezing of funds and financial assets.[58] Described as one of the most strongly worded resolutions in the history of the Security Council[59], it also requires countries to cooperate on extradition matters and the sharing of information about terrorist networks.[60]

As a decision made under Chapter VII of the United Nations Charter, compliance with Resolution 1373 is mandatory for UN members, imposing certain obligations upon those members.[61] Those obligations can be viewed in two parts. The first is the imposition of specific counter-terrorist

---

[55] United Nations General Assembly Resolution 58/136 of 22 December 2003, *Strengthening international cooperation and technical assistance in promoting the implementation of the universal conventions and protocols related to terrorism within the framework of the activities of the Centre for International Crime Prevention*, A/RES/58/136.

[56] United Nations Security Council Resolution 1368, S/RES/1368, 12 September 2001 – Appendix 2C herein.

[57] Ibid, paragraph 3.

[58] Above, n 24.

[59] Richard Rowe, "Key Developments: Year of International Law in Review", A paper presented at the 10th Annual Meeting of the Australian & New Zealand Society of International Law, *New Challenges and New States: What Role for International Law?*, 15 June 2002, Australian National University, Canberra. Richard Rowe at that time worked in the International Organisations and Legal Division of the Australian Department of Foreign Affairs and Trade. He was the Australian representative and Vice-Chairman of the Ad Hoc Committee Established by General Assembly Resolution 51/210 during its Sixth Session, which followed the September 11 attacks.

[60] Above, n 58, para 3.

[61] Article 25 of the Charter of the United Nations.

obligations, as follows:

Acting under Chapter VII of the Charter of the United Nations,

1. *Decides* that all States shall:
(a) Prevent and suppress the financing of terrorist acts;
(b) Criminalize the wilful provision or collection, by any means, directly or indirectly, of funds by their nationals or in their territories with the intention that the funds should be used, or in the knowledge that they are to be used, in order to carry out terrorist acts;
(c) Freeze without delay funds and other financial assets or economic resources of persons who commit, or attempt to commit, terrorist acts or participate in or facilitate the commission of terrorist acts; of entities owned or controlled directly or indirectly by such persons; and of persons and entities acting on behalf of, or at the direction of such persons and entities, including funds derived or generated from property owned or controlled directly or indirectly by such persons and associated persons and entities;
(d) Prohibit their nationals or any persons and entities within their territories from making any funds, financial assets or economic resources or financial or other related services available, directly or indirectly, for the benefit of persons who commit or attempt to commit or facilitate or participate in the commission of terrorist acts, of entities owned or controlled, directly or indirectly, by such persons and of persons and entities acting on behalf of or at the direction of such persons;

2. *Decides also* that all States shall:
(a) Refrain from providing any form of support, active or passive, to entities or persons involved in terrorist acts, including by suppressing recruitment of members of terrorist groups and eliminating the supply of weapons to terrorists;
(b) Take the necessary steps to prevent the commission of terrorist acts, including by provision of early warning to other States by exchange of information;
(c) Deny safe haven to those who finance, plan, support, or commit terrorist acts, or provide safe havens;
(d) Prevent those who finance, plan, facilitate or commit terrorist acts from using their respective territories for those purposes against other States or their citizens;
(e) Ensure that any person who participates in the financing, planning, preparation or perpetration of terrorist acts or in supporting terrorist acts is brought to justice and ensure that, in addition to any other measures against them, such terrorist acts are established as serious criminal offences in domestic laws and regulations and that the punishment duly reflects the seriousness of such terrorist acts;

(f) Afford one another the greatest measure of assistance in connection with criminal investigations or criminal proceedings relating to the financing or support of terrorist acts, including assistance in obtaining evidence in their possession necessary for the proceedings;

(g) Prevent the movement of terrorists or terrorist groups by effective border controls and controls on issuance of identity papers and travel documents, and through measures for preventing counterfeiting, forgery or fraudulent use of identity papers and travel documents;

This set of obligations expands upon and significantly strengthens the Council's earlier Resolution 1269 of 1999.[62] While Resolution 1269 considered steps to be taken by States to suppress terrorism, deny safe haven to terrorists and cooperate with others in the bringing to justice of perpetrators of terrorist conduct, the language of the Resolution is weaker for two principal reasons.[63] First, paragraphs 1 and 2 of Resolution 1373 are considerably more specific in the steps to be taken in countering terrorism. Second, the instructive words of the more recent Resolution provides that "all States *shall*", whereas the earlier Resolution used a less forceful provision *calling upon* States to take *appropriate steps* to achieve the stated objectives. In short, then, Resolution 1373 takes a considerable step forward in the imposition of counter-terrorism obligations upon members of the United Nations.

The second obligation is a more general requirement to enter into what might be described as a reporting and monitoring dialogue between States and a special committee of the Security Council established under the Resolution, the Counter-Terrorism Committee. Paragraph 6 of the Resolution provides as follows:

6. *Decides* to establish, in accordance with rule 28 of its provisional rules of procedure, a Committee of the Security Council, consisting of all the members of the Council, to monitor implementation of this resolution, with the assistance of appropriate expertise, and *calls upon* all States to report to the Committee, no later than 90 days from the date of adoption of this resolution and thereafter according to a timetable to be proposed by the Committee, on the steps they have taken to implement this resolution;

Since Resolutions 1368 and 1373, there have been further resolutions of the Security Council dealing with the issue of international terrorism.[64]

---

[62] Above, n 22.

[63] Para 4.

[64] Interestingly, though, the only resolution of the United Nations Security Council prior to September 11 and dealing with terrorism in the international context, rather than relating to

Recognizing the considerable burden upon States in the implementation process to become a party to the 12 international conventions and in complying with Resolution 1373, the Council tasked the Counter-Terrorism Committee with exploring ways in which States could be assisted.[65] Resolutions 1452 and 1455 concerned themselves specifically with the Taliban and al-Qaida.[66]

Further obligations upon States? One further issue arises from the Security Council's Resolution 1373 and its later Resolution 1456.[67] Adopted in January 2003, Resolution 1456 calls upon the Counter-Terrorism Committee to intensify its efforts to promote the implementation of Resolution 1373, which is discussed further below.[68] It also contains the following provisions:

The Security Council therefore calls for the following steps to be taken:

1.   All States must take urgent action to prevent and suppress all active and passive support to terrorism, and in particular comply fully with all relevant resolutions of the Security Council, in particular resolutions 1373 (2001), 1390 (2002) and 1455 (2003);

2.   The Security Council calls upon States to:
(a) become a party, as a matter of urgency, to all relevant international conventions and protocols relating to terrorism, in particular the 1999 international convention for the suppression of the financing of terrorism and to support all international initiatives taken to that aim, and to make full use of the sources of assistance and guidance which are now becoming available;
(b) assist each other, to the maximum extent possible, in the prevention, investigation, prosecution and punishment of acts of terrorism, wherever they occur;
(c) cooperate closely to implement fully the sanctions against terrorists and their associates, in particular Al-Qaeda and the Taliban and their

---

and restricted to specific events, is Security Council Resolution 1189 of 13 August 1998, S/RES/1189 (1998). Although the resolution was adopted in response to the 1998 bombings in Nairobi, Kenya and Tanzania, it called upon all States "to adopt, in accordance with international law and as a matter of priority, effective and practical measures for security cooperation, for the prevention of such acts of terrorism, and for the prosecution and punishment of their perpetrators" (para 5).

[65] United Nations Security Council Resolution 1377 of 12 November 2001, S/RES/1377 (2001).

[66] Discussed in Chapter 4.

[67] United Nations Security Council Resolution 1456 of 20 January 2003, S/RES/1456 (2003) – Appendix 2H herein.

[68] See para 4.

associates, as reflected in resolutions 1267 (1999), 1390 (2002) and 1455 (2003), to take urgent actions to deny them access to the financial resources they need to carry out their actions, and to cooperate fully with the Monitoring Group established pursuant to resolution 1363 (2001);

The content of paragraph 1 and paragraphs 2(b) and 2(c), by themselves, do not cause any particular concern. Indeed, they are entirely consistent with earlier resolutions of the Council. It is paragraph 2(a), building upon paragraph 3(d) of Resolution 1373, that raises some issues about the proper role of the Security Council. By calling upon States to become a party to all counter-terrorist conventions and protocols, is the Council over-stepping its function and impinging upon State sovereignty?

This is an interesting constitutional question that warrants at least some consideration. On the one hand, member States of the United Nations have surrendered their sovereignty by becoming a party to the United Nations Charter, to the extent that they have agreed to be bound by decisions of the Security Council.[69] At the same time, however, it could hardly have been intended by those becoming party to the Charter to grant the Security Council the authority to direct members in their treaty-making decision processes. A considerable number of States have involved constitutional rules concerning the executive's treaty-making power which must be complied with before a State can ratify or accede to a treaty. Is the Security Council, by issuing the directions contained in paragraph 3(f) of Resolution 1373 and paragraph 2(a) of Resolution 1456, able to override such domestic constitutional safeguards?

Answering that question appears to lie in one further enquiry: whether any such resolution is indeed binding within the terms of article 25 of the Charter. There appear to be two bases upon which this second question might be answered. The first is to consider whether the resolution has been made within the mandate of the Security Council, since the various powers given to the Council, conferred under article 24, are so conferred to discharge its duties for the maintenance of international peace and security and for no other reason. Thus, if a resolution is not made for that purpose, the resolution would be made outside the authority of the Security Council and could not then be binding upon member States. In the context of the resolutions at hand, the subject matter concerns the suppression of terrorism which, as repeatedly stated by both the Security Council and General Assembly, is seen as one of the most serious threats to peace and security. Resolutions 1373 and 1456 were made, it is therefore concluded, within the proper authority of the Security Council.

---

[69] Article 25 of the Charter of the United Nations.

The second consideration is whether the provisions at hand are "decisions" within the meaning of article 25 of the Charter, which provides that:

> The Members of the United Nations agree to accept and carry out the decisions of the Security Council in accordance with the present Charter.

The answer turns on whether exhortatory provisions constitute "decisions" within the meaning of article 25 and, in turn, whether the provisions at hand are exhortatory. This issue was considered by the International Court of Justice in the *Namibia Advisory Opinion*, where the Court took the position that a resolution couched in non-mandatory language should not be taken as imposing a legal duty upon a member State.[70] Turning to the paragraphs in issue, if the Security Council "calls upon States" to become party to counter-terrorism treaties, is this mandatory or exhortatory? The phrase is certainly not as forceful as "all States shall/must", but it is at the same time more compelling than "requesting" or even "strongly encouraging" States to do so.[71]

Bearing in mind that the more forceful terms "shall" or "must" were not used (whereas they were used within other provisions of the resolutions) and that the provisions concern the treaty-making process (a matter that has always been regarded as within the sole purview of State executives), it is posited that a restrictive interpretation must be given to the provisions. The provisions must be seen as exhortatory and, following the *Namibia Advisory Opinion*, do not impose a legal duty upon States to become signatories to the various international counter-terrorism conventions.

Revitalization of the Counter-Terrorism Committee. Notable terrorist events since September 11, drawing the condemnation of the Security Council and prompting it to reiterate its earlier resolutions, include the bomb attacks in Bali, Indonesia on 12 October 2002;[72] the taking of hostages in Moscow, the Russian Federation, on 23 October 2002;[73] the bombing of the Paradise Hotel in Kikambala, Kenya, and the attempted

---

[70] *Legal Consequences for States of the Continued Presence of South Africa in Namibia (South-West Africa) notwithstanding Security Council Resolution 276 (1990), (1970-1971),* Advisory Opinion of the International Court of Justice of 21 June 1971, 53.

[71] Both terms/phrases being commonly used in Security Council resolutions.

[72] United Nations Security Council Resolution 1438 of 14 October 2002, S/RES/1438 (2002).

[73] United Nations Security Council Resolution 1440 of 24 October 2002, S/RES/1440 (2002).

missile attack on Arkia Israeli Airlines flight 582 departing Mombasa, Kenya (al-Qaida claiming responsibility for those acts);[74] and the bombing by the terrorist group ETA[75] in Madrid, Spain, on 11 March 2004.[76]

With these events in mind, the Counter-Terrorism Committee (CTC) has undergone revitalization under Security Council Resolution 1535.[77] The Committee's reform has been implemented to give it further means to fulfil its mandate of monitoring the implementation of Resolution 1373. The Committee now consists of two main organs. The first, the "Plenary", is composed of the Security Council member States and acts to monitor the second part of the Committee and provide it with policy guidance. The functional part of the Committee is the "Bureau" composed of the Chair and Vice-Chairs of the Security Council and a renamed "Counter-Terrorism Committee Executive Directorate" (which comprises, in real terms, those members of the CTC that had worked in the Committee up to its restructuring).[78]

---

[74] United Nations Security Council Resolution 1450 of 13 December 2002, S/RES/1450 (2002).

[75] The ETA, *Ezukadi Ta Askatasuna* (roughly translated as "Basque Fatherland and Liberty") was founded in 1959 with the aim of establishing an independent homeland in the northern Spanish provinces based on Marxist principles and operating primarily in the Basque autonomous regions of northern Spain and south-western France: see Appendix A "Background Information on Designated Foreign Terrorist Organizations" in Howard, R.D. and Sawyer, R.L. (eds), *Terrorism and Counterterrorism. Understanding the New Security Environment (Revised and Updated)*, McGraw-Hill (2003), 507.

[76] United Nations Security Council Resolution 1530 of 11 March 2004, S/RES/1530 (2004).

[77] United Nations Security Council Resolution 1535 of 26 March 2004, S/RES/1536 (2004). It should be noted, however, that the proposal to revitalize the Committee pre-dated the Madrid Bombing: see United Nations Information Service, "Security Council Considers Proposal to Revitalize Counter-Terrorism Committee", 5 March 2004, SC/8020. Interestingly, the Council was briefed on the work of the Counter-Terrorism Committee by the CTC's Chairman, Inocencio Arias, Permanent Representative of Spain to the United Nations.

[78] A very useful website has been established by the Counter-Terrorism Committee, explaining the mandate, practices and assistance programme of the Committee and containing State reports to the Committee and other useful documents and papers: see URL <http://www.un.org/Docs/sc/committees/1373>.

Human Rights and Counter-Terrorism

The reaction of States to Resolution 1373 has been, almost invariably, to introduce or amend counter-terrorist legislation and to take various other policy or regulatory steps in support of the obligations under the Resolution and the associated Suppression of Financing Convention. The scope of and the manner in which those steps have been taken has, however, been of concern to politicians, civil liberties groups and various non-governmental organizations throughout the world. On the basis of their international counter-terrorist obligations and comparative domestic security concerns, many States have extended executive authority, raising concerns about executive powers, due process, and privacy.[79] Against that background, a conflict of wills is exposed: the desire to eradicate terrorism versus the maintenance of human rights standards. The question is whether the two objectives are compatible: can human rights be limited, at international law and within free and democratic societies, in the pursuit of counter-terrorist objectives and, if so, to what extent?

The words of the United Nations Secretary-General, Kofi Annan, when addressing the issue of terrorism before the General Assembly of the United Nations in 1999 are no less relevant today. He said:[80]

> We are all determined to fight terrorism and to do our utmost to banish it from the face of the earth. But the force we use to fight it should always be proportional and focused on the actual terrorists. We cannot and must not fight them by using their own methods – by inflicting indiscriminate violence and terror on innocent civilians, including children.

His comments focus on the more physical aspects of countering terrorism. They are just as relevant, however, to the issue of striking a balance between counter-terrorism and the protection of civil rights. Some time

---

[79] See, for example, Conte, A., "A Clash of Wills: Counter-Terrorism and Human Rights", *New Zealand Universities Law Review*, 20 (2003) 338; Donohue, L.K., "Fear Itself. Counterterrorism, Individual Rights, and US Foreign Relations Post 9-11" in Howard, R.D. and Sawyer RL (eds), *Terrorism and Counterterrorism. Understanding the New Security Environment (Revised and Updated)*, McGraw-Hill (2003) 313; and Michaelsen, C., "International Human Rights on Trial – The United Kingdom's and Australia's Legal Response to 9/11" 25 (2003) *The Sydney Law Review* 275.

[80] Address of the United Nations Secretary General to the General Assembly, 18 November 1999.

before him, Aristotle made an equally relevant observation:[81]

> For man, when perfected, is the best of animals, but when separated from law and justice, he is worst of all.

When may Human Rights be Limited?

The starting point in examining the relationship between counter-terrorism and human rights is that, notwithstanding the importance of the objective of counter-terrorism and the very strong wording of Resolution 1373, implementation of counter-terrorist measures must comply with existing international human rights obligations. To do otherwise would be to allow the United Nations Security Council, with a membership of fifteen, to effectively override international human rights treaties, including the United Nations Charter and the Universal Declaration of Human Rights, the founding documents of the United Nations.[82]

At the same time, it must be acknowledged that not all human rights are absolute. The right to life, freedom from torture and slavery, and freedom of thought, conscience and religion, for example, are recognized in various documents as being absolute and non-derogable.[83] Other rights, in certain circumstances however, can (and indeed sometimes must) be qualified in order to achieve other pressing objectives. Typically, this occurs in two scenarios. The first is where a right or freedom conflicts with or must be measured against another right or freedom.[84] For example, freedom of expression does not carry with it the right to incite violence or racial hatred, defame others or engage in commercial fraud.[85] A further example is commonly seen in questions concerning the medical treatment of children. In such cases and for various reasons including religious belief, the parents of a child may choose not to permit their child to receive medical treatment,

---

[81] Aristotle, *Politics* (350BC), as translated by Benjamin Jowett, Book One, Chapter II.

[82] A point made by Treasa Dunworth in her address "New Zealand's Legislative Responses to September 11", paper presented at the 10th Annual Meeting of the Australian and New Zealand Society of International Law, *New Challenges and New States: What Role for International Law?*, 16 June 2002, Australian National University, Canberra.

[83] See, for example, article 4 of the International Covenant on Civil and Political Rights 1966, adopted 16 December 1966, 999 UNTS 171 (entered into force 23 March 1976).

[84] As recognized in the preamble of the International Covenant on Civil and Political Rights.

[85] An example made in the New Zealand Department of Justice report, *A Bill of Rights for New Zealand – A White Paper*, Government Printer, Wellington, 1985, 71.

which exposes a conflict between the rights of the child[86] and the right to religious belief.[87]

The next category of permissible derogation of rights is within the context of a conflict between a right or freedom and some important objective, whether of the international community at international law or of a State in its domestic law. This, in turn, can be viewed within the framework of two categories: derogation of rights because of a state of emergency, as permitted by article 4 of the International Covenant on Civil and Political Rights for example; and/or where there is some other pressing objective that needs to be met for the maintenance of society itself. The latter qualified guarantee, effectively limited by the notion that a cure should never be worse than the disease, is given effect within many domestic human rights instruments.[88]

The purpose of achieving counter-terrorist objectives would appear, at face value, to be an objective that can justify limitations upon rights and freedoms. It is very useful, in that regard, to consider the views and positions espoused within the international arena on the question of terrorism and human rights. What follows is a brief appraisal of the International Covenant on Civil and Political Rights (ICCPR), and the work and comments of the UN General Assembly and Commission on Human Rights on the subject.[89]

---

[86] More specifically, the right to life, as reflected in article 6 of the United Nations Convention on the Rights of the Child, 1577 UNTS 44 (entered into force 2 September 1990); and the requirement in article 3 of the Convention to give effect to the best interests of the child.

[87] See article 18(1) of the International Covenant on Civil and Political Rights.

[88] See, for example, the qualification in New Zealand legislation through section 5 of the New Zealand Bill of Rights Act 1990, which provides that "Subject to section 4 of this Bill of Rights, the rights and freedoms contained in this Bill of Rights may be subject only to such reasonable limits prescribed by law as can be demonstrably justified in a free and democratic society". Similarly, article 1 of the Canadian Charter of Rights and Freedoms, upon which New Zealand's section 5 is based, provides that "[t]he Canadian Charter of Rights and Freedoms guarantees the rights and freedoms set out in it subject only to such reasonable limits prescribed by law as can be demonstrably justified in a free and democratic society".

[89] In all fairness to the issue of the interface between human rights and counter-terrorism, this chapter only endeavours to introduce the issue and give some thought to it in the context of the United Nations role in the maintenance of peace and security. Substantial work has been undertaken in this field. Some articles have already been mentioned (above, n 88) and of considerable use also is the report of the Advisory Council of Jurists for the Asia Pacific Forum, *Reference on the Rule of Law in Combating Terrorism*, publication of the Asia Pacific Forum of National Human Rights Institutions, 2004.

The International Covenant on Civil and Political Rights. The ICCPR recognizes within its preamble and article 4 that not all rights are absolute. The preamble to the Covenant reads:

> The States Parties to the present Covenant,
> *Considering* that, in accordance with the principles proclaimed in the Charter of the United Nations, recognition of the inherent dignity and of the equal and inalienable rights of all members of the human family is the foundation of freedom, justice and peace in the world,
> *Recognizing* that these rights derive from the inherent dignity of the human person,
> *Recognizing* that, in accordance with the Universal Declaration of Human Rights, the ideal of free human beings enjoying civil and political freedom and freedom from fear and want can only be achieved if conditions are created whereby everyone may enjoy his civil and political rights, as well as his economic, social and cultural rights,
> *Considering* the obligation of States under the Charter of the United Nations to promote universal respect for, and observance of, human rights and freedoms,
> *Realizing* that *the individual, having duties to other individuals and to the community to which he belongs*, is under a responsibility to strive for the promotion and observance of the rights recognized in the present Covenant,
> *Agree upon* the following articles... [emphasis added]

In turn, article 4 of the Covenant permits certain limitations upon rights and freedoms:[90]

> In time of public emergency which threatens the life of the nation and the existence of which is officially proclaimed, the States Parties to the present Covenant may take measures derogating from their obligations under the present Covenant to the extent strictly required by the exigencies of the situation, provided that such measures are not inconsistent with their other obligations under international law and do not involve discrimination solely on the ground of race, colour, sex, language, religion or social origin.

Thus, when a public emergency arises which is officially proclaimed to threaten the life of a nation, a State party to the ICPPR can derogate from a number of rights to the extent strictly required by the situation. The State party cannot, however, derogate from certain specific rights and may not take discriminatory measures on a number of grounds.[91] States are also

---

[90] Article 4(1).

[91] Article 4(2) qualifies the ability to derogate by stating that "No derogation from articles 6, 7, 8 (paras 1 and 2), 11, 15, 16 and 18 may be made under this provision". Those articles relate to the right to life (art 6), freedom from torture or to cruel, inhuman or degrading

under an obligation to inform other States parties immediately, through the United Nations Secretary-General, of the derogations it has made including the reasons for such derogations and the date on which the derogations are terminated.[92]

As the treaty-monitoring body for the ICCPR, the Human Rights Committee has issued a General Comment[93] on the application of article 4.[94] The document clearly considers that article 4(1) is limited to states of emergency, as provided for within municipal legislation setting out grounds upon which a state of emergency may be declared.[95] While the Committee does not explain its rationale in coming to this view, it seems to be based upon the wording of the provision and upon the idea of certainty and the rule of law: the idea that there be certainty in the law, reasonably ascertainable by the people within a State so that they are able to regulate their conduct accordingly and know the basis upon which the State can act. At paragraph 3 of its General Comment, the Committee said:

> [I]n times of emergency, the protection of human rights becomes all the more important, particularly those rights from which no derogations can be made.

The Committee has also expressed the view that measures taken under article 4 are of an exceptional and temporary nature and can only last as long as the life of the nation concerned is threatened. In the context of counter-terrorism, the question is whether this serves as an appropriate mechanism (at least for the purpose of the Covenant) by which counter-terrorist measures infringing human rights might be justified? One might

---

treatment or punishment (art 7), the prohibition of slavery and servitude (art 8(1) and (2)), freedom from imprisonment for failure to fulfil a contract (art 11), freedom from retrospective penalties (art 15), the right to be recognized as a person before the law (art 16) and freedom of thought, conscience and religion (art 18).

[92] Article 4(3) of the Covenant.

[93] General Comments are intended to be used by States parties as a tool for interpretation and implementation of rights commented upon.

[94] *Derogation of Rights (Art 4)*, CCPR General Comment 5 (31/07/81).

[95] The term "*state* of emergency", rather than "*public* emergency" is that adopted by the Human Rights Committee within its General Comment 5 (ibid, para 2). It does not, however, reflect the actual wording of art 4(1), which refers to "public emergency" only. This is an important distinction, since (in the author's view) the latter phrase has a wider meaning than "state of emergency". Ultimately, it should be noted that General Comments of the Human Rights Committee are made by the Committee for the purpose of assisting interpretation and application of ICCPR provisions and are without legal standing. While they certainly might indicate the way in which the Committee might address a complaint presented to it, General Comments do not function as a binding interpretation or direction. In fact, the making of General Comments is not even set out within the ICCPR or its optional protocols as part of the Human Rights Committee's functions.

argue that such measures will only in very limited circumstances be said to be within the context of a state of emergency which threatens the life of the State, i.e., during the period of the terrorist activity itself, where this is directed at the State or its people or territory, as occurred in New York and Washington DC on September 11, 2001. To counter this, one might equally say that acts of terrorism do strike at the heart of a nation and that the activation of such measures is only temporary (during the emergency period alone) and thus in satisfaction of the Human Rights Committee's conditions.

European Convention on Human Rights. Similar limitation provisions exist under Europe's Convention for the Protection of Human Rights and Fundamental Freedoms.[96] Of considerable relevance to the issue of terrorism and human rights for States parties to that Convention is the 2002 directive of the Council of Europe on the subject (the first international directive of its kind).[97]

United Nations General Assembly and Commission on Human Rights

The following examination of resolutions of the General Assembly and Commission on Human Rights, albeit brief for the purpose of this chapter, reveals that a link between terrorism and human rights is not a new one. Significantly, there are a number of statements that preceded the September 11 attacks and cannot therefore be criticized as being a knee-jerk reaction to that event. What is interesting, though, is that the focus of this earlier link between counter-terrorism and human rights was (in the main) one-directional: that is, primarily focused upon the impact of *terrorism* on human rights, rather than the impact of *counter*-terrorism on human rights. Clearly, however, the resolutions recognize that counter-terrorism is a pressing objective due to the adverse affect that terrorist acts have upon human rights.

The adverse affects of terrorism upon human rights. On the fiftieth anniversary of the United Nations, the General Assembly adopted Resolution 50/6, in which it set out certain principles by which it would be guided in its future endeavours with respect to peace, development,

---

[96] Adopted 4 November 1950, 213 UNTS 222 (entered into force 3 September 1953): see article 15 concerning permissible derogations of the rights set out within the Convention.

[97] Council of Europe, *Guidelines on Human Rights and the Fight Against Terrorism*, Council of Europe Publishing (2002).

equality and justice.[98] Within the category of peace, the maintenance of which is the principal objective of the United Nations, the General Assembly resolved that United Nations members should act together to defeat threats to States and people posed by terrorism, in all its forms and manifestations.[99]

Of the more recent resolutions on the interrelationship between counter-terrorism and human rights prior to September 11 is General Assembly Resolution 54/164.[100] The preamble to Resolution 54/164 affirms that it is guided by the Charter of the United Nations and the Universal Declaration of Human Rights and the International Covenants on Human Rights. It also reaffirms the position that terrorism undermines human rights, fundamental freedoms and democracy.[101] More specifically, it characterizes terrorism as something aimed at the destruction of human rights, the right to life being the most basic of those rights. It expresses the view that terrorism creates an environment that destroys the right of people to live in freedom from fear,[102] the right to liberty and security[103] and, more broadly, is described in the following terms:[104]

> ...activities aimed at the destruction of human rights, fundamental freedoms and democracy, threatening the territorial integrity and security of States, destabilizing [sic] legitimately constituted Governments, undermining pluralistic civil society and having adverse consequences for the economic and social development of States.

---

[98] United Nations General Assembly Resolution 50/6, *Declaration on the Occasion of the Fiftieth Anniversary of the United Nations*, A/RES/50/6, 24 October 1995.

[99] Ibid, para 1(4).

[100] United Nations General Assembly Resolution 54/164, *Human Rights and Terrorism*, A/RES/54/164, 24 February 2000 – Appendix 2K herein. The Resolution is very similar to its three predecessors: A/RES/49/185 of 23 December 1994; A/RES/50/186 of 22 December 1995; and A/RES/52/133 of 27 February 1998. Its contents were similarly reaffirmed within subsequent resolutions of the General Assembly: A/RES/56/160 of 13 February 2002; and A/RES/58/174 of 10 March 2004.

[101] As adopted at the World Conference on Human Rights of 1993 through the Vienna Declaration and Programme of Action of 25 June 1993.

[102] See the preamble, which reads (in part): "*Seriously concerned* about the gross violations of human rights perpetrated by terrorist groups, *Profoundly deploring* the increasing number of innocent persons, including women, children and the elderly, killed, massacred and maimed by terrorists in indiscriminate and random acts of violence and terror, which cannot be justified under any circumstances".

[103] Ibid, para 2.

[104] Ibid, para 3.

When reading the Resolution as a whole, with its successors,[105] it is clear that the General Assembly regards terrorism as a direct threat to two principles of the United Nations: the maintenance of peace and security and the protection of human rights.

The UN Commission on Human Rights has made similar comments. In the preamble to its Resolution 1999/27, which was specifically mentioned in General Assembly Resolution 54/164, the Commission stated:[106]

Regretting that the negative impact of terrorism, in all its dimensions, on human rights continues to remain alarming, despite national and international efforts to combat it,
Convinced that terrorism, in all its forms and manifestations, wherever and by whomever committed, can never be justified in any instance, including as a means to promote and protect human rights,
Conscious of the increasing importance of the role played by the United Nations in combating terrorism,
Bearing in mind that the most essential and basic human right is the right to life,
Bearing in mind also that terrorism in many cases poses a severe challenge to democracy, civil society and the rule of law,
Bearing in mind further that terrorism creates an environment that destroys the freedom from fear of the people.

Two common themes emerge from these resolutions by the General Assembly and Commission. First, terrorism is seen as a threat to peace and security, the maintenance of which is a paramount priority for the United Nations and its members.[107] Second, it is also seen as a threat to human rights, through the impact it has upon its physical targets.

Thus, counter-terrorism can and should be seen as a pressing objective which may, by proportional and necessary means, call for the limitation of rights.

---

[105] See resolution of the Assembly with the same title, *Human Rights and Terrorism*: A/RES/56/160 of 13 February 2002; and A/RES/58/174 of 10 March 2004.
[106] Resolution 1999/27 of the United Nations Economic and Social Council's Commission on Human Rights, *Human Rights and Terrorism*, E/CN.4/RES/1999/27 – Appendix 2L herein. The resolution contains nine operative paragraphs, through which the General Assembly called upon States, inter alia, to take all necessary and effective measures to prevent, combat and eliminate terrorism in all its forms and manifestations, wherever and by whomever committed (para 4). The resolution was similarly restated in the Commission's resolution on *Human Rights and Terrorism* of 23 April 2001, E/CN.4/RES/2001/37.
[107] Currently being 191, with the admission of Switzerland and East Timor in 2002.

The impact of counter-terrorism upon human rights. As has been discussed, the focus of resolutions prior to September 11, as well as Security Council Resolution 1373, was upon the impact of terrorist conduct upon human rights. Since that time, however, there has been considerable attention paid to the potentially adverse affect that *counter*-terrorist measures can have upon human rights. Having said that, a provision of an early General Assembly resolution, Resolution 54/164 did mandate that counter-terrorist measures must be taken:

> ...in accordance with relevant provisions of international law, including international human rights standards...

Similarly, Security Council Resolution 1373 calls on States to:[108]

> 3(f) Take appropriate measures *in conformity with the relevant provisions of national and international law, including international standards of human rights*, before granting refugee status, for the purpose of ensuring that the asylum-seeker has not planned, facilitated or participated in the commission of terrorist acts; [emphasis added]

Those very brief qualifications have been expanded upon by the General Assembly in two resolutions entitled *Protection of Human Rights and Fundamental Freedoms While Countering Terrorism*, adopted in late 2002 and 2003.[109] Likewise, Commission on Human Rights Special Rapporteur Kalliopi Koufa released a detailed report in June 2004, *Specific Human Rights Issues: New Priorities, In Particular Terrorism and Counter-Terrorism.*[110]

Conclusion

International terrorism has been identified by both the UN General Assembly and Security Council as one of the most serious threats to peace and security. The terrorist attacks of September 11, 2001, ultimately prompted the intervention in Afghanistan. They also shook the United Nations into concerted action in the fight to eradicate terrorism. Due to a

---

[108] At para 3(f).

[109] United Nations General Assembly Resolution 57/219 of 18 December 2002, A/RES/57/129, and 58/187 of 22 December 2003, A/RES/58/187.

[110] Final report of the Special Rapporteur, Kalliopi K. Koufa, *Specific Human Rights Issues: New Priorities, In Particular Terrorism and Counter-Terrorism*, E/CN.4/Sub.2/2004/40, 25 June 2004.

lack of international consensus on the meaning of the terms terrorism, however, that action has failed to produce a comprehensive convention on terrorism. Despite the considerable work of the Security Council Counter-Terrorism Committee and the Ad Hoc Committee established under General Assembly Resolution 51/210, the international law on counter-terrorism is mainly based upon twelve very specific conventions that do not have general application and are limited in their binding nature to States parties to those treaties. Having said this, the Suppression of Financing Convention does have potentially wider application in its description of conduct that may not be financed. While Security Council Resolutions 1269 and 1373 also fail to define the term, Resolution 1269 makes it clear that the Council has adopted an objective understanding of the term, condemning all acts of terrorism regardless of their motivation.

Both the General Assembly and Security Council have issued numerous resolutions on the topic of counter-terrorism. Although not binding, the General Assembly has built on various guiding principles and expectations in its declarations on measures to eliminate international terrorism. The Security Council established a Counter-Terrorism Committee very soon after the terrorist attacks of September 11, 2001, with the role of liaising with UN members on the implementation of Resolution 1373 and the twelve counter-terrorism conventions, as well as to provide means by which States could be assisted in doing so. The Council has imposed various specific obligations upon States under Resolutions 1373 and 1456. It has been posited, however, that the requirement to become a party to each of the treaties on terrorism remains within the sole privilege of State executives and is not a binding provision of Resolution 1456.

An important issue to remember in the implementation of the various obligations considered is that the maintenance of peace and security (through, in this example, the elimination of terrorism) is not the only principle and purpose of the United Nations. Article 1(3) of the Charter also establishes the organization as one to maintain and promote human rights. An interesting and complex relationship is thus exposed in the setting of counter-terrorism. On the one hand, terrorism is a threat to both peace and security (by virtue of the violent and fear-inducing nature of such conduct) and also a threat to human rights (by the taking of life, or its imposition upon liberty and security, and undermining civil society). Equally, however, the General Assembly and Commission on Human Rights, and the Security Council to a lesser extent, have recognized and expressed that counter-terrorist measures must be implemented in a way that is consistent with States' international human rights obligations.

Chapter 3

Operation Enduring Freedom

Introduction

Self-defence involves measures taken by one or more States in the defence of self or their neighbours. *Operation Enduring Freedom* is a multinational operation in the exercise of self-defence under article 51 of the United Nations Charter. Various obligations come with such action, and this chapter will consider the nature and extent of such obligations and also the important question of whether *Operation Enduring Freedom* is indeed a valid exercise of article 51. Also considered is the role to be played by the Security Council when self-defence action is taken by a State or States under article 51.

Jus Ad Bellum – Activating Article 51 of the UN Charter

Article 51 of the Charter of the United Nations retains the inherent right of a State to act in defence of itself, and extends the principle to one of "collective self-defence", whereby members of the United Nations are also permitted to use force in the defence of a State seeking the assistance of others to defend itself:[1]

> Article 51
> Nothing in the present Charter shall impair the inherent right of individual or collective self-defence if an armed attack occurs against a Member of the United Nations, until the Security Council has taken measures necessary to maintain international peace and security. Measures taken by Members in the exercise of this right of self-defence shall be immediately reported to the Security Council and shall not in any way affect the authority and responsibility of the Security Council under the present Charter to take at any time such action as it deems necessary in order to maintain or restore international peace and security.

---

[1] This relationship with, and extension of, customary international law at the time of the adoption of the United Nations Charter is discussed by the International Court of Justice in the *Case Concerning Military and Paramilitary Activities in and Against Nicaragua (Nicaragua v United States)*, Merits Phase [1986] ICJ Reports 4, 534–536.

The US-led coalition forces involved in *Operation Enduring Freedom*, which commenced on 7 October 2001, relied upon article 51 as the basis of the intervention.[2] The provision, and its wording, raises various questions to be considered within this part of the chapter. One is whether the terrorist attacks of September 11 fall within the meaning of "armed attack" in the first sentence of the article. Another issue that has been of interest to the international community is that of notice to the United Nations Secretary-General. For the purpose of this chapter, these issues are dealt with in reverse order.

Notice of Exercise of Self-Defence

Measures taken in reliance upon article 51 must, according to the second sentence of that article, be immediately notified to the United Nations Secretary-General. The essential nature of this requirement was addressed by the International Court of Justice in *Nicaragua v US*, where the Court made adverse comments about the failure of the United States to give such notice in its purported exercise of self-defence.[3]

Nicaragua v US concerned the support by military forces of the United States to insurgents within Nicaragua who unsuccessfully sought to overthrow the established, communist, government of that State. In a memorandum filed by the United States during the jurisdiction phase of the litigation,[4] the US put forward the argument that, even if the ICJ did have jurisdiction, the conduct of the United States was justified under article 51 of the UN Charter as being in defence of its neighbour El Salvador. During the merits phase of the case, the Court gave consideration to the question of whether the US conduct could fall within article 51.[5] In a somewhat

---

[2] See, for example, International Affairs and Defence Section of the UK House of Commons Library, "Operation *Enduring Freedom* and the Conflict in Afghanistan: An Update", Research Paper 01/81 of 31 October 2001, 9.

[3] Above, n 1, 121.

[4] The United States claimed that the International Court of Justice had no jurisdiction to determine the claim by Nicaragua (for various reasons that do not bear relevance to the issue at hand).

[5] In protest against the decision of the International Court of Justice concerning its jurisdiction to adjudicate over the dispute, the United States declined to lodge memoranda during the merits phase of the litigation. The Court was therefore unable to refer to official counter arguments by the United States and was compelled to refer to the relevant statements contained within the US memoranda on jurisdiction.

scathing judgment, the Court said:[6]

> At no time, up to the present, has the United States Government addressed to the Security Council, in connection with the matters the subject of the present case, the report which is required by Article 51 of the United Nations Charter in respect of measures which a State believes itself bound to take when it exercises the right of individual or collective self-defence ... the Court is justified in observing that this conduct of the United States hardly conforms with the latter's avowed conviction that it was acting in the context of collective self-defence as consecrated by Article 51 of the Charter. This fact is all the more noteworthy because, in the Security Council, the United States has itself taken the view that failure to observe the requirement to make a report contradicted a State's claim to be acting on the basis of collective self-defence.

The resultant position is quite clear. If a State wishes to act in reliance upon article 51, it must make its report to the Security Council, failing which adverse deductions will be made. In the case of *Operation Enduring Freedom*, notifications were duly made to the Council. In a letter addressed to the President of the Security Council on the same day as the commencement of the intervention in Afghanistan, the US Ambassador to the United Nations, John Negroponte, wrote:[7]

> ...my Government has obtained clear and compelling information that the Al-Qaeda organization, which is supported by the Taliban regime in Afghanistan, had a central role in the attacks...
>
> ...the attacks on 11 September 2001 and the ongoing threat to the United States and its nationals posed by the Al-Qaeda organization have been made possible by the decision of the Taliban regime to allow parts of Afghanistan that it controls to be used by this organization as a base of operations. Despite every effort by the international community, the Taliban regime has refused to change its policy. From the territory of Afghanistan, the Al-Qaeda organization continues to train and support agents of terror who attack innocent people throughout the world and target United States nationals and interests in the United States and abroad.
>
> In response to these attacks, and in accordance with the inherent right of individual and collective self-defence, United States armed forces have initiated actions designed to prevent and deter further attacks on the United States.

---

[6] Above, n 1, 121-122.

[7] Letter from the United States Ambassador to the United Nations, John Negroponte, to the President of the United Nations Security Council, 7 October 2001.

Similarly, the United Kingdom Mission to the UN wrote:[8]

...the United Kingdom has military assets engaged in operations against targets we know to be involved in the operation of terror against the United States of America, the United Kingdom and other countries around the world, as part of an international effort.

These forces have now been employed in exercise of the inherent right of individual and collective self-defence, recognised in Article 51, following the terrorist outrage of 11 September, to avert the continuing threat of attacks from the same source."

Was September 11 an "Armed Attack"?

Because terrorist acts fall outside the scope of what one would normally consider to be an act of State aggression or war, the question of whether the terrorist attacks of 9/11 constituted an "armed attack" within the meaning of article 51 is not as simple as it might seem at first instance. The first consideration is whether a "terrorist attack" is an armed attack in the abstract sense, that is, whether terrorist conduct has the type of aggressive elements that constitute an armed attack. The second question is whether and how a terrorist attack by a non-State actor (a terrorist organization, namely al-Qaida) constitutes an "armed attack" for the purpose of article 51.

Are terrorist acts "armed attacks"? The precise meaning of "armed attack" is, in the context of terrorism, unclear. Professor Arend asks a series of pertinent questions in that regard.[9] When does a terrorist action constitute an armed attack? Must it occur in the territory of the aggrieved State? Must it be of a particular intensity? Would an isolated terrorist action amount to an armed attack, or would it have to be part of an ongoing effort?

In the case of the events of September 11, the answer seems to be clearly in the affirmative: yes, the attacks of 9/11, in their entire context, amounted to an "armed attack" within the meaning of article 51. In coming to that conclusion, the judgment of the ICJ in *Nicaragua*, as well as Security Council resolutions following September 11, are of assistance.

---

[8] Letter from the United Kingdom Mission to the United Nations, Stewart Eldon, to the President of the United Nations Security Council, 7 October 2001.

[9] Arend, A.C., "Terrorism and the Just War Doctrine", in Howard, R.D. and Sawyer, R.L. (eds), *Terrorism and Counterterrorism. Understanding the New Security Environment* (Revised and Updated), McGraw-Hill (2003), 347.

In *Nicaragua v US*, the Court considered the concept of an "armed attack" and how one is to determine whether such an attack has occurred:[10]

...it is the State which is the victim of an armed attack which must form and declare the view that it has been so attacked. There is no rule in customary international law permitting another State to exercise the right of collective self-defence on the basis of its own assessment of the situation. Where collective self-defence is invoked, it is to be expected that the State for whose benefit this right is used will have declared itself to be a victim of an armed attack.

In the context of September 11, it is clear that the United States considered itself to have been subject to an armed attack. As seen from the article 51 notice from Ambassador Negroponte, the United States saw September 11 as constituting armed attacks against it. United States President Bush had earlier referred, in his address to the Joint Session of Congress after September 11, to the attacks as an "act of war".[11] He referred to "a collection of loosely affiliated terrorist organizations known as Al-Qaeda" as having attacked the United States and said:[12]

They are the same murderers indicted for bombing American embassies in Tanzania and Kenya, and responsible for bombing the USS *Cole* [in Yemen in 2000].

Likewise, it seems that the Security Council considered that the attacks on September 11 were in respect of which self-defence could be exercised and, furthermore, that all acts of terrorism constituted a threat to international peace and security. Security Council Resolution 1368, which was adopted on the day after the September 11 attacks, provided:[13]

The Security Council,

Recognizing the inherent right of individual or collective self-defence in accordance with the Charter,

1. *Unequivocally condemns* in the strongest terms the horrifying terrorist attacks which took place on 11 September 2001 in New York, Washington DC

---

[10] Above, n 1, 104.
[11] Address to Joint Session of Congress, 20 September 2000.
[12] Ibid.
[13] United Nations Security Council Resolution 1368 of 12 September 2001, S/RES/1368 (2001) – Appendix 2C herein.

and Pennsylvania and *regards* such acts, like any act of international terrorism, as a threat to international peace and security;

These classifications of the events of 9/11 should not, however, be read in isolation. In a statement of the World Islamic Front of 28 February 1998, a decree of jihad was issued to all Muslims:[14]

...the killing of Americans and their civilian and military allies is a religious duty for each and every Muslim to be carried out in whichever country they are until Al Aksa mosque has been liberated from their grasp and until their armies have left Muslim lands ... We – with God's help – call on every Muslim who believes in God and wishes to be rewarded to comply with God's order to kill Americans and plunder their money whenever and wherever they find it. We also call on Muslims . . . to launch the raid on Satan's U.S. troops and the devil's supporters allying with them, and to displace those who are behind them.

This statement, when read together with the statements of the US President, the US Ambassador to the UN and the Security Council itself, demonstrate that the events of September 11 were attacks upon the State of America for the purpose of article 51 of the Charter. They were not an isolated incident, but clearly part of an ongoing action by al-Qaida against America and its allies.

Do terrorist acts, perpetrated by non-State actors, trigger article 51? What is less certain is whether the 9/11 attacks triggered article 51, not from the perspective of constituting acts of aggression, but in terms of attributing responsibility for the acts (by al-Qaida, a non-State actor) upon Afghanistan and thereby allowing self-defence action to be taken against Afghanistan.

Attribution of Responsibility to Afghanistan

The question of attributing responsibility upon Afghanistan, as a State, for the terrorist attacks of September 11 by al-Qaida, a non-State entity, has drawn criticism and is by far the most controversial aspect of determining the legitimacy or otherwise of *Operation Enduring Freedom*.

---

[14] *The New York Times*, 'Britain's Bill of Particulars: "Planned and Carried out the Atrocities"', 5 October 2001. The "fatwa", as it is known, was issued and signed by Usama bin Laden and other prominent members of al-Qaida and associated terrorist entities under the World Islamic Front for Jihad Against the Jews and Crusaders, which merged with the Egyptian Islamic Jihad in June 2001.

State Responsibility

Attributing responsibility upon a State for conduct of individuals and State officials has been a subject of concern for the international community for as long as States have existed. The subject has drawn the attention of the International Law Commission over the past several years, resulting in the drawing up of Articles on State Responsibility.[15] The articles provide that every wrongful act of a State entails the responsibility of that State, whether to make reparations or to cease and desist the wrongful conduct.[16] "Internationally wrongful acts" comprise conduct that constitutes a breach of an international obligation that is attributable to the State.[17]

Chapter II of the Articles sets out the means by which attribution is made. The conduct of any State organ is deemed to constitute an act of the State, whether within or in excess of authority or instructions.[18] Likewise, attribution arises where a person or entity acts under State legislative or governmental authority or is acting on the instructions of or under the direct control of the State.[19] Conduct of a non-State actor that is subsequently acknowledged and adopted by the State as its own naturally also results in the attribution of responsibility.[20]

There is evidence, in the present context, that the attacks were organized and perpetrated by al-Qaida, a terrorist organization established by Usama bin Laden in the late 1980s to bring together Arabs who fought in Afghanistan against the Soviet Union (and with the then support and assistance of the United States).[21] Its current goal, it is said, is to establish a pan-Islamic Caliphate throughout the world by working with allied Islamic extremist groups to overthrow non-Islamic regimes and expelling Westerners and non-Muslims from Muslim countries.[22] On 11 September 2001, 19 al-Qaida suicide attackers have been identified as being

---

[15] The final version of these articles were adopted by the International Law Commission at its fifty-third session in May 2001. These were, in turn, considered by the United Nations General Assembly and commended for the attention of member State governments: see United Nations General Assembly Resolution 56/83 of 12 December 2001, A/RES/56/83.

[16] See articles 1, 30 and 31 of the Articles on the Responsibility of States for Internationally Wrongful Acts.

[17] Article 2.

[18] Articles 4 and 7.

[19] Articles 5 and 8.

[20] Article 11.

[21] Appendix A "Background Information on Designated Foreign Terrorist Organizations" in Howard, R.D. and Sawyer, R.L. (eds), *Terrorism and Counterterrorism. Understanding the New Security Environment* (Revised and Updated), McGraw-Hill (2003), 521.

[22] See, for example, the statement of 28 February 1998 under the World Islamic Front for Jihad Against the Jews and Crusaders, above, n 14.

responsible for the hijacking of four US commercial jets and crashing them, two into the World Trade Center in New York City, one into the Pentagon near Washington DC and a fourth into a field in Shanksville Pennsylvania,[23] leaving almost 3,000 individuals dead or missing.[24]

According to those accounts, al-Qaida perpetrated the 9/11 attacks and was a non-State extremist organization. If that is correct, then (at least at face value), the September 11 attacks do not seem to bear the hallmarks of conduct for which Afghanistan could be held responsible. Al-Qaida is not, nor has it ever been, an organ of the Afghan State, nor is there evidence that it acted under legislative or governmental authority or under the instructions or direct control of Afghanistan.[25] While the Taliban, the de facto but non-recognized government authority of Afghanistan, did not assist the United States to apprehend Usama bin Laden or other members of al-Qaida, neither did it adopt the September 11 attacks as its own.[26]

Attribution of Responsibility upon the Taliban

A notable absence in the various documents alleging Taliban responsibility for the conduct of al-Qaida is mention and application of the principles on State responsibility. This might partly rest on the fact that the Articles on State Responsibility have not yet been adopted in any formal sense, nor incorporated into a treaty to which States have become parties. It is troubling to the author, however, that open consideration of these principles has not occurred. The Articles reflect a decade of consideration and deliberation by the International Law Commission, a body established in 1947 by the UN General Assembly to promote the progressive development of international law and its codification.[27] The articles are significant not only because of that, but also due to the fact that the International Court of Justice is likely to give great weight to the principles enumerated, the Articles often reflecting or stemming from decisions or observations of the Court through litigation between States on the question of responsibility for wrongful acts.

---

[23] This aircraft having been taken into the control of passengers from the hijackers, but regrettably crashing in the process, and suspected to be headed towards the White House in Washington DC.

[24] Above, n 21.

[25] Thus ruling out attribution under the principles articulated within articles 4, 5, 7 and 8 of the Articles on State Responsibility.

[26] Ruling out application of the principle within article 11 of the Articles on State Responsibility.

[27] United Nations General Assembly Resolution 94(I) of 31 January 1947, A/RES/94(I).

If the Articles on State Responsibility have not been the express means by which Taliban, and Afghani, responsibility for al-Qaida's conduct has been attributed, how has such accountability been apportioned? The answer lies in a series of Security Council resolutions directed towards the Taliban and the notion that, but for the protective mantle afforded by the Taliban, al-Qaida could never have perpetrated the heinous attacks on 11 September 2001.

That view was reflected within a report of Her Majesty's Government, tabled before the British Parliament on 4 October 2001 (just three days prior to the commencement of *Operation Enduring Freedom*):[28]

Usama Bin Laden's Al Qaida and the Taleban régime have a close and mutually dependent alliance. Usama Bin Laden and Al Qaida provide the Taleban régime with material, financial and military support. They jointly exploit the drugs trade. The Taleban régime allows Bin Laden to operate his terrorist training camps and activities from Afghanistan, protects him from attacks from outside, and protects the drugs stockpiles. Usama Bin Laden could not operate his terrorist activities without the alliance and support of the Taleban régime. The Taleban's strength would be seriously weakened without Usama Bin Laden's military and financial support.

The report concluded:[29]

The attacks of the 11 September 2001 were planned and carried out by Al Qaida, an organisation whose head is Usama Bin Laden. That organisation has the will, and the resources, to execute further attacks of similar scale. Both the United States and its close allies are targets for such attacks. *The attack could not have occurred without the alliance between the Taleban and Usama Bin Laden*, which allowed Bin Laden to operate freely in Afghanistan, promoting, planning and executing terrorist activity. [emphasis added]

Security Council Resolutions. Resolutions of the UN Security Council, both before and after September 11, also add to the idea of what might be termed "but for" responsibility.[30] Indeed, treating the Taliban accountable

---

[28] Her Majesty's Government, *Responsibility for the Terrorist Atrocities in the United States, 11 September 2001*, 4 October 2001, para 4 (background).

[29] Ibid, para 70.

[30] That is, responsibility on the basis that, but for the relationship between the Taliban and al-Qaida, the September 11 attacks could not have been perpetrated (as reflected in the British report mentioned earlier). Interestingly, the notion of a "but for" test for attributing criminal responsibility in various municipal jurisdictions has been rejected as lacking a sufficiently cogent chain of causation between perpetrator and accused. This is due to the need to take into account various factors, including the significance of an actor's

for the conduct of al-Qaida is also evident in the earlier resolutions of the Council. The language and tenor of Resolution 1267 is a classic example.[31] It condemns the use of the Afghan territory within the control of the Taliban for the "sheltering and training of terrorists and planning of terrorist acts"[32] and proving safe haven to Usama bin Laden (who had, by that time, been indicted for the 1998 bombings of the United States embassies in Nairobi, Kenya, and Dar es Salaam, Tanzania, and for conspiring to kill American nationals outside the United States).[33] As well as imposing sanctions upon the Taliban regime,[34] the Resolution made the following mandatory demands of the Taliban:

1. *Insists* that the Afghan faction known as the Taliban, which also calls itself the Islamic Emirate of Afghanistan, comply promptly with its previous resolutions and in particular cease the provision of sanctuary and training for international terrorists and their organizations, take appropriate effective measures to ensure that the territory under its control is not used for terrorist installations and camps, or for the preparation or organization of terrorist acts against other States or their citizens, and cooperate with efforts to bring indicted terrorists to justice;

2. *Demands* that the Taliban turn over Usama bin Laden without further delay to appropriate authorities in a country where he has been indicted, or to appropriate authorities in a country where he will be returned to such a country, or to appropriate authorities in a country where he will be arrested and effectively brought to justice;

Issued in December 2000, Resolution 1333 condemned the Taliban's failure to comply with the latter stipulations and also demanded that the Taliban close all camps where terrorists were trained within the territory

---

contribution; how salient that action is; the complexity caused by multiples causes; and intervening causes, such as natural events and third parties.

[31] United Nations Security Council Resolution 1267 of 15 October 1999, S/RES/1267 (1999) – Appendix 2A herein.

[32] Preambular para 3. The Security Council had earlier demanded, through para 13 of United Nations Security Council Resolution 1214 of 8 December 1998, S/RES/1214 (1998), that "the Taliban stop providing sanctuary and training for international terrorists and their organizations, and that all Afghan factions cooperate with efforts to bring indicted terrorists to justice".

[33] Preambular paras 4 and 5.

[34] Para 4. On the issues of sanctions, see also United Nations Security Council Resolutions 1452 of 20 December 2002, S/RES/1452 (2002), and 1526 of 30 January 2004, S/RES/1526 (2004).

under its control.[35] Following the September 11 attacks, and the refusal by the Taliban to assist in surrendering Usama bin Laden to US authorities, the Council issued Resolution 1378 which contains probably the most damning inference (by the Council, at least) that the Taliban bore responsibility for the attacks.[36] In calling for the establishment of a new, broad-based, multi-ethnic and fully representative government, it condemned the Taliban for allowing Afghanistan to be used as "a base for the export of terrorism by the Al-Qaida network and other terrorist groups and for providing safe haven to Usama Bin Laden, Al-Qaida and others associated with them".[37] Reiterating this condemnation, and earlier demands, Security Council Resolution 1390 imposed further sanctions on Usama bin Laden, al-Qaida and the Taliban.[38]

The level and significance of the link between the Taliban and international terrorism has become so entrenched that, in a resolution of the Security Council issued in January 2004, States were urged to provide the Counter-Terrorism Committee[39] with the names of members of al-Qaida and the Taliban to assist the Committee in its task of identifying international terrorists.[40]

Jus In Bello – The Exercise of Self-Defence

Although the introductory chapter to this text indicated that *jus in bello* issues would not be considered in any detail, it is worth mentioning at least *some* principles about international humanitarian law, or the law of armed conflict.[41] The guiding principles are those of necessity and proportionality: what is done in the conduct of war must be necessary to

---

[35] United Nations Security Council Resolution 1333 of 19 December 2000, S/RES/1333 (2000). Paras 1 and 2 restated the demands already included in paras 1 and 2 of Resolution 1267. Para 3 added the demand to shut down terrorist training camps.

[36] United Nations Security Council Resolution 1378 of 14 November 2001, S/RES/1378 (2001).

[37] Preambular para 4.

[38] United Nations Security Council Resolution 1390 of 16 January 2002, S/RES/1390 (2002).

[39] The Security Council Counter-Terrorism Committee, established under United Nations Security Council Resolution 1373 of 28 September 2001, S/RES/1373 (2001), Appendix 2D herein, is discussed within Chapter 2, pages 26–29.

[40] United Nations Security Council Resolution 1526 of 30 January 2004, S/RES/1526 (2004), para 16.

[41] This is, by no means, meant to provide a thorough review of the law of armed conflict but simply to give an overview of the guiding principles to highlight some issues raised by the intervention in Afghanistan.

achieve proper military objectives and exercised in a proportional manner. Following the Second World War, and building upon the 1899 and 1907 Hague Conventions, duties on States and individuals were codified under the four Geneva Conventions of 1949.[42] The Conventions have since been added to by the first and second Protocols of 1977.[43] The Geneva Conventions and *Nuremberg List* of war crimes have been subsequently used as the basis for the crimes set out in the Rome Statute of the International Criminal Court.[44]

Cluster Bombs

Within the war crimes set out in the Rome Statute are those of:

• wilfully causing great suffering, or serious injury to body and health;[45]
• extensive destruction and appropriation of property not justified by military necessity;[46]
• intentionally directing attacks against the civilian population or civilian objects;[47] and
• intentionally launching an attack in the knowledge that such attack will cause incidental loss of life or injury to civilians.[48]

Potentially falling within the classification of those crimes, and a criticism of the International Committee of the Red Cross (ICRC), was the use of

---

[42] Geneva Convention for the Amelioration of the Condition of the Wounded and Sick in Armed Forces in the Field, opened for signature 12 August 1949, 75 UNTS 32 (entered into force 21 October 1950); Geneva Convention for the Amelioration of the Condition of the Wounded, Sick and Shipwrecked Members of Armed Forces at Sea, opened for signature 12 August 1949, 75 UNTS 85 (entered into force 21 October 1950); Geneva Convention Relative to the Treatment of Prisoners of War, opened for signature 12 August 1949, 75 UNTS 136 (entered into force 21 October 1950); and the Geneva Convention Relative to the Protection of Civilian Persons in Time of War, opened for signature 12 August 1949, 75 UNTS 288 (entered into force 21 October 1950).

[43] Protocol Additional to the Geneva Conventions of 12 August 1949 and Relating to the Protection of Victims of International Armed Conflicts (Protocol I), opened for signature 8 June 1977, 1125 UNTS 4 (entered into force 7 December 1978); and the Protocol Additional to the Geneva Conventions of 12 August 1949 and Relating to the Protection of Victims of Non-International Armed Conflicts (Protocol II), opened for signature 8 June 1977, 1125 UNTS 610 (entered into force 7 December 1978).

[44] Rome Statute of the International Criminal Court, opened for signature 17 July 1998, 2187 UNTS 90 (entered into force 1 July 2002).

[45] Article 8(2)(a)(iii).

[46] Article 8(2)(a)(iv).

[47] Articles 8(2)(b)(i) and 8(2)(b)(ii).

[48] Article 8(2)(b)(iv).

form of munition aimed at scattering a large number of smaller submunitions over an area (a useful means by the military to impact upon tanks, vehicles and the like travelling in groups). Cluster bombs may be delivered by surface artillery and rockets or by air. Each bomb releases a large number (usually between 150 to 200) of submunitions (called *bomblets* or *grenades*). These are delivered over a large area, each activated by an internal fuse and can, depending on the type, detonate above ground, at impact, or in delayed mode.[49]

The use of cluster bombs has been controversial in a number of conflicts, including *Operation Enduring Freedom* in Afghanistan and during *Operation Allied Force* in Kosovo. The controversy surrounds the regular failure rate of submunitions to detonate, leaving bomblets "alive" and liable to explode after the intended targets have passed. The United Kingdom Ministry of Defence estimated that there was a five percent failure rate during *Operation Allied Force*, although the UN Mine Action Coordinating Centre on Kosovo gave a much higher figure.[50] Even at five percent, the number of unexploded submunitions in Kosovo and Afghanistan is of considerable concern.

Following the death of 50 people, and injury of 101, through NATO's use of cluster bombs in the Kosovo Crisis, the ICRC called for a worldwide moratorium on the use of cluster bombs.[51] Another non-governmental organization, Human Rights Watch, called for the suspension of the use of cluster bombs in Afghanistan soon after the commencement of *Operation Enduring Freedom* until effective measures were put in place to lessen their impact upon civilian populations.[52] Both Human Rights Watch and the ICRC have raised concern over the use of cluster bombs near populated areas, and concerning the fact that unexploded cluster bombs (bright yellow

---

[49] See WordiQ.com Encyclopedia, *Cluster Bomb*, URL <http://www.wordiq.com/definition/cluster_bomb> at 9 August 2004.

[50] Norton-Taylor, R., 'Cluster Bombs: the Hidden Toll', *The Guardian International*, United Kingdom, 8 August 2000, URL <http://www.guardian.co.uk/international/story/0,,351742,00.html>.

[51] The Acronym Institute for Disarmament Diplomacy, 'ICRC Calls for Cluster Bomb Moratorium", September 2000, URL <http://www.acronym.org.uk/dd/dd50/50icrc.htm> at 9 August 2004.

[52] Human Rights Watch Backgrounder, 'Cluster Bombs in Afghanistan', October 2001, URL <http://www.hrw.org/backgrounder/arms/cluster-bck1031.htm> at 1 May 2004. Human Rights Watch recommended: that cluster bombs should be banned until the failure rate was reduced to a level of no more than 1%; that their use in or near populated areas or urban areas be prohibited; that accurate recording and mapping of cluster bomb use be kept to facilitate post-conflict clearance of unexploded submunitions; and assessment of the feasibility of including self-deactivating mechanisms.

with miniature parachutes attached) made them similar in appearance to humanitarian aid packages and especially attractive to young children.[53]

The controversial nature of the use of cluster bombs, and reference to their use in Afghanistan, was officially acknowledged within a research paper of the United Kingdom House of Commons.[54] It is yet to be seen whether the use of cluster bombs by coalition forces that are parties to the Rome Statute will be the subject of prosecution. However, given the level of knowledge of the potential impact of cluster bombs upon civilian populations, those forces may well face difficult questions to answer.

Overthrow of the Taliban Regime

A further issue arising in the conduct of *Operation Enduring Freedom* is whether the targeted overthrow of the Taliban regime fell within the elements of necessity and proportionality. Was it necessary to overthrow the regime as part of the self-defence action? This is an important issue and one with significant ramifications for the international community and, in particular, for States in which terrorist organizations operate.

As a starting point, there must be a presumption against regime change as a motive for conflict, based upon the non-intervention norm and the sovereign integrity of all States, or at the very least a restrictive approach taken to this. Article 2 reflects the following purposes of the United Nations:

> Article 2
> The Organization and its Members, in pursuit of the Purposes stated in Article 1, shall act in accordance with the following Principles.
> 1.   The Organization is based on the principle of the sovereign equality of all its Members.
> ...
> 7.   Nothing contained in the present Charter shall authorize the United Nations to intervene in matters which are essentially within the domestic jurisdiction of any state or shall require the Members to submit such matters to settlement under the present Charter; but this principle shall not prejudice the application of enforcement measures under Chapter VII.

These provisions have implications not just for the manner in which *Operation Enduring Freedom* was conducted in the targeting of the Taliban, but also in the conduct of the Security Council. As mentioned

---

[53] Above, notes 51 and 52.
[54] Above, n 2, 23–24.

earlier, the Security Council itself called for regime change under Resolution 1378 in November 2001, albeit that this was after the commencement of *Operation Enduring Freedom* and in the face of the declining stability and authority of the Taliban.[55]

Nevertheless, the question, having regard to article 2(7) of the Charter, is whether this was appropriate and within the proper role of the Security Council. The Security Council's sole mandate is over peace and security and Chapter VII resolutions may only be made where there is a determination that there has been a breach to, or there is a threat to, international peace and security. To that extent, having regard to the pattern of resolutions already discussed,[56] the Council has assessed the Taliban's link with terrorist organizations, training camps, al-Qaida and Usama bin Laden as constituting a threat to peace and security. In this very specific instance, then, the Council's call for regime change might be seen as acceptable. This must, however, be treated with extreme care in any attempt to establish precedent.

The same argument is applicable, and was relied upon, in the coalition conduct under *Operation Enduring Freedom*.[57] That is, that due to the intimate link and bilateral support between the Taliban and al-Qaida, elimination of the Taliban was necessary to eliminate the threat posed to America and its allies. On 16 October 2001, for example, the UK Foreign Secretary outlined a hierarchy of campaign objectives, listing the following as the third and fourth most immediate objectives at that time:[58]

(c) ...to ensure that Afghanistan ceases to harbour and sustain international terrorism...

(d) Assuming that Mullah Omar will not comply with the US ultimatum we require sufficient change in the leadership to ensure that Afghanistan's links to international terrorism are broken.

The Role of the United Nations Security Council

Consideration of the Security Council's role when a State or States are conducting self-defence operations, such as in *Operation Enduring Freedom* brings some very interesting issues to bear. Other than requiring

---

[55] Para 1.

[56] Resolutions 1214, 1267, 1333 and 1390 in particular, as discussed above.

[57] See the notices of the United States and United Kingdom to the President of the Security Council: above, notes 7 and 8.

[58] United Kingdom Foreign Secretary Jack Straw, *Defeating International Terrorism: Campaign Objectives*, Dep 01/1460, 16 October 2001.

notice to be given to the Security Council of action being taken in reliance upon article 51 of the Charter, self-defence largely involves unilateral conduct. In other words, it does not require any act of approval by the Security Council before self-defence measures can be taken (although the Council could in theory retrospectively declare purported self-defence measures to constitute an act of aggression). Does this mean that the United Nations is devoid of any responsibility once valid self-defence action is initiated and notified to the Council? The mandate of the UN Security Council is clear. The members of the United Nations have conferred upon the Security Council, under article 24(1) of the Charter, primary responsibility for the maintenance of international peace and security.

What, then, is the role of the Security Council when self-defence action is taken by a State or States under article 51? In the context of Security Council action in Afghanistan, this question is considered in two settings: peacekeeping operations; and the role of the Council in monitoring the exercise of self-defence action.

Peacekeeping: The Maintenance of Security in Kabul

Between September 11, 2001, and mid-2004, a total of fifteen resolutions were made by the Security Council concerning the situation in Afghanistan and including initial responses to the attacks by al-Qaida against the United States of America.[59] The issue of peace and security within Afghanistan was addressed under Security Council Resolution 1378.[60] The day prior to the making of that Resolution, the Special Representative to Afghanistan met with the Security Council and outlined three options concerning the establishment and maintenance of security in the area: an all-Afghan security force; a multinational component; or a United Nations peacekeeping presence.[61] He indicated that there appeared to be a general preference for the first option, so long as this could be established in a speedy manner. Given that the speedy establishment of an all-Aghani

---

[59] S/RES/1368 (2001), S/RES/1373 (2001), S/RES/1378 (2001), S/RES/1383 (2001), S/RES/1386 (2001), S/RES/1388 (2002), S/RES/1390 (2002), S/RES/1401 (2002), S/RES/1413 (2002), S/RES/1419 (2002), S/RES/1444 (2002), S/RES/1453 (2002), S/RES/1471 (2003), S/RES/1510 (2003), and S/RES/1536 (2004).

[60] United Nations Security Council Resolution 1378 of 14 November 2001, S/RES/1378 (2001).

[61] United Nations Press Release 'Special Representative outlines plans for political transition; thirty-eight speakers stress UN involvement, broad-based future (Statement by Special Representative) government', SC/7210, 13 November 2001.

security force was not likely, however, consideration of an international presence (through options two and three) would have to be given. Of those options, and against the background of past experiences of peacekeeping operations in Kosovo, Rwanda and East Timor, he warned that a United Nations peacekeeping presence should only be committed to with a mandate to implement an existing political settlement. Given the absence of a political administration, let alone an agreement for peace, this effectively left the Security Council with one option: the re-establishment and maintenance of security through a multinational force.

In the preamble to its next Resolution, 1386, the Security Council expressed its "recognition" that the ultimate responsibility for providing security and law and order throughout the country rested with the Afghan people themselves.[62] To that end, Annex I to the Bonn Agreement[63] called for the international community to assist the new Afghan authorities in the establishment and training of new Afghan security and armed forces. The Bonn Agreement itself recognized that some time would be required for a new Afghan security force to be fully constituted and functional and that other interim security provisions would therefore need to be put in place.[64] Annex I accordingly set out a request that the Security Council consider authorizing the deployment to Afghanistan of a United Nations mandated force to assist with the maintenance of security for Kabul and its surrounding areas. It indicated that such a force could, as appropriate, be progressively expanded to other urban centres and other areas.

The International Security Assistance Force

The response of the Security Council was to authorize a multinational security force, the International Security Assistance Force (ISAF), under the initial leadership and command of the United Kingdom.[65] ISAF was

---

[62] United Nations Security Council Resolution 1386 of 20 December 2001, S/RES/1386 (2001).

[63] Agreement on Provisional Arrangements in Afghanistan Pending the Re-Establishment of Permanent Government Institutions, the "Bonn Agreement", signed at Bonn on 5 January 2001 – Appendix 3 herein.

[64] See the preamble to the Bonn Agreement and Annex I to the Agreement, ibid.

[65] United Nations Security Council Resolution 1386 of 20 December 2001, S/RES/1386 (2001), para 1. The United Kingdom led the multinational force, comprising 18 UN member States, for the first period of its deployment. Turkey took over the lead from the United Kingdom in organizing and commanding the International Security Assistance Force from 20 June 2002: as reflected in United Nations Security Council Resolution 1444 of 27 November 2002, S/RES/1444 (2002), preamble. As anticipated within resolution 1444, and proposed in a joint letter of 21 November 2002 from the Foreign Ministers of Germany and

established for an initial period of six months, with the intention of renewing this term periodically, and tasked with the role of assisting the Afghan Interim Authority in the maintenance of security in Kabul and its surrounding areas.[66]

The use of force by ISAF. In the role of maintaining peace and security, the ability to use force where necessary is a requisite element for the achievement of that mandate. To that end, ISAF was established with an accompanying authority from the Security Council to take "all necessary measures" to fulfil its functions.[67]

United Nations control over ISAF. The delegation of responsibility for maintenance of peace and security by the Security Council to ISAF, as a multinational force, is not the first of its kind. It is in fact borne out of necessity given the lack of a standing army as had been envisaged by the drafters of the United Nations Charter under article 43. It does illustrate, however, the dependence of the Security Council upon UN members to provide the finance, personnel and equipment for security operations. Resolution 1386 in fact "stresses" that the expenses of the ISAF were to be borne by the participating UN members of the multinational force and "called upon", rather than required, all UN members to contribute to a trust fund for ISAF operations, as well as the contribution of personnel, equipment and other resources.[68]

The particular wording of Resolution 1386 also illustrates the reduced level of authority that the Security Council has come to expect it can hold over such a multinational force. Paragraph 3 of the Resolution authorized

---

the Netherlands to the Secretary-General (S/2002/1296, annex), leadership of ISAF was then passed from Turkey to Germany and the Netherlands on 10 February 2004. On 11 August 2003, the North Atlantic Treaty Organization (NATO) assumed strategic command, control and coordination of ISAF: see the letter dated 2 October 2003 from the Secretary-General of the North Atlantic Treaty Organization addressed to the Secretary-General of the United Nations, set out as an Annex to the letter dated 7 October 2003 from the United Nations Secretary-General to the President of the United Nations Security Council, S/2003/970.

[66] The authority of ISAF was extended to 20 December 2002 under United Nations Security Council Resolution 1413 of 23 May 2002, S/RES/1413 (2002), para 1; it was extended for a further period of twelve months beyond 20 December 2002 under United Nations Security Council Resolution 1444 of 27 November 2002, S/RES/1444 (2002), para 1; and for a further period of twelve months under Resolution 151 of 13 October 2003, para 3.

[67] See Resolution 1386, above n 62, para 3; Resolution 1413 of 23 May 2002, S/RES/1413 (2002), para 2; Resolution 1444, above n 65, para 2; and Resolution 1510 of 13 October 2003, S/RES/1510 (2003), para 4.

[68] United Nations Security Council Resolution 1386 of 20 December 2001, S/RES/1386 (2001), paras 2 and 8.

members of the UN participating in ISAF to take all necessary measures to fulfil its mandate. The Resolution did not, however, identify or seek to place limits upon the mandate of ISAF other than the general authorisation set out in paragraph 1:

> ...to assist the Afghan Interim Authority in the maintenance of security in Kabul and its surrounding areas, so that the Afghan Interim Authority as well as the personnel of the United Nations can operate in a secure environment;

Again in non-mandatory language, Resolution 1386 called upon the International Security Assistance Force to work in consultation with the Afghan Interim Authority and with the UN Special Representative. The general rule concerning the status of Security Council resolutions is that decisions of the Council are, under article 25 of the Charter, binding upon members of the United Nations and, therefore, upon members participating in a UN-mandated multinational force.

The question raised by this provision, in the context of the non-mandatory language used concerning ISAF, is whether the resolutions concerned had a binding effect upon participating member States under article 25. As discussed within Chapter 2, the answer turns on the issue of whether exhortatory provisions constitute "decisions" within the meaning of article 25.[69] Applying the reasoning discussed to the Security Council "calling upon" ISAF to work with the Afghan Interim Authority, it seems clear that there is and was no legal obligation upon members participating in ISAF in that regard. The resolution simply "calls upon" ISAF to do work "in consultation with" the Interim Authority.

The language of Resolution 1386, and the absence of a precise mandate for ISAF within the resolution, means that the level of authority held by the United Nations over the multinational force is weak. As events have transpired, this does not appear to have caused problems and, as indicated earlier, such arrangements are not unprecedented in the history of UN operations. Similar exhortatory language was later employed: as in Resolution 1401, "requesting" ISAF to work in close consultation with the Secretary-General and his Special Representative;[70] Resolution 1413, "requesting" the leadership of ISAF to provide monthly reports through the

---

[69] Pages 27–28.
[70] United Nations Security Council Resolution 1401 of 28 March 2002, S/RES/1401 (2002) – Appendix 2E herein, para 6. See also United Nations Security Council Resolution 1471 of 28 March 2003, S/RES/1471 (2003), para 8.

UN Secretary-General;[71] and Resolution 1444, again "requesting" reports from ISAF, this time on a quarterly basis.[72]

Diminishing Control?

Albeit prudent from a practical perspective, does the delegation of peacekeeping functions by the Security Council to multinational forces such as ISAF signal an erosion of the Council's mandate? It certainly seems that this is the way in which such devolution is put into effect through the language employed, and this is not altogether surprising. Given that the United Nations does not have a standing army at its disposal, it has no choice but to request member States to provide miliary personnel and resources to implement the Council's decisions on peace and security. The corollary of such a request is that the contributing members naturally wish to retain control over those forces. It is difficult to envisage that UN members contributing to a multinational peacekeeping or security force would want their personnel to be under the direct and unfettered command and control of the United Nations.

For the practical reasons discussed, this is a weakness in the exercise of UN security operations that is unlikely to change. The drafters of the Charter may well have envisaged that the Council would be vulnerable to such a weakness, prompting them to provide for a UN army under article 43:

Article 43
1. All Members of the United Nations, in order to contribute to the maintenance of international peace and security, undertake to make available to the Security Council, on its call and in accordance with a special agreement or agreements, armed forces, assistance, and facilities, including rights of passage, necessary for the purpose of maintaining international peace and security.
2. Such agreement or agreements shall govern the numbers and types of forces, their degree of readiness and general location, and the nature of the facilities and assistance to be provided.
3. The agreement or agreements shall be negotiated as soon as possible on the initiative of the Security Council. They shall be concluded between the Security Council and Members or between the Security Council and groups of Members and shall be subject to ratification by the signatory states in accordance with their respective constitutional processes.

---

[71] United Nations Security Council Resolution 1413 of 23 May 2002, S/RES/1413 (2002), para 4.
[72] Resolution 1444, above, n 65, para 4.

Although article 43 was adopted by the drafters by 36 to 0 votes, the concept of a permanent international army as one that is superior to national armed forces has not been popular. Participating governments at the Dumbarton Oakes Conference favoured the idea of putting national contingents at the disposal of an international command.[73] This is reflected within the structure of article 43, which does not obligate members to provide military contingents to the United Nations, but merely obligates them to negotiate agreements. As a necessary pre-requisite for such agreement, the Military Staff Committee (a body established under article 47 of the Charter to advise the Security Council on military requirements and strategic decisions) was instructed to consider article 43.[74] The Committee's report[75] contained 41 articles, of which only 25 were accepted by all members of the Committee. There was disagreement on a considerable number of important issues, such as levels of contributions by members and the location of such an army. The result was that agreements under article 43 could not, at that time, be concluded.

Reconsideration of article 43 has been prompted by both the General Assembly[76] and UN Secretary-General[77] since then, but nothing has come of this. The result is that the weakness identified continues to be felt by the Security Council, as is evident through the language of the resolutions concerning the International Security Assistance Force in Afghanistan.

The International Conflict Outside Kabul

A fact recognized by the UN Secretary-General at a relatively early stage in the Afghan intervention, and reported to the Security Council, was the

---

[73] For a discussion of the historical origins of article 43, see Simma B (ed), *The Charter of the United Nations. A Commentary*, (1995) Oxford University Press, 636–638.

[74] United Nations Security Council Resolution 1 of 25 January 1946, S/RES/1 (1946).

[75] Report of the United Nations Military Staff Committee, *General Principles Governing the Organization of the Armed Forces Made Available to the Security Council by Members Nations of the United Nations*, 30 April 1947, *United Nations Yearbook* (1946–7), 424.

[76] See United Nations General Assembly Resolution 25/2734, *Declaration on the Strengthening of International Security*, 16 December 1970, in which the General Assembly recommended that "the Security Council take steps to facilitate the conclusion of agreements envisaged in Article 43 of the Charter in order to fully develop its capacity for enforcement action as provided for under Chapter VII of the Charter;" (para 9).

[77] United Nations Secretary-General Boutros-Ghali, *An Agenda for Peace*, 1992, S/24111, in which the Secretary-General recommended that the Security Council initiate article 43 negotiations (para 43).

volatile situation in areas outside Kabul.[78] Juxtaposed to the progress made by the UN in assisting the establishment of the Interim Authority and bringing a level of security to Kabul through ISAF, the situation across the rest of Afghanistan remained unstable and unpredictable. Even by the end of March 2002, pockets of Taliban and al-Qaida resistance remained; factional clashes were erupting between rival political and military actors; and banditry continued, this having developed under the war economy of the past two decades in Afghanistan. In his report to the General Assembly and Security Council of 28 March 2002, the Secretary-General called for urgent action to bridge the gap between the insecure situation that was then presented and the eventual deployment of an effective security force.[79] As summarized by the Secretary-General:[80]

> At present, the Force [ISAF] remains limited to Kabul, while the main threats to the Interim Administration emanate from the provinces. There is a continuing danger that existing security structures, both Afghan and international, will not adequately address the security threats that are currently discernible and that are likely to increase as the convening of the emergency *loya jirga* approaches. I hope that the Security Council will consider these factors and support the wish of the Afghan people for the expansion of the Force.

Expansion of the ISAF Role in Afghanistan

In the Security Council resolution that followed the Secretary-General's call for expansion of ISAF, Resolution 1401, no mention was made of such expansion. ISAF was simply requested to work in close consultation with the Secretary-General and his Special Representative.[81]

Security was again identified by the Secretary-General as the most serious challenge facing the peace process in Afghanistan, in his report to the General Assembly and Security Council in March 2003.[82] However, it was not until late 2003, following the assumption of strategic command and control of ISAF by the North Atlantic Treaty Organisation (NATO), that any serious discussion was entered into concerning a longer-term and

---

[78] United Nations Secretary-General, *Report on the Situation in Afghanistan and its Implications for International Security*, 6 December 2001, A/56/681, S/2001/1157, Part III.
[79] United Nations Secretary-General, *Report on the Situation in Afghanistan and its Implications for International Security*, 18 March 2002, A/56/875, S/2002/278, para 53.
[80] Ibid, para 59.
[81] Above, n 70, para 6.
[82] Above, n 79, Part IIC.

expanded role for ISAF.[83] On 1 October 2003, the North Atlantic Council agreed upon a strategy for NATO in its ISAF role in Afghanistan and produced this to the UN Secretary-General.[84] The proactive action of NATO saw the Afghan Minister for Foreign Affairs request the assistance of ISAF outside Kabul[85] and the Security Council respond under Resolution 1510.[86] Resolution 1510 authorized:[87]

> ...expansion of the mandate of the International Security Assistance Force to allow it, as resources permit, to support the Afghan Transitional Authority and its successors in the maintenance of security in areas of Afghanistan outside of Kabul and its environs, so that the Afghan Authorities as well as the personnel of the United Nations and other international civilian personnel engaged, in particular, in reconstruction and humanitarian efforts, can operate in a secure environment, and to provide security assistance for the performance of other tasks in support of the Bonn Agreement;

Even still, what should be noted about the Resolution is that the latter authorization is restricted to the issue of political and economic reconstruction. The Security Council made no mention whatsoever of the continuing international conflict outside Kabul.

Due Deference or Neglect?

The United Nations role in Kabul, aimed at the secure political and economic reconstruction of the State, seems relatively uncontroversial. Clearly those are aims that go to the first-stated principle of the United

---

[83] International peacekeepers, in the form of ISAF, numbered approximately 5,500 personnel at time, although the United Nations stated that at least double that number would be needed to guarantee safe and transparent elections: United Nations Foundation, 'NATO to Discuss Afghan Security Expansion on Friday', *UN Wire*, <http://www.unwire.org/UNWire>, 5 February 2004.

[84] Letter dated 2 October 2003 from the Secretary-General of the North Atlantic Treaty Organization addressed to the Secretary-General of the United Nations, set out as an Annex to the letter dated 7 October 2003 from the United Nations Secretary-General to the President of the United Nations Security Council, S/2003/970 – Appendix 4 herein.

[85] Letter dated 10 October 2003 from the Minister for Foreign Affairs of Afghanistan to the United Nations Secretary-General, annexed to the letter dated 13 October 2003 from the United Nations Secretary-General to the President of the United Nations Security Council, S/2003/986. The Minister identified the instability outside Kabul as an impediment to the reconstruction and stability of Afghanistan and requested the Security Council to expand the mandate of ISAF in accordance with the NATO proposals.

[86] United Nations Security Council Resolution 1510 of 13 October 2003, S/RES/1510 (2003).

[87] Ibid, para 1.

Nations Charter, to maintain peace and security. The only issue of debate, it seems, is whether this is a role that should be undertaken by the Security Council.[88]

What is less clear is the medium- to long-term role of the United Nations, through the Security Council, when faced with a continuing armed conflict that began as self-defence action. Two principal issues arise. First, is there a time limitation upon the exercise of self-defence under article 51 of the United Nations Charter? Next, and linked with the first, what is the role of the UN Security Council where self-defence action is taken? In other words, does the Security Council have a duty to monitor the exercise of self-defence and itself take measures under Chapter VII of the Charter?

These questions are important for all actors. From a UN perspective, they raise issues concerning the interpretation of article 51 of the Charter and the role of the Security Council in maintaining peace and security. From the perspective of those involved in self-defence action, the questions bear upon the lawfulness or otherwise of continuing miliary operations and, consequently, on State responsibility issues for contributing forces.

Careful consideration of the wording of article 51, and the concept and nature of self-defence, needs to be given:

> Nothing in the present Charter shall impair the inherent right of individual or collective self-defence if an armed attack occurs against a Member of the United Nations, *until* the Security Council has taken measures necessary to maintain international peace and security. Measures taken by Members in the exercise of this right of self-defence shall be immediately reported to the Security Council and shall not in any way affect the authority and *responsibility of the Security Council* under the present Charter to take at any time such action as it deems necessary in order to maintain or restore international peace and security. [emphasis added]

Is There a Time Limit on the Exercise of Article 51 Self-Defence?

The wording of article 51, permitting self-defence measures to be taken "*until* the Security Council has taken measures necessary to maintain international peace and security", is not overly helpful. This does not say whether there is a time limitation upon the exercise of article 51. Equally, there are no other time limitations expressed or implied within the provision.

---

[88] The question of political and economic reconstruction in Afghanistan is addressed in Chapter 4.

That being the case, this enquiry requires consideration of the nature of self-defence. Kelsen has described self-defence as a remedy of self-help and, subsequently, the International Law Commission has extended this to the idea of "armed self-help".[89] What, then, is the *purpose* of such self-help? Put simply, self-defence is an exercise of miliary self-help in response to an armed attack in order to prevent further attacks against the victim State.

This position is reflected within the notices of article 51 action lodged with the United Nations. The US Ambassador's notice referred to the need to take self-defence action due to "the ongoing threat to the United States and its nationals".[90] Likewise, Stewart Eldon for the United Kingdom wrote of the need to take measures "to avert the continuing threat of attacks".[91] It is also consistent with what the International Court of Justice had to say about the exercise of self-defence in the *Nicaragua* case:[92]

...the reaction of the United States in the context of what it regarded as self-defence was continued long after the period in which any presumed attacks by Nicaragua [on El Salvador] could reasonably be contemplated.

...[US measures] were only taken, and began to produce their effects, several months after the major offensive of the armed opposition against the Government of El Salvador had been completely repulsed and the actions of the opposition considerably reduced in consequence. Thus it was possible to eliminate the main danger of the Salvadorian Government without the United States embarking on activities in and against Nicaragua. Accordingly, it cannot be held that these activities were undertaken in the light of necessity.

Clearly, then, the right to exercise self-defence is limited: not just "until the Security Council has taken measures" (according to the wording of article 51); but also only for as long as the exercise of armed self-help is *necessary* to prevent further attacks against the victim State.

Applying this to the intervention in Afghanistan in areas outside Kabul, in respect of which coalition forces purport to be continuing to act under article 51, there are some serious concerns about the legitimacy of such action. Rephrasing the conclusion made within the preceding paragraph: is the continued military action in Afghanistan necessary to prevent further attacks against the United States and its nationals/allies? The author doubts that the answer can be in the affirmative, given that the Taliban is no longer in power (the Taliban, as discussed, having been identified as the means by

---

[89] Kelsen, H., *The Law of the United Nations* (1950), 914.
[90] Above, n 7.
[91] Above, n 8.
[92] Above, n 1, 122–123.

which al-Qaida was able to operate) and that it is highly questionable whether Afghanistan remains (even without Taliban support) a base of al-Qaida operations. That being so, it is difficult to see how the continued international conflict in Afghanistan could be necessary to avert threats against the US and, thus, how it could be lawful.

The only potential contention is to argue that the forces involved in the continuing international conflict are there with the consent of the Afghan State. There are two problems with such an argument, however. The first is that coalition forces purport to be involved in the conflict under the authority of article 51, rather than at the behest of Afghan authorities. The second problem has wider implications and requires, it is the view of the author, a presumption against accepting such an argument. Care should be taken with such a position where there has been regime change, as in the case of Afghanistan. If such an argument is readily accepted, there is a danger that States will consider themselves free to intervene in the territory of another State, perhaps on dubious political or economic grounds, and then seek to achieve *ex post facto* validation of their conduct by effecting regime change and implementing a regime that is sympathetic to the intervening State and willing to "consent" to the continued presence of that State.

Does the Security Council have a Duty to Monitor?

The wording of article 51 also appears to imply, based on the time limitation in the wording, and also upon the reference within article 51 of the continued responsibility of the Council to take action necessary to maintain or restore peace and security, that the Security Council must be proactive in taking collective security measures. There are three particular aspects of the provision's wording that are relevant in that regard: first, the provision permits self-defence action "until the Security Council has taken measures"; self-defence action "shall not in any way affect the authority" of the Security Council; and such action "shall not in any way affect the ...responsibility of the Security Council under the present Charter to take at any time such action as it deems necessary in order to maintain and restore peace and security".

Together with the article 24 mandate of the Security Council, those parts of article 51 mentioned raise questions that all point, in the author's view, to a duty on the part of the Security Council to monitor the conduct of self-defence action. If the right of self-defence remains "until the Security Council has taken measures", how does the Security Council determine *when* it should take such measures? If the *authority* of the

Security Council "shall not in any way" be affected by self-defence action, how should the Security Council go about exercising its authority and/or determine *when* to exercise that authority? If article 51 action does not avert the Council's *responsibility* under the Charter, how is it to decide what action is necessary to maintain peace and security? It seems obvious that the only way is by monitoring the self-defence measures taken. Not only that, but because article 51 talks of the Council's *responsibility* under the Charter, it seems that this is a duty upon the Security Council, rather than a merely permissive authority.

Indeed, to otherwise approach the issue would be to allow a State(s) to unilaterally and finally determine the legality of its own action in self-defence, a notion that must be, and has been, rejected.[93] As stated by the International Military Tribunal at Nuremberg:[94]

> It was further argued that Germany alone could decide, in accordance with the reservations made by many of the Signatory Powers at the time of the conclusion of the Kellog-Briand Pact, whether preventive action was a necessity, and that in making her decision her judgment was conclusive. But whether action taken under the claim of self-defence was in fact aggressive or defensive must ultimately be subject to investigation and adjudication in international law is ever to be enforced.

Practice of the Security Council. An argument against such a reading of article 51 might be based upon the practice of the Security Council when States have undertaken self-defence measures. Applying article 31(3)(b) of the Vienna Convention on the Law of Treaties, one might argue that a prior lack of monitoring self-defence action amounts to a practice in the application of article 51 which establishes an agreement on the interpretation of the provision:[95]

SECTION 3: INTERPRETATION OF TREATIES
Article 31 General Rules of Interpretation
3. There shall be taken into account, together with the context:
b. Any subsequent practice in the application of the treaty which establishes the agreement of the parties regarding its interpretation;

---

[93] A notion which has been rejected by several commentators including Bowett, D.W., *Self-Defence in International Law* (1958), 263; and Dinstein, Y., *War, Aggression and Self-Defence* (2nd ed. 1994), 203–204.
[94] International Military Tribunal (Nuremberg), Judgment (1946), 1 IMT 171, 208.
[95] Opened for signature 23 May 1969, 1155 UNTS 331 (entered into force 27 January 1980).

This argument fails, in the view of the author, on several grounds. First, it seems highly dubious that an organization or body can, by its conduct, interpret away *obligations* upon it under its constitutive charter. As indicated already, article 51 talks of the Security Council's responsibility, thus concerning itself with a duty rather than a permissive authority.

More importantly, careful consideration has to be given to whether the practice of the Council in fact amounts to an "agreement of the parties" regarding the interpretation of article 51 of the United Nations Charter. It is, in turn, posited that there are three reasons that such an agreement does not exist. The first is that it is doubtful that the conduct of the Security Council, a limited membership of fifteen UN members, can have the effect of influencing the interpretation and application of Charter provisions which dictate the manner in which the Council is to conduct itself in discharge of its mandate under article 24. In other words, it is difficult to see that Security Council conduct can amount to an "agreement of the [Charter] *parties*". The second reason to cast doubt on any inferences to be drawn from the conduct of the Council is that most instances in which self-defence action has been taken have involved multinational forces. Those forces have included contributions from permanent members of the Security Council and, accordingly, those permanent members have had a vested interest in avoiding any adverse comment about the conduct of operations by the Council. The power of veto under article 27(3) of the Charter has guaranteed that any move to monitor self-defence conduct can be avoided, thus evading the possibility of adverse comments or findings being made. If that is indeed the reason behind the lack of Security Council monitoring, then this cannot be taken to be evidence of "agreement" on the interpretation of article 51.[96]

The final issue is that the Security Council has not in fact been consistent and *has* shown a willingness to consider and make comments upon the conduct of self-defence action. In January 1980, the Security Council met to consider developments in Afghanistan. The Permanent Representative of Afghanistan advised the Council that, in order to remove threats to its independence, sovereignty and territorial integrity posed by continued armed attacks and interventions from abroad, Afghanistan had been compelled to invoke article 51 by requesting assistance from the

---

[96] This is illustrated by the Security Council's consideration of the situation in Afghanistan in 1980, discussed in the following paragraphs, where the Soviet Union prevented adoption of a resolution pertaining to military deployments which were said to be part of the USSR's contribution to self-defence action.

Soviet Union based on a mutual defence treaty between the two States.[97] Soviet forces were accordingly dispatched, but 52 member States of the United Nations, by letter dated 3 January 1980, challenged whether this was indeed an exercise of self-defence under article 51.[98] Afghanistan's response was that the Security Council was prohibited from considering the question, since the forces were dispatched at Afghanistan's request and the Council was therefore prevented from considering the issue or deciding upon any measures since this would amount to a breach of the prohibition of the non-intervention norm under article 2(7) of the Charter:

> 7. Nothing contained in the present Charter shall authorize the United Nations to intervene in matters which are essentially within the domestic jurisdiction of any state or shall require the Members to submit such matters to settlement under the present Charter; but this principle shall not prejudice the application of enforcement measures under Chapter VII.

The United Nations Repertory of Practice records that, even if article 51 had been correctly invoked, the Council would have had the authority to take measures deemed necessary to maintain international peace and security.[99] Ultimately, however, lack of unanimity on the part of the permanent members prevented the Security Council from adopting a draft resolution which would have called for the immediate and unconditional withdrawal of all foreign (Soviet) troops from Afghanistan.[100]

Conclusion

The intervention in Afghanistan under *Operation Enduring Freedom* raises important and difficult questions concerning the interpretation and application of article 51 of the UN Charter, the codified right of inherent and collective self-defence.

On the question of the legitimacy of the self-defence action, a *jus ad bellum* issue, it has been made clear through the International Court of Justice that a party seeking to take such action must give immediate notice of the same to the UN Secretary-General. Apart from this procedural but

---

[97] The Afghan-Soviet Treaty of Friendship, Good Neighbourliness and Co-operation of 5 December 1978.

[98] S/13724/Add.1 and 2.

[99] United Nations, *Repertory of Practice of United Nations Organs Supplement No 6*, Volume III (1979-1984) Article 51, para 27.

[100] Ibid, para 28. The draft resolution, document S/13729, received 13 votes in favour, 2 against (with application of article 27(3) of the Charter preventing adoption).

nevertheless important step, the action must be in response to an "armed attack" which is attributable to the State against which action is being taken. In the context of *Operation Enduring Freedom*, there seems little doubt that September 11 was an "armed attack" and one that was part of an ongoing jihad action brought by al-Qaida against America and its allies. What is less certain is whether that action was properly attributed to the Afghan State, although the argument employed by coalition forces and apparently endorsed by the Security Council has been that, but for the intimate link and support structures between the Taliban regime and al-Qaida, the September 11 attacks could not have been perpetrated. It has been argued that although such an argument might hold weight, it should be very carefully assessed based on evidence and on a strictly case-by-case basis.

Turning to *jus in bello*, and whether the conduct of the intervention has been proper, two matters illustrating the type of issues involved in the law of war have been explored. The use of cluster bombs raises concerns about their impact upon the civilian population and whether such an impact is, in all the circumstances, proportional. The overthrow of the Taliban regime, rather than concerning proportionality, is linked with the question of necessity. Again dependent on evidence of the link between the Taliban and al-Qaida, it seems plausible that the removal of the Taliban was necessary for the removal of the terrorist threats against the United States.

Linked with this is the question of the Security Council's role when intervention occurs within a State in reliance upon article 51. Peacekeeping operations, through the delegation of a peacekeeping mandate to a multinational force (the International Security Assistance Force), were conducted at an early stage within Kabul and immediately surrounding areas with a view to supporting the establishment of a democratic government in Afghanistan. Such delegation of authority comes with a reduced level of UN governing influence, although the absence of article 43 agreements necessitates this. The Security Council also has a positive duty to monitor the conduct of self-defence action to ascertain whether the action remains justified under article 51 and the notions of necessity and proportionality, something it has seemingly failed to do concerning the conduct of *Operation Enduring Freedom*.

Chapter 4

Political and Economic Reconstruction in Afghanistan

Introduction

As seen through the foregoing chapter, self-defence involves measures taken by one or more States in the defence of self or their international neighbours. Consideration was given, in that chapter, to the Security Council's role in maintaining peace and security, through the International Security Assistance Force in Afghanistan. Criticism was made of the lack of scrutiny in the continued exercise of self-defence action under *Operation Enduring Freedom*.

This chapter considers what has become an expanded role of the United Nations, generally post-conflict, in the political and economic reconstruction of war-torn regions. This is an issue of relevance to the interventions in both Afghanistan and Iraq. This text only considers the UN post-conflict role in Afghanistan, to avoid repetition of common issues and since the situation in Iraq at the time of writing this text is far from resolved.

Political Reconstruction

At a meeting of the Security Council on 13 November 2003, by which time *Operation Enduring Freedom* had just entered its second month, Secretary-General Kofi Annan opened by calling for a sustained engagement of the Security Council to ensure that Afghanistan achieved lasting peace.[1] The terrorist attacks of September 11 and the consequent military action in Afghanistan, he said, created an environment presenting daunting challenges to the international community, as well as new opportunities. First and foremost, he emphasized the need for the United Nations to do everything possible to help meet the humanitarian needs of the Afghan

---

[1] United Nations Press Release, "Secretary-General says sustained engagement of Security Council needed to get Afghanistan on path to lasting peace", SG/SM/8031, AFG/164, SC/7211, 13 November 2001.

people, who had been suffering from decades of man-made and natural disasters. Next, he called upon focus to be placed upon the challenge of a post-Taliban period to avoid a political and security vacuum.

Just days before the commencement of *Operation Enduring Freedom*, the UN Secretary-General reappointed Mr Lakhdar Brahimi as Special Representative to Afghanistan to oversee the organization's humanitarian work and political rehabilitation in the region.[2]   The humanitarian assistance coordinated by the United Nations was significant, despite being faced with the usual hurdles in delivering assistance to a war-torn location and the desperation of those in need of aid.   For the purposes of this chapter, however, discussion will be limited to the United Nations' role in the political reconstruction of Afghanistan.   As emphasized by the Secretary-General in his address to the Security Council, the political stability of Afghanistan was seen as an essential element in ensuring that the State would be in a continuing position to carry out its international obligations and not pose a threat to its neighbours.[3]

Security Council Resolution 1378

Under the chairmanship of the UN Secretary-General, a meeting of representatives of the six nations neighbouring Afghanistan (China, Iran, Pakistan, Tajikistan, Turkmenistan and Uzbekistan) as well as the United States and Russian Federation was held on 12 November 2003.   The representatives (collectively known as the "Six plus Two" Group), through a joint declaration, pledged their support to efforts of the Afghan people to find a political solution to the Afghan crisis, and agreed that there should be the establishment of a "broad-based, multi-ethnic, politically balanced, freely chosen Afghan administration representative of their aspirations and at peace with its neighbours".[4]

By the time of the Security Council's meeting on 13 November 2001, Special Representative Brahimi had returned from Pakistan, Iran and Saudi Arabia and reported that there was a real opportunity to create a fully

---

[2] United Nations Foundation, "Annan to Reappoint Special Representative; More", *UN Wire*, <http://www.unwire.org/UNWire>, 4 October 2001.
[3] United Nations Press Release "Special Representative outlines plans for political transition; thirty-eight speakers stress UN involvement, broad-based future government", SC/7210, 13 November 2001. For a useful appraisal of early humanitarian relief efforts in Afghanistan under the coordination of the United Nations, see the Secretary-General's *Report on the Situation in Afghanistan and its Implications for International Security*, 18 March 2002, A/56/875, S/2002/278.
[4] Declaration on the Situation in Afghanistan by the Foreign Ministers and other Senior Representatives of the Six plus Two, 12 November 2001.

representative government in Afghanistan. Based on discussions with representatives from those States and with Afghans, including women and children, Mr Brahimi moved to convene a meeting with representatives of the Northern Alliance and other groups, in order to ensure fair representation, and work towards a long-term framework for political representation.[5] He reported that Afghans were united in the belief that only such a government could free the country from the grips of international terrorist groups.

Against that background, the Security Council issued Resolution 1378 in which it expressed support for the establishment by the Afghan people of a transitional administration leading to the formation of a government, both of which:[6]

- should be broad-based, multi-ethnic and fully representative of all the Afghan people and committed to peace with Afghanistan's neighbours,
- should respect the human rights of all Afghan people, regardless of gender, ethnicity or religion,
- should respect Afghanistan's international obligations, including by cooperating fully in international efforts to combat terrorism and illicit drug trafficking within and from Afghanistan, and
- should facilitate the urgent delivery of humanitarian assistance and the orderly return of refugees and internally displaced persons, when the situation permits;

As well as expressing a commitment on the part of the United Nations to playing a central role in the establishment of such administrations, the Council called upon members of the UN to lend their support, provide humanitarian assistance and long-term assistance for the social and economic reconstruction of Afghanistan.[7]

The Bonn Agreement

Following Resolution 1378, lengthy negotiations were conducted between concerned parties with the assistance of the UN Special Representative.

---

[5] United Nations Press Release "Special Representative outlines plans for political transition; thirty-eight speakers stress UN involvement, broad-based future government (Statement by Special Representative)", SC/7210, 13 November 2001.

[6] United Nations Security Council Resolution 1378 of 14 November 2001, S/RES/1378 (2001), para 1. See also the preamble to United Nations General Assembly Resolution 56/200A, *The Situation in Afghanistan and its Implications for International Peace and Security*, in which the General Assembly expressed the need for the formation of such a government

[7] At paras 3 and 4.

The result was the signing of the Agreement on Provisional Arrangements in Afghanistan Pending the Re-establishment of Permanent Government Institutions (the "Bonn Agreement") in December 2001, at Bonn, Germany.[8] On the day after the signing of that agreement, the Security Council adopted Resolution 1383, endorsing the agreement and calling on all Afghan groups to implement it. The Bonn Agreement set out various objectives, primarily to establish an Afghan Interim Authority (AIA) as a first step toward the setting up of a fully representative government in accordance with the principles of Islam, democracy, pluralism and social justice.[9]

The AIA consisted of an Interim Administration (the political arm of the Interim Authority), a Special Independent Commission and a Supreme Court of Afghanistan. The Interim Authority took power on 22 December 2001 as the repository of Afghan sovereignty, capable of representing Afghanistan in its external relations and occupying the seat of Afghanistan at the United Nations.[10] The Interim Administration, as detailed in Annex IV of the Agreement, was composed of the Chairman, Hamid Karzai, five Vice-Chairs and twenty-four further members. Each member took a particular portfolio, much as ministers of a government cabinet office might in a western democratic State, with detailed provisions concerning procedures and functions set out in the Bonn Agreement.[11]

The Special Independent Commission was tasked with convening an Emergency Loya Jirga (roughly translated to mean an emergency consultative meeting) within six months, to decide on an Afghan Transitional Authority (ATA).[12] The Transitional Authority would, in turn, replace the Interim Authority and undertake its mandate until the establishment of a fully representative, elected government. By convening an Emergency Loya Jirga to establish the Transitional Authority, however, the aim was to provide for a broader base of support for and input into the composition of what would in essence be the "transitional government" of

---

[8] Agreement on Provisional Arrangements in Afghanistan Pending the Re-establishment of Permanent Government Institutions, S/2001/1154, 5 December 2001: see Appendix 3 herein.

[9] See the preamble to the Bonn Agreement, ibid.

[10] See Part I of the Bonn Agreement, para 3.

[11] See Part III of the Bonn Agreement.

[12] The *loya jirga* is a forum which is centuries old and unique to Afghanistan in which, traditionally, tribal elders (Pashtuns, Tajiks, Hazaras and Uzbeks) come together to debate and settle national affairs or rally behind a particular (normally national) cause, often with reference to the Qu'ran. In Pashto, the phrase means "grand council". See BBC News Online, "Q&A: What is a loya jirga?", <http://news.bbc.co.uk/1/hi/world/south?asia/1782079.stm> at 16 March 2004.

Afghanistan.[13] The Bonn Agreement then provided for a Constitutional Loya Jirga, to be convened within eighteen months of the establishment of the Transitional Authority, for the adoption of a new constitution for Afghanistan.[14] The Special Independent Commission was established with the assistance of the United Nations and based upon lists of candidates submitted by participants in the UN Talks on Afghanistan (the "Six plus Two" Group). The United Nations also assisted with the functioning of the Commission.[15]

All branches of the Interim and Transitional Authorities were, under the Bonn Agreement, bound to act in accordance with international human rights and humanitarian treaty obligations; to cooperate with the international community's fight against terrorism, drugs and organized crime; and to maintain peaceful and friendly relations with neighbouring countries and the rest of the international community.[16]

Under Annex II to the Bonn Agreement, Special Representative Brahimi was tasked with responsibility for all aspects of the UN's work in Afghanistan and with monitoring and assisting in the implementation of the Agreement. Annex III called upon the United Nations to conduct a census and a registration of voters for the eventual general elections to be held upon the adoption of the new constitution by the Constitutional Loya Jirga.

The United Nations Special Mission to Afghanistan

Well before September 11 and the ensuing military conflict in Afghanistan, a Special Mission to Afghanistan was established under General Assembly Resolution 48/208 of 21 December 1993. The Resolution came out of the reconstruction and international assistance needs of Afghanistan coming out of the ten-year Soviet occupation between 1979 and 1989.[17] In particular, it was borne out of concern that the unstable situation in Afghanistan following the Soviet occupation posed a continuing threat to peace and security in the region. The response of the UN General Assembly was to request the Secretary-General to establish a United Nations Special Mission to Afghanistan (UNSMA). The Special Mission

---

[13] See Part I of the Bonn Agreement, paras 4 and 5.

[14] See Part I of the Bonn Agreement, para 6.

[15] See Part IV of the Bonn Agreement, para 1.

[16] See Part IV of the Bonn Agreement, paras 2 and 3.

[17] Two useful texts dealing with the history of and issues within the Soviet/Afghan war are: Bradsher, H.S., *Afghanistan and the Soviet Union*, Durham, Duke University Press, 1985; and Krivosheev, G.F., *The Lessons of the Soviet/Afghan War*, London, Greenhill Books, 1997.

was tasked with a broad range of responsibilities, from facilitating political security to mobilizing financial, technical and material assistance for the reconstruction of the State.[18]　The following discussion concerns the reactivation of the Special Mission's mandate within the post-September 11 era.　The General Assembly's role in establishing the Special Mission also warrants discussion, highlighting the dynamics between the Security Council and General Assembly in the UN's role of maintaining peace and security.

The General Assembly and the Security Council.　As discussed in Chapter 1, the first-stated principle of the United Nations is to maintain international peace and security.　This is a shared role between the General Assembly and Security Council, although the Security Council has the primary responsibility to act in this regard.[19]　The General Assembly has what might be described as a "subordinate" role in the maintenance of peace and security.　Articles 11, 12 and 14 of the Charter provide:

Article 11
1.　The General Assembly may consider the general principles of co-operation in the maintenance of international peace and security, including the principles governing disarmament and the regulation of armaments, and may make recommendations with regard to such principles to the Members or to the Security Council or to both.
2.　The General Assembly may discuss any questions relating to the maintenance of international peace and security brought before it by any Member of the United Nations, or by the Security Council, or by a state which is not a Member of the United Nations in accordance with Article 35, paragraph 2, and, except as provided in Article 12, may make recommendations with regard to any such questions to the state or states concerned or to the Security Council or to both. Any such question on which action is necessary shall be referred to the Security Council by the General Assembly either before or after discussion.
3.　The General Assembly may call the attention of the Security Council to situations which are likely to endanger international peace and security.
4.　The powers of the General Assembly set forth in this Article shall not limit the general scope of Article 10.

Article 12
1.　While the Security Council is exercising in respect of any dispute or situation the functions assigned to it in the present Charter, the General

---

[18] United General Assembly Council Resolution 48/208 of 21 December 1993, A/RES/48/208, para 4.
[19] See article 24 of the United Nations Charter.

Assembly shall not make any recommendation with regard to that dispute or situation unless the Security Council so requests.
2.   The Secretary-General, with the consent of the Security Council, shall notify the General Assembly at each session of any matters relative to the maintenance of international peace and security which are being dealt with by the Security Council and shall similarly notify the General Assembly, or the Members of the United Nations if the General Assembly is not in session, immediately the Security Council ceases to deal with such matters.

Article 14
Subject to the provisions of Article 12, the General Assembly may recommend measures for the peaceful adjustment of any situation, regardless of origin, which it deems likely to impair the general welfare or friendly relations among nations, including situations resulting from a violation of the provisions of the present Charter setting forth the Purposes and Principles of the United Nations.

The General Assembly therefore has the ability to make various recommendations to remedy situations posing a threat to international peace and security (articles 11 and 14), unless the Security Council is deliberating upon the same situation (article 12). The reality is that the General Assembly rarely makes resolutions concerning peace and security but, instead, goes about its roles under article 11 through its First Committee on Disarmament and International Security and the various programmes being administered under the First Committee. Resolutions concerning peace and security are generally made by the Security Council, by virtue of the responsibility conferred upon it under article 24 of the Charter.

General Assembly Resolution 48/208 therefore stands out as an exception to the general conduct of the United Nations. The question is *why*. The answer lies in power of veto within the decision-making process of the Security Council;   namely, that any decision of the Council (including resolutions under Chapter VII of the Charter) must be by at least nine affirmative votes, including the concurring votes of the permanent members.[20] With one of the permanent members of the Council being the USSR (now Russia), this explains why there was no hope of the Security Council making a resolution pertaining to Afghanistan, the former occupied territory of the Soviet Republic. Any resolution would have been blocked by an exercise of the veto power by the USSR.

This was borne out by the fact that only one resolution concerning Afghanistan was made from the time of the Soviet withdrawal from

---

[20] See article 27(3) of the United Nations Charter.

Afghanistan in 1989 and well after the General Assembly's resolution in 1993. Security Council Resolution 647 of 11 January 1990 did not, however, deal with the issue of security within Afghanistan or in relation to neighbouring USSR but instead concerned itself with relations between Afghanistan and Pakistan.[21] The General Assembly was therefore able to make a resolution concerning peace and security issues in Afghanistan, free from the restraints under article 12(1) of the Charter.

This reflects both well and negatively upon the functioning of the United Nations as the guardian of international security. It reflects the negative aspect of what has been termed the "abuse of the veto right",[22] where a permanent member of the Security Council (the USSR in this case) has acted to prevent the Council from undertaking its responsibilities under the Charter. This issue is considered in more detail within Chapter 8, *Security Council Reform and Accountability*. It also reflects positively upon the institution of the UN, however, illustrating that even where the Security Council is rendered ineffective by the power of veto, the General Assembly is capable and willing to act.

Reactivation and replacement of the UN Mission to Afghanistan. In response to a report of the UN Secretary-General,[23] the General Assembly adopted Resolution 56/200A in 2002 supporting the Secretary-General's recommendation for an enhanced role of the UN Special Mission to Afghanistan in helping the interim authority to implement the Bonn Agreement.[24] Due primarily to security issues pertaining to the Special Mission and the Special Representative, those offices found themselves having a very limited capacity to monitor and assist in the implementation of the Bonn Agreement throughout the country.[25] In June 2001, the Taliban seized the UNSMA office building. Although returned to the United Nations by the Afghan Interim Administration, the building was severely damaged and in need of extensive repair.

Partly against that background, and also in an effort to coordinate all elements of UN operations in Afghanistan, the Secretary-General recommended to the Security Council the establishment of a single mission,

---

[21] United Nations Security Council Resolution 647 of 11 January 1990, S/RES/647 (1990).

[22] See, for example, Simmer, B. (ed), *The Charter of the United Nations. A Commentary*, 2nd edition, Oxford University Press, 2002, 514.

[23] Report of the Secretary-General on the Situation in Afghanistan and its Implications for International Peace and Security, 6 December 2001, A/56/681, S/2001/1157, Part IV.

[24] United Nations General Assembly Resolution 56/200A of 28 February 2002, A/RES/56/200.

[25] Above, n 23, para 91.

the United Nations Assistance Mission in Afghanistan (UNAMA).[26] The Security Council responded unanimously by doing just that under Resolution 1401, establishing UNAMA for an initial period of twelve months with the intention of considering periodic extensions to its authority.[27] The Mission was established with what the Secretary-General described as two main "pillars": the first to monitor and support the implementation of the Bonn Agreement;[28] and the second to coordinate and undertake relief, recovery and reconstruction.[29]

Establishment of the Transitional Authority

As envisaged under the Bonn Agreement, an Emergency Loya Jirga was held between 11 and 19 June 2002, opened by former King Mohammed Zaher. All ethnic and religious communities were represented at the loya jirga, as well as a large number of women participating in the forum. Early on in the process of the Emergency Loya Jirga, and again as anticipated under the Bonn Agreement, votes were taken to elect a Head of State, pending full elections and the establishment of a new constitution.[30] Hamid Karzai (who had acted as Chairman of the Interim Authority) was, as a result, elected President and Head of State of Afghanistan as part of the Afghan Transitional Authority. Following further talks, a ministerial cabinet was created to form the Transitional Administration (the political arm of the ATA).[31]

---

[26] Above, n 23, Part VI.

[27] United Nations Security Council Resolution 1401 of 28 March 2002, S/RES/1401 (2002) – Appendix 2E herein. The authority of UNAMA was indeed extended in March 2003 for a further period of 12 months (under United Nations Security Council Resolution 1471 of 28 March 2003, S/RES/1471 (2003), para 1); and again in Resolution 1536 of 26 March 2004, S/RES/1536 (2004), para 1.

[28] Above, n 23, paras 104 and 105.

[29] Ibid, paras 106 to 108.

[30] President Karzai was elected to the position on 13 June 2002.

[31] The Transitional Administration was established with the following membership. President: Hamid Karzai. Vice Presidents: General Mohammad Fahim (Tajik), Karim Khalili (Hazara Shia), and Haji Abdul Qadeer (Pashtun), all of whom were warlords who had belonged to the former Northern Alliance. Special Adviser: Younis Qanooni, as adviser on Internal Security to the President and Education Minister (Tajik). Main Cabinet posts: General Mohammed Fahim, Minister of Defence, Tajik (no change) and also Vice President; Taj Mohammad Khan Wardak, Minister of Interior, Pashtun (replacing Yunus Qanooni); Abdullah Abdullah, Minister of Foreign Affairs, Tajik (no change); Ashraf Ghani, Minister of Economy and Finance, Pashtun (replacing Hedayat Arsala); Haji Mohammad Mohaqiq, Minister of Planning, Hazara Shia (no change); Masoum Stanakzai, Minister of Communications, Pashtun (replacing Abdul Rahim); Suheila Siddiq, Minister of Health, Pashtun Woman (no change); Younis Qanooni, Minister for Education, Tajik (also Special

Shortly after this process, the Security Council expressed support for the establishment of the ATA and called for all Afghan groups to cooperate with the ATA and to implement the decisions of the Emergency Loya Jirga.[32] It also called upon the Transitional Authority to strengthen central government and establish an independent Constitutional Commission for the purpose of holding full elections in June 2004.[33] Some months later, the Council expressed "recognition" of the ATA as the sole legitimate Government of Afghanistan, pending democratic elections in 2004.[34]

Through the Afghan Transitional Authority, Afghanistan held talks with neighbouring States on the status and future of relations between them, ultimately leading to the Kabul Declaration on Good-Neighbourly Relations, signed by the Transitional Administration of Afghanistan and the Governments of China, Iran, Pakistan, Tajikistan, Turkmenistan and Uzbekistan.[35]

National Elections

The aim of the Bonn Agreement of December 2001 was, through the temporary vehicles of the Interim Authority and the broader-based

---

Adviser); Mohammed Amin Farhang, Minister of Reconstruction, Pashtun (no change); Abdul Qadir, Minister of Public Works, Pashtun (also Vice President); Sayed Hussain Anwari, Minister of Agriculture, Tajik Shia (no change); Raihalla Sarabi. Minister for Womens Affairs, Hazara. Other Cabinet posts: Arif Noorzai, Minister of Frontier Areas, Pashtun (replacing Amanullah Zadran); Syed Mustafa Kasemi, Minister of Trade, Tajik Shia (no change); Mir Wais Sadeq, Minister for Civil Aviation and Tourism; Herati Tajik (son of warlord Ismael Khan); Alim Razim, Minister of Light Industry, Uzbek (replacing Mohammad Khan Noorzai); Enyatullah Naziri, Minister of Refugees, Tajik (no change); Juma Mohammad Mohammedi, Mines and Heavy Industry, Pashtun (replacing Alim Razim); Abbas Karimi, Minister of Justice, Uzbek; Sayed Makhdoom Rahin, Minister for Information and Culture, Tajik (no change); Mohammed Amin Nasiryar, Minister for Haj and Mosques, Pashtun; Mohammed Yousuf Pashtun, Minister for Urban Affairs, Pashtun; Noor Ahmed Qarqeen, Minister for Labour and Social Affairs, Turkmen; Ahmed Shakar Kargar, Minister for Water and Power, Uzbek; Yousuf Nuristani, Minister for Irrigation and Environment, Nuristani; Abdullah Wardak, Minister of Martyrs and Disabled, Pashtun; Sharif Faez, Minister of Higher Education, Tajik (no change); Syed Ali Jawed, Minister for Transport, Shia Tajik; and Hanif Atmar, Minister for Rural Development, Pashtun.
[32] United Nations Security Council Resolution 1419 of 26 June 2002, S/RES/1419 (2002), paras 1 and 5 – Appendix 2F herein.
[33] Ibid, para 4.
[34] United Nations Security Council Resolution 1453 of 24 December 2002, S/RES/1453 (2002), preamble – Appendix 2G. It did so again within the preamble to United Nations Security Council Resolution 1471 of 28 March 2003, S/RES/1471 (2003).
[35] The Kabul Declaration on Good-Neighbourly Relations, signed at Kabul on 22 December 2002, S/2002/1416, Appendix 5 herein.

Transitional Authority, to ultimately hold national elections to establish a "broad-based, multi-ethnic, politically balanced, freely chosen Afghan administration representative of their aspirations and at peace with its neighbours".[36]

At the request of President Karzai, by recommendation of the Secretary-General, and with the endorsement of the Security Council, an electoral unit independent of the Afghan Transitional Authority was established under the auspices of UNAMA.[37] According to the Secretary-General's report in March 2003, the ATA had made progress in the consolidation of government authority through various means, including the adoption of a national development budget, the successful completion of a currency reform operation, and steps taken towards public consultations and the holding of a Constitutional Loya Jirga later that year. He also reported that the Electoral Assistance Division of the Department of Political Affairs (part of the UN Secretariat) was working with UNAMA on the process for holding elections to be held in June 2004. The UNAMA electoral unit would, again at the suggestion of the Secretary-General, be headed by an internationally recognized senior expert, supported by a team in Kabul and in the provinces.[38]

Despite the work of the electoral unit, it was indicated by the Transitional Authority that elections in Afghanistan would not be held before September 2004.[39] By mid-March 2004, just 1.5 million of Afghanistan's 10 million eligible voters were registered, although a voter registration drive was planned for May 2004.[40] Notwithstanding the fact

---

[36] As expressed within the Declaration on the Situation in Afghanistan by the Foreign Ministers and other Senior Representatives of the Six plus Two, above, n 4.

[37] See the Report of the Secretary-General on the Situation in Afghanistan and its Implications for International Peace and Security, 18 March 2003, A/57/762 and S/2003/333 (which was completed and presented to coincide with the completion of UNAMA's initial mandate of one year); and United Nations Security Council Resolution 1471 of 28 March 2003, S/RES/1471 (2003), para 2. The letter from President Karzai to the United Nations Secretary-General dated 15 February 2003 is referred to within the Secretary-General's report, at para 15, in which the President requested that "UNAMA be entrusted with the mission to help prepare and organize the electoral process and to coordinate international electoral assistance".

[38] Ibid, para 66(c).

[39] Astill J, "Afghan Elections Put Back to September", *Guardian Unlimited*, 29 March 2004, URL <http://www.guardian.co.uk/afghanistan/story/0,1284,1179967,00.html> at 2 August 2004. See also United Nations Foundation, "Afghanistan's Elections Postponed Until September", *UN Wire*, 29 March 2004, URL <http://www.unwire.org/UNWire> at 5 April 2004.

[40] United Nations Foundation, "Karzai Suggests Afghan Election Delay as Late as August", *UN Wire*, URL <http://www.unwire.org/UNWire>, 18 March 2004.

that a date of 9 October 2004 has since been set for the elections,[41] considerable instability remains, particularly in outlying areas of Afghanistan.[42] The Taliban is said to be conducting daily attacks on voter registration venues, killing at least 650 people to the end of August 2004.[43] In urging the Afghan people to boycott the elections, the Taliban has claimed that the presidential candidates are representatives of the United States and United Kingdom, not of the Afghan people.[44]

Economic Reconstruction

Having considered the political reconstruction of the Afghan State, some regard should be had to the closely linked issue of economic reconstruction. A close examination of this issue is not intended, save to highlight the Conference on Reconstruction Assistance to Afghanistan, the role and function of the World Bank and International Monetary Fund, the United Nations Development Programme, and the question of UN Economic Sanctions.

International Conference on Reconstruction Assistance to Afghanistan

The International Conference on Reconstruction Assistance to Afghanistan, a ministerial-level conference, was held at Tokyo in late January 2002, with the participation of the Chairman of the Afghan Interim Authority Hamid Karzai and other representatives of the Administration. The Conference was convened for the primary goal of facilitating the international donor community, represented by 61 countries and 21 international organizations, to meet with the AIA and consider reconstruction assistance to Afghanistan.[45]

---

[41] Francis J, "Afghanistan Elections: the US Agenda", *Afgha.com*, 15 August 2004, URL <http://www.afgha.com/index.php?af=printnews&sid=45350> at 18 August 2004.

[42] Leading to the expanded role of the International Security Assistance Force, discussed in Chapter 3, 62-63.

[43] Above, n 41.

[44] Reuters, "Taliban Ally Urges Afghans to Boycott Elections", *Reuters Foundation*, 1 September 2004, URL <http://www.alertnet.ord/thenews/newsdesk/L015126.htm> at 2 September 2004. See also United Nations Foundation, 'Study Finds Political Intimidation in Afghanistan', *UN Wire*, 19 July 2004, URL <http://www.unwire.org/UNWire> at 26 July 2004; and Francis, J., above, n 41.

[45] Experts also met to discuss military demobilization, military and police training, de-mining, counter-narcotics issues and alternative development: see the Co-Chairs' Summary of Conclusions on the International Conference on Reconstruction Assistance to

Several key priority areas requiring reconstruction were identified by both the Interim Authority and the UN Secretary-General, including: the enhancement of administrative capacity; education; health and sanitation; infrastructure (roads, electricity and telecommunications in particular); reconstruction of the economic and currency systems; agriculture and rural development; and the provision of a fairer justice system.[46] In response, the Conference participants expressed their readiness to provide assistance to Afghanistan, with pledges and contributions of over US$1.8 billion for 2002 announced. With some donors making commitments of various time frames, the cumulative amount was more than US$4.5 billion, although Kofi Annan indicated in his address to the Conference that an estimated US$10 billion would be needed over the following five years to meet the challenges of reconstruction. An Implementation Group was established, to be chaired by the AIA, with vice-chairs, including representatives of the World Bank and the United Nations Development Programme.

World Bank and International Monetary Fund

During the latter stages of the Second World War, allied governments began discussing the issue of post-conflict reconstruction and the establishment of an international economic order. International economists and financial experts from those allied States met at Bretton Woods, New Hampshire, US. The Bretton Woods Conference resulted in the establishment of what are described as two of the three pillars of the Bretton Woods international economic system: the International Monetary Fund (IMF) and the International Bank for Reconstruction and Development (World Bank).[47] Each of these financial institutions was designed to play distinct roles in the post-conflict era. The IMF was created to establish and maintain international liquidity by creating foreign exchange reserves and, by allowing States to borrow from those reserves when experiencing temporary balance of payment problems, aimed at allowing the continuing functioning and international trading of member States. The World Bank, as apparent from its full name, was instead aimed

---

Afghanistan, Ministry of Foreign Affairs of Japan, <http://www.mofa.go.jp/region/middle_e/afghanistan/min0201/summary.html> at 10/03/04.

[46] Ibid. See also the Address of the Secretary-General to the International Conference on Reconstruction Assistance to Afghanistan, <http://www.un.org/News/dh/latest/afghan/sg-tokyo21.htm> at 10/03/04.

[47] The third "pillar", negotiated at about the same time in Geneva, was the General Agreement on Tariffs and Trade, opened for signature 30 October 1947, 55 UNTS 187 (entered into force 30 May 1950).

at establishing funds through which States could be assisted in post-conflict reconstruction, or in their development.

The first year of the World Bank's re-engagement in Afghanistan, after a gap of more than two decades, was the implementation of four International Development Assistance Post-Conflict grants totalling US$100 million.   The Bank also facilitated the establishment of the Afghanistan Reconstruction Trust Fund, a multi-donor fund with pledges of US$200 million within the first year.[48] The grants and Trust Fund were accompanied by a Transitional Support Strategy, the main aim of which was and continues to be the construction of national administrative capacity in Afghanistan.[49] Since January 2002, the IMF has also had considerable input at the request of the AIA, providing policy advice and technical assistance "to ensure that sound foundations for economic management and macroeconomic stability be established".[50]

United Nations Development Programme

Linked with the latter organizations, but within the framework of the UN, is the United Nations Development Programme (UNDP) which is a special programme of the UN General Assembly. It aims to assist developing States by assisting States to gain access to information and expertise. The UNDP has participated at a considerable level in post-conflict reconstruction in Afghanistan, with focus upon its Millennium Development Goals[51] (eradicating extreme poverty and hunger; achieving universal primary education; promoting gender equality and empowerment of women; reducing child mortality; improving maternal health; combating HIV/AIDS, malaria and other diseases; ensuring environmental sustainability; and developing a global partnership for development). Given the level of poverty in Afghanistan, the UNDP is playing a significant role.   It has been involved in the establishment and implementation of the Bonn process and, according to the UNDP, seeks to

---

[48] See the *Report of the World Bank on the Afghanistan Transitional Support Strategy*, 14 February 2003, i.

[49] Ibid, Part V.

[50] International Monetary Fund, *Islamic State of Afghanistan. Rebuilding a Macroeconomic Framework for Reconstruction and Growth*, 5 September 2003, para 6.

[51] The Millennium Development Goals were adopted by the United Nations Development Programme at the Millennium Summit in September 2000, see URL <http://www.undp.org/mdg> at 3 August 2004.

provide a bridge between immediate recovery mechanisms and long-term development needs.[52]

Economic Sanctions

The final point worth mentioning is the status of Security Council economic sanctions imposed against Afghanistan during Taliban rule. The Security Council, upon determining that any situation constitutes a breach of or threat to peace and security, is able to impose economic sanctions upon the State concerned with the aim of alleviating the breach or threat. Article 41 reads:

> The Security Council may decide what measures not involving the use of armed force are to be employed to give effect to its decisions, and it may call upon the Members of the United Nations to apply such measures. These may include complete or partial interruption of economic relations and of rail, sea, air, postal, telegraphic, radio, and other means of communication, and the severance of diplomatic relations.

Acting under article 41, and in response to conduct on the part of the Taliban that was considered to constitute a threat to peace and security, the Security Council issued various resolutions imposing economic sanctions against Afghanistan. Two such resolutions were made in 1999 (Resolution 1267) and 2000 (Resolution 1333), in response to the humanitarian needs of the Afghan people; the conduct of warring factions within Afghanistan; the sheltering and training by the Taliban regime of terrorists and terrorist organisations; the exploitation of Afghanistan for illicit drug operations; and to the treatment of Afghan people, particularly women, by the Taliban regime.[53]

In January 2002, Resolution 1388 saw sanctions lifted against Ariana Afghan Airlines on the basis that the airline was no longer owned, leased or operated by or on behalf of the Taliban. In particular, sanctions under paragraph 8(b) of Resolution 1333 were terminated (which had required UN members to close all offices of the airline within their territories).[54]

---

[52] United Nations Development Programme, "About the UNDP in Afghanistan", 10 May 2004, URL <http://www.mirror.undp.ord/afghanistan/undpafghanistan.html> at 2 September 2004.
[53] United Nations Security Council Resolutions 1267 of 15 October 1999, S/RES/1267 (1999), Appendix 2A herein, and 1333 of 19 December 2000, S/RES/1333 (2000).
[54] The termination of this sanction was done under paragraph 2 of Resolution 1267, ibid.

The sanctions under paragraph 4(a) and 4(b) of Resolution 1267 were also lifted, those provisions having required States to:[55]

(a) Deny permission for any aircraft to take off from or land in their territory if it is owned, leased or operated by or on behalf of the Taliban as designated by the Committee[56] established by paragraph 6 below, unless the particular flight has been approved in advance by the Committee on the grounds of humanitarian need, including religious obligation such as the performance of the Hajj;

(b) Freeze funds and other financial resources, including funds derived or generated from property owned or controlled directly or indirectly by the Taliban, or by any undertaking owned or controlled by the Taliban, as designated by the Committee established by paragraph 6 below, and ensure that neither they nor any other funds or financial resources so designated are made available, by their nationals or by any persons within their territory, to or for the benefit of the Taliban or any undertaking owned or controlled, directly or indirectly,

In contrast to Resolution 1388, which lifted certain economic sanctions against the State of Afghanistan, Resolution 1390[57] saw the Security

---

[55] The lifting of those sanctions was done under paragraph 1 of Resolution 1267, ibid.

[56] The "Committee", established under paragraph 6 of Resolution 1267 and in accordance with rule 28 of the Security Council's Rules of Procedure, was created to undertake and report on the following matters: "(a) To seek from all States further information regarding the action taken by them with a view to effectively implementing the measures imposed by paragraph 4 above; (b) To consider information brought to its attention by States concerning violations of the measures imposed by paragraph 4 above and to recommend appropriate measures in response thereto; (c) To make periodic reports to the Council on the impact, including the humanitarian implications, of the measures imposed by paragraph 4 above; (d) To make periodic reports to the Council on information submitted to it regarding alleged violations of the measures imposed by paragraph 4 above, identifying where possible persons or entities reported to be engaged in such violations; (e) To designate the aircraft and funds or other financial resources referred to in paragraph 4 above in order to facilitate the implementation of the measures imposed by that paragraph; (f) To consider requests for exemptions from the measures imposed by paragraph 4 above as provided in that paragraph, and to decide on the granting of an exemption to these measures in respect of the payment by the International Air Transport Association (IATA) to the aeronautical authority of Afghanistan on behalf of international airlines for air traffic control services;" and (g) To examine the reports submitted by States under paragraph 9 of the Resolution.

[57] The latter Resolution was made by the United Nations Security Council on the day after it had lifted economic sanctions pertaining to Ariana Afghan Airlines under Resolution 1388: see United Nations Security Council Resolution 1390 of 16 January 2002, S/RES/1390 (2002).

Council issue further economic sanctions against the Taliban and al-Qaida:

...all States shall take the following measures with respect to Usama bin Laden, members of the Al-Qaida organization and the Taliban and other individuals, groups, undertakings and entities associated with them...

(a) Freeze without delay the funds and other financial assets or economic resources of these individuals, groups, undertakings and entities, including funds derived from property owned or controlled, directly or indirectly, by them or by persons acting on their behalf or at their direction, and ensure that neither these nor any other funds, financial assets or economic resources are made available, directly or indirectly, for such persons' benefit, by their nationals or by any persons within their territory;

(b) Prevent the entry into or the transit through their territories of these individuals, provided that nothing in this paragraph shall oblige any State to deny entry into or require the departure from its territories of its own nationals and this paragraph shall not apply where entry or transit is necessary for the fulfilment of a judicial process or the Committee determines on a case by case basis only that entry or transit is justified;

(c) Prevent the direct or indirect supply, sale and transfer, to these individuals, groups, undertakings and entities from their territories or by their nationals outside their territories, or using their flag vessels or aircraft, of arms and related materiel of all types including weapons and ammunition, military vehicles and equipment, paramilitary equipment, and spare parts for the aforementioned and technical advice, assistance, or training related to military activities;

In a move that might be seen as one of the more proactive approaches of the Security Council in the implementation of economic sanctions, the Council charged the Security Council Committee Established under Resolution 1267 with various implementation and monitoring responsibilities.[58] It also called on members of the UN to report to the Committee on the steps taken to implement the new economic sanctions imposed against the Taliban and al-Qaida.[59]

---

[58] Resolution 1390, above, n 57, para 5.
[59] Such reports were to be furnished within 90 days and, thereafter, according to a timetable set by the Committee: see para 6 of Resolution 1390, above, n 57. Similar steps were taken by the Security Council, relating to the responsibilities of the Committee and duty upon States to report, under the earlier Resolution 1267 sanctions, above, n 53.

Westernization of the Middle East

With the support of and monitoring by the United Nations, the progress made towards the re-establishment of political and economic structures within Afghanistan is a remarkable feat. Even with recent doubts about the timing of nation wide elections in Afghanistan, the institution of structures to bring together disparate ethno-linguistic groups is seen by most as a positive step towards the future of a stable environment in Afghanistan and within the Middle East. What remains to be seen is whether this positive step is based upon a strong enough foundation to bring lasting stability to the region. Afghanistan has been ravaged by wars through internal conflict and external intervention for decades. It has a myriad of ethnic, linguistic and regional groupings.[60] As a result, the country and its people have survived through loyalty to tribal, regional, ethnic and warlord structures rather than any sense of national identity. The only aspect of life truly shared by all Afghans has been the Islamic religion, although different subsets do exist.

Of particular concern to future stability, and therefore peace and security, is the imposition of Western values upon Afghanistan through the political and economic structures being established, including the democratization of Afghanistan. It is interesting to note in this regard that, at least in theory, international law is neutral on the question of the political structures of a nation. As far as statehood is concerned a "State" must, to be an international person, possess a permanent population, a defined territory, a government, and the capacity to enter into relations with other States.[61] The Montevideo Convention does not purport to specify the type of government required for the establishment or continuance of statehood, whether democratic, religious, communist, or other. Indeed, the UN General Assembly has declared that every State has "an inalienable right to choose its political, economic, social and cultural systems, without interference in any form by another State".[62] The United Nations Charter itself expresses itself to be based upon the respect for the principle of equal

---

[60] Ethno-linguistic groups in Afghanistan include Baloch, Aimak, Hazara, Pashtun (Durrani and Ghilzai), Qizilbash, Tajik, Kirghiz, Turkmen, Uzbek, Brahui and Nuristani.

[61] Montevideo Convention on the Rights and Duties of States, 1933, art 1.

[62] United Nations General Assembly Resolution 2625 (XXV), Declaration on Principles of International Law Concerning Friendly Relations and Cooperation Among States in Accordance with the Charter of the United Nations, adopted 24 October 1970 at the 1883rd plenary meeting during the General Assembly's 25th Session, set out within the text of the Declaration under the title *The principle concerning the duty not to intervene in matters within the domestic jurisdiction of any State, in accordance with the Charter.*

rights and self-determination of peoples[63] and the principle of the sovereign equality of all its members.[64]

The question is whether there is an emerging norm requiring a democratic government. This might be taken to be the case from certain provisions of the "International Bill of Rights"[65] and from the conduct of the United Nations in post-conflict reconstruction operations. The International Covenant on Civil and Political Rights (ICCPR) for example, one of the three instruments comprising the International Bill of Rights, provides as follows through article 25(b):

> Every citizen shall have the right and the opportunity, without any of the distinctions mentioned in article 2 and without unreasonable restrictions:
> (b) To vote and to be elected at genuine periodic elections which shall be by universal and equal suffrage and shall be held by secret ballot, guaranteeing the free expression of the will of the electors;

Article 4(2) of the ICCPR does not permit derogation from this right, one that clearly envisages a democratic government. Added to this is the conduct of reconstruction operations. As can be seen through the Bonn Agreement and the endorsement of it by the UN Security Council and the UN Special Representative to Afghanistan, it has been assumed from the outset that the only path forward in the political reconstruction of Afghanistan is through democratic elections. That may well be the correct approach for Afghanistan, a nation comprised of various groups, all of which need to be part of, or at least represented within, any workable central administration. What some critics appear to be concerned with, however, is the alleged dismissal of a monarch or religious leadership of Afghanistan. The former King of Afghanistan, Mohammed Zaher Shah, expressed that he had no intention of restoring the monarchy, nor to stand as a candidate for any position in the Emergency Loya Jirga, although it is said that this was a decision of the US Special Envoy to Afghanistan, Zalmay Khalilzad.[66]

---

[63] Article 1(1).

[64] Article 2(1).

[65] The International Bill of Rights comprises the Universal Declaration of Human Rights, 1948; the International Covenant on Civil and Political Rights 1966; and the International Covenant on Economic, Social and Cultural Rights 1966.

[66] See, for example, Ingalls J., "The United States and the Afghan Loya Jirga. A Victory for the Puppet Masters", *Z Magazine*, <http://www.zmag.org/Zmag/articles/sep02ingalls.html> at 17/03/04.

Should the Security Council be Concerned with Political and Economic Reconstruction?

Evident through this chapter is the fact that, although there have been a considerable number of participants in post-conflict reconstruction issues in Afghanistan, from the Secretary-General to the World Bank and UNDP, the lead role has been taken by the Security Council. The question is whether this is appropriate.

In an early examination of the United Nations system, Vallat discussed the separation of functions under the Charter of the United Nations and the idea that the Security Council and General Assembly usually operate independently of one another, in different modes and in different areas.[67] Koskenniemi more recently challenged whether that separation is being maintained under the modern functioning of the UN.[68] He described the Charter as dealing with international order on the one hand and international justice on the other, using the two main organs of the United Nations so that both types of problems can be simultaneously addressed and to ensure that neither issue is overtaken by or collapsed into the other:[69]

> The competence, composition and procedures of each organ is justifiable only as a separation of powers arrangement which seeks to provide optimal efficiency in policing the world as well as a forum for seeking agreement on various economic, social and humanitarian policies, while trying to keep both in check so as to avoid the dangers inherent in establishing a full precedence of one over the other.

Although both the General Assembly and Security Council are concerned with international peace and security,[70] they each have a different authority, a distinct set of powers and responsibilities and dramatically contrasting membership. This combination of factors means that each organ has and should maintain discrete roles: the Security Council functions to police the world and maintain international order, whereas the General Assembly serves to promote international justice through broadly represented debates and action on economic, social and humanitarian issues. To achieve the overall objectives of the United Nations, one should not usurp the other.

---

[67] Vallat, "The General Assembly and Security Council of the United Nations", (1952) XXIV *British Yearbook of International Law* 78.

[68] Koskenniemi M, "The Police in the Temple. Order, Justice and the UN: A Dialectical View", (1995) 6 *European Journal of International Law* 1.

[69] Ibid, 13–14.

[70] As a result of the principles and purposes of the United Nations and the more specific directions upon each organ under articles 11 and 24 of the Charter.

That position holds considerable merit. The political and economic reconstruction of Afghanistan has been characterized by the Security Council, and to a lesser extent by the Secretary-General, as an issue vital to the maintenance of peace and security in the region. That certainly seems to be an accurate assessment of the position. The challenge is whether the Security Council should, in the way it has in Afghanistan, direct the issue or defer to the General Assembly as the appropriate body to deal with political and economic reconstruction. Reconstruction of that type concerns economic, social and humanitarian issues, all of which are identified by Koskenniemi as matters of international justice, this falling within the proper role of the General Assembly. By having such issues dealt with by the General Assembly, a broader base of input can be guaranteed, as opposed to directions made or plans approved by a Council of 15 members (and in circumstances where, due to the power of veto, those directions or approvals must meet with the consent of an even more limited membership of the five permanent members). To the author's mind, therefore, the Security Council should have limited its post-conflict involvement to peacekeeping and security issues within Afghanistan, as well as the policing of the international conflict in areas outside Kabul.[71]

Conclusion

The post-conflict political and economic reconstruction of a State, from a medium- to long-term perspective, is a matter of considerable relevance to the maintenance of peace and security within a region. The political stability of a nation, as expressed by the UN Secretary-General, is a matter essential to the ability of a State to be in a continuing position to carry out its international obligations and not pose a threat to its neighbours. The United Nations has responded to this by taking a proactive role in addressing those issues, as well as issues involved in restoring security within the State. In Afghanistan, a Special Representative to Afghanistan was appointed to oversee the UN's humanitarian work and political rehabilitation. With the assistance of the Special Representative, the Bonn Agreement was adopted, establishing a framework for the incremental introduction of a broad-based representative government. The process was assisted by the United Nations Special Mission to Afghanistan, subsequently replaced by the United Nations Assistance Mission in

---

[71] On the latter point, see the discussion in Chapter 3 concerning the role of the Security Council under article 51 of the United Nations Charter, 66–69.

Afghanistan (UNAMA), established to monitor and support the implementation of the Bonn Agreement and coordinate relief, recovery and physical reconstruction.

As envisaged under the Bonn Agreement, an Emergency Loya Jirga was held in June 2002, resulting in the formation of the Afghan Transitional Authority (ATA) and the Transitional Administration, the ministerial cabinet and political arm of the ATA. The Transitional Authority was formally recognized by the Security Council as the sole legitimate Government of Afghanistan, pending nation wide democratic elections. To that end, UNAMA and the United Nations Electoral Assistance Division have begun a process of voter registration within Afghanistan. Due to security issues within Afghanistan, particularly in areas outside Kabul and due to warring factions and a recent resurgence in Taliban activities, that process has been marred by violent attacks and the initial election date of June 2004 postponed to October 2004.

On the economic front, the UN Secretary-General and Special Representative to Afghanistan enlisted the support of the World Bank, International Monetary Fund and United Nations Development Programme, each contributing to the establishment and application of funds for the political, social, economic and physical reconstruction of the nation. The Security Council at the same time took steps to lift non-military sanctions directed against the State of Afghanistan, but maintaining and increasing sanctions against the Taliban, al-Qaida and Usama bin Laden.

While all this has been generally positive, issues have arisen about the manner in which the United Nations has conducted itself. The first concerns the assumption, predicated by the United Nations' own human rights framework, that the political reconstruction of Afghanistan must be by way of the Western notion of democratic government. In a somewhat ironic twist, it is that human rights framework (which, in part, advocates tolerance and respect for political and religious expression) which assumes that rights and freedoms may only be enjoyed within a democratic system. The second concern relates to the interaction of, and roles adopted by, the General Assembly and Security Council in reconstruction issues, challenging whether the Security Council should take the lead role it has adopted in such matters.

Chapter 5

Pre-emptive Strikes in the War on Terror

Introduction

The tragic events of September 11, 2001 have prompted much recent action and debate on the issue of preventing and dealing with terrorism. The "War on Terror" has evidenced itself in two main ways. The first might be loosely labelled "counter-terrorism", in terms of initiating, consolidating and improving upon measures that can detect, deter and deal with terrorists and associated entities. This was the issue of consideration within Chapter 2. The second strategy forming part of the War on Terror, and that of focus in this chapter, is of more concern to inter- rather than intra-state conduct and relations: the policy of using pre-emptive strikes against States harbouring or assisting terrorists and associated entities.

The Rhetoric of Pre-Emptive Strikes in the War on Terror

To place this matter in its proper context, and thereby draw out issues to be considered, it is useful to have regard to various statements made concerning the War on Terror. Pre-emptive action was signalled by President Bush as early as 1 June 2002 when he said:[1]

> We must take the battle to the enemy, disrupt his plans, and confront the worst threats before they emerge. ... our security will require all Americans to be forward-looking and resolute, to be ready for pre-emptive action when necessary.

Referring to the President's remarks, Vice-President Cheney[2] soon after

---

[1] Remarks by United States President George W. Bush at the 2002 Graduation Exercise of the United States Military Academy, Washington, 1 June 2002.

[2] Remarks by United States Vice-President Richard Cheney to the National Association of Home Builders, Washington, 6 June 2002. Commenting on this speech, the BBC noted that it "was the latest in a series by top administration officials promoting what is emerging as a new doctrine of the Bush administration – that the US must be prepared to take pre-emptive action against new security threats": BBC News, 7 June 2002.

said this:

> Wars are not won on the defensive. We must take the battle to the enemy –
> and, where necessary, pre-empt grave threats to our country before they
> materialize.

These expressions of policy, in what has come to be known as The Bush
Doctrine on the pre-emptive use of force, were relatively shortly followed
by similar statements by the Prime Minister of Australia, John Howard:[3]

> ...it stands to reason that if you believed that somebody was going to launch
> an attack against your country, either of a conventional kind or of a terrorist
> kind, and you had a capacity to stop it and there was no alternative other than
> to use that capacity, then of course you would have to use it.

Australia's position on the War on Terror was, not surprisingly, received
well by the United States, Ari Fleischer (White House Spokesperson),
saying this:[4]

> The President did announce a new doctrine that recognises that the threats we
> face are no longer from known enemies, nations that have fleets or missiles or
> bombers that we can see come to the Unites States, nations that can be
> deterred through previous notions such as mutually assured destruction or any
> other previous defence notions. It requires a fresh approach to protect the
> country. Other nations think it through as well, and come to similar
> conclusions. Australia has been a stalwart ally of the United States in the war
> on terror.

In contrast, New Zealand's Prime Minister was more vague in her reaction
to Prime Minister Howard's remarks,[5] stating in an interview the day after

---

[3] This statement was made by Prime Minister Howard on Sunday 1 December 2002, as
reported by Catherine McGrath, "ALP, Greens Question Howard Pre-emptive Strike
Comments", *The World Today on ABC Radio*, Australia, 2 December 2002, transcript
<http://www.abs.net.au/worldtoday/s738997.htm> at 9 February 2004.
[4] John Shovelan, "Bush Backs Howard's Pre-emptive Strike Approach", *The World Today
on ABC Radio*, Australia, 3 December 2002, transcript <http://www.abs.net.au/worldtoday/
s739439.htm> at 9 February 2004.
[5] New Zealand Press Association, "NZ Supports Howard Terror Doctrine", *The Sydney
Morning Herald*, Sydney, Australia, 2 December 2002, through <http://www.smh.com.au/
articles/2002/12/02/1038712877389.html> at 9 February 2004. It should be noted that the
title of that article is misleading. Prime Minister Clark said, in interview, that she did not
believe Australia had committed to any intervention, nor to any desire to breach of

his comments:

> We don't read Mr Howard's comments as indicative of Australia wanting to
> be in breach of international law ... I haven't inferred from anything that I've
> read that Australia is about to go off and attack anybody.

It has to be recognized that the statements considered above were made,
more or less, within a year of the September 11 attacks. It should also be
borne in mind that there has been no subsequent use of force against a State
in express (or at least *sole*) reliance upon what might be termed the anti-
terror pre-emptive strike policy. The question nevertheless needs
answering: can pre-emptive strikes be used against States that harbour or
assist terrorists and associated entities? Indeed, the issue remains alive. A
substantial basis of the US justifications for intervention in Iraq in 2003,
under *Operation Iraqi Freedom*, was intervention for the purpose of self-
defence.[6] Within that, as could be seen in the address of US Secretary of
State Colin Powell to the Security Council, was reliance not just upon
threats posed by Iraq through weapons of mass destruction, but also upon
purported links between the State of Iraq and terrorist groups and facilities.[7]
President Bush had himself identified that link in his earlier address to the
United Nations General Assembly, when he singled out Iraq and said this:[8]

> In the attacks against America a year ago, we saw the destructive intentions of
> our enemies ... [Our] greatest fear is that terrorists will find a shortcut to their
> mad ambitions when an outlaw regime supplies them with the technologies to
> kill on a massive scale ... In one place – in one regime – we find all these
> dangers, in their most lethal and aggressive forms, exactly the kind of
> aggressive threat the United Nations was born to confront.

The policy of pre-emption was further confirmed within the Bush
Administration's National Security Strategy of September 2002.[9]
     What should be noted at this stage is that there appears to be a
difference between the policies of the Unites States and Australia. The US

---

international law. The statements of the Prime Minister do not appear to support a pre-
emptive strike policy in the War on Terror.
[6] The National Security Strategy of the United States, September 2002,
<http://www.whitehouse.government/nsc/nss.html> at 9 February 2004.
[7] Remarks of US Secretary of State Colin Powell to the United Nations Security Council on
5 February 2003.
[8] Remarks of United States President George W. Bush at the United Nations General
Assembly, New York, 12 September 2002, transcript <http://www.whitehouse.government/
news/releases/2002/09/20020912-1.html> at 9 February 2004.
[9] Above, n 6.

has tended to express a relatively broad and imprecise policy of "confronting threats before they emerge", "pre-empting grave threats" and "fresh approaches" to self-defence. Prime Minister Howard's statement on 1 December 2002 seems to be more limited, envisaging the pre-emptive use of force only where there is evidence of an impending terrorist attack[10] and no alternative other than the use of force is available or appropriate in response.[11]

From all this emerge the following issues to be considered: first, this paper will consider the post-1945 prohibition against the use of force between States and the potential arguments for and against, and restrictions upon, the pre-emptive use of force *per se*. Consideration will then be given to the particular context of anticipatory self-defence in the War on Terror, having regard to particular difficulties posed by such a war and the fact that terrorist conduct is generally perpetrated by non-State actors.

Self-Defence and the United Nations Charter

As discussed in Chapter 1, the international law on the use of force can be summarized as follows. The use of force between States, or threat of such, is prohibited by the United Nations Charter, except in two situations: first, where authorized by a decision of the Security Council, acting under Chapter VII of the Charter, in response to a threat to or breach of peace; second, where a State is acting by way of individual and collective self-defence, within the terms of article 51. It is the latter exception that requires further examination, in the context of pre-emptive strikes.

Article 51 of the UN Charter

The operative part of the article 51 right of individual and collective self-defence provides:

> Nothing in the present Charter shall impair the inherent right of individual or collective self-defence if an armed attack occurs against a Member of the United Nations, until the Security Council has taken measures necessary to maintain international peace and security.

---

[10] The Prime Minister referred to belief "...that somebody was going to launch an attack against your country, either of a conventional kind or of a terrorist kind", above, n 3.

[11] The Prime Minister continued "...and you had a capacity to stop it and there was no alternative other than to use that capacity, then of course you would have to use it", above, n 3.

What should be recognized at the outset is that article 51 stands as the only exception to the prohibition against the use of force whereby States can themselves, without any need to obtain prior consent or authority from the UN Security Council,[12] use force against an aggressor in defence of themselves, or a State requesting assistance.[13] It is the only instance where a State may unilaterally use force. There are questions concerning the activation and scope of article 51 that require consideration: what is meant by *inherent* self-defence; does this mean that there is a parallel customary law right to act in self-defence that might be somehow different to the right under article 51; and when is an *armed attack* deemed to have occurred?[14]

The only judgment of the International Court of Justice, in which the substance and meaning of article 51 was considered by the Court, is to be found in *Nicaragua v US*.[15] It was recognized in that decision that article 51 codified an existing "inherent" customary right of self-defence, although largely replacing that right with another, more developed, norm of customary law.[16] Significantly, however, the Court took the view that the two expressions of self-defence (inherent and codified) did not overlap exactly, while at the same time emphasising that customary law may continue to exist alongside codifications of the customary law.[17] As Shaw points out, for example, the customary rule of proportionality within *jus in bello*[18] was not set out within article 51 but has clearly continued to exist.[19] Although this fact was recognized by the Court in *Nicaragua*, no majority agreement was reached on whether the customary norm permitted a wider

---

[12] The only recourse required is that the State(s) that are to act under article 51 must give notice to the Security Council, as set out within the wording of that article and confirmed by the International Court of Justice in *Case Concerning Military and Paramilitary Activities in and Against Nicaragua (Nicaragua v United States)*, Merits Phase [1986] ICJ Reports 4, 121.

[13] Defence of another falls within the concept of "collective self-defence" within article 51, as discussed within the *Nicaragua v US*, ibid, 536 (Judge Jennings).

[14] Also attached to article 51 is the issue of whether there is a time limitation on the exercise of article 51 (i.e. linked to the last part of the first sentence of article 51 which qualifies the right by adding "until the Security Council has taken measures necessary to maintain international peace and security"). The latter is a very interesting question, but one that does not pertain to the subject of this paper – whether pre-emptive action can be taken in the War on Terror.

[15] Above, n 12.

[16] Ibid. See, in particular, the judgment of Judge Jennings, 518–536, where he discusses the view that article 51 extended the 1945 customary norms on self-defence to "collective self-defence" and, thereby, potentially replaced the former.

[17] Ibid, 176.

[18] Customary international law rules pertaining to the *conduct* of war, rather than the ability to use force (*jus ad bellum*).

[19] Shaw, M., *International Law*, 4th ed. (1997), 788–789.

authority to use force than the provisions of the United Nations Charter.[20] It is thus not surprising that two views have arisen and continue to be debated concerning the scope of self-defence.

The Opposing Views in Brief

The broad view of self-defence rests on two main arguments. The first, as advocated by Bowett for example, holds that article 51 was not intended to limit the pre-1945 customary international law right to self-defence.[21] This relies on evidence in the *travaux préparatoires* that the intention of article 51 was to reassure regional organizations (such as the Organization of American States) that the Security Council would not prejudice their arrangements for collective security, rather than being drafted for the purpose of defining the full limits of self-defence.[22] The second argument in favour of a broad approach rests on developments in customary international law since the Charter, pointing to events such as the 1962 Cuban Missile Crisis, the Six Day War of 1967 and the attack on the Osirak reactor by Israel in 1981.[23]

Adopting a restrictive view on self-defence, commentators such as Kelsen read article 51 as meaning that, for United Nations members, the right of self-defence has no other content than the one defined by article 51.[24] A further argument is that the prohibition against the use of force, enunciated in article 2(4) of the Charter, is a norm of *jus cogens*: a peremptory norm of customary international law from which no derogation is permitted.[25] If that is correct, then inconsistent pre-1945 norms were extinguished when the Charter was adopted, and subsequent inconsistent State practice cannot be seen as establishing a new customary norm unless itself a *jus cogens* norm.

Assessing those views, there is indeed evidence in the records of the San Francisco Conference on the adoption of the United Nations Charter that the term "inherent" was inserted into draft article 51 to clarify that regional security measures should be allowed to continue. It is a stretch,

---

[20] As discussed by Dixon, M. and McCorquodale, R. in *Cases and Materials on International Law* (Australian Supplement, 1991), 561.

[21] Bowett, D.W., *Self-Defence in International Law* (1958) 185.

[22] See Harris, D.J., *Cases and Materials on International Law*, 4th Ed (1991), 849-850.

[23] As discussed by Arend, A.C., in "International Law and the Preemptive Use of Military Force", *The Washington Quarterly*, 2003 Vol 26(2), 89, 93-96.

[24] Kelsen, H., *The Law of the United Nations* (1950), 914.

[25] See, for example, the judgment of Sir Ivor Jennings in *Nicaragua v US*, above n 12, 518–524; and Henkin, Pugh, Schachter and Smit, *International Law Cases and Materials*, 1980, 910.

however, to say that this was *the* purpose of the inclusion of article 51. The Charter regime was clearly intended by the drafters, against the backdrop of two world wars, to prohibit the use of force between States and be very clear about the permissible exceptions to that prohibition. What is more, Chapter VIII of the UN Charter specifically provides for the continued existence of regional arrangements for the maintenance of peace and security. Likewise, it is far from clear that post-Charter events amount to developments in, or the continuation of, anticipatory self-defence as a doctrine that has remained alive under customary international law.[26] As stated by the International Court of Justice in *Nicaragua v US*:[27]

> In order to deduce the existence of customary rules, the Court deems it sufficient that the conduct of states should, in general, be consistent with such rules, and that instances of state conduct inconsistent with a given rule *should generally have been treated as breaches of that rule not as indications of the recognition of a new rule. [emphasis added]*

Turning to an evaluation of the restrictive approach, it seems unlikely that Kelsen's approach (limiting self-defence to the words of article 51 by virtue of States' membership in the United Nations) can be correct in view of the ICJ's ruling in *Nicaragua v US* that the codified right of self-defence under the Charter does not overlap exactly with customary self-defence, and that treaty and custom can lie side by side.[28] Perhaps the most persuasive argument is the one relying upon the *jus cogens* status of the prohibition against the use of force. If article 2(4) of the Charter is indeed a reflection of a *jus cogens* prohibition, to be read in conjunction with the balance of the Charter, then any pre-1945 custom allowing for the use of force became extinguished, since *jus cogens* does not permit derogation. Adopting the same argument, any purported development of customary law since 1945 to allow for the use of force would require the unanimous acceptance of States to permit variation of the *jus cogens* prohibition.[29] Since the doctrine of

---

[26] The adverse comments of the Security Council concerning the bombing of the Osirak reactor are considered, by way of example, in the paragraphs that follow.

[27] Above, n 12.

[28] Ibid.

[29] This requirement for unanimity in the amendment of peremptory norms is taken from the definition of *jus cogens* provided in the Vienna Convention on the Law of Treaties, opened for signature 23 May 1969, 1155 UNTS 331 (entered into force 27 January 1980), article 53, which reads in part "For the purposes of the present Convention, a peremptory norm of general international law is a norm accepted and recognized by the international community of States as a whole as a norm from which no derogation is permitted and which can be modified only by a subsequent norm of general international law having the same character".

anticipatory self-defence is one of considerable controversy, it cannot be said that it has attained that level of acceptance.

It is also relevant to note, in that regard, the guidelines of the Council of Europe on the fight against terrorism:[30]

> In their fight against terrorism, States may never act in breach of peremptory norms of international law nor breach international humanitarian law, where applicable.

Actual versus Imminent Attack

If a restrictive approach is taken, one is left with the words of article 51 as the extent to which self-defence measures are permitted. One must then determine whether the words of that provision permit anticipatory self-defence. Brownlie and Henkin focus on the phrase "if an armed attack occurs" within article 51 and conclude that the ordinary meaning of the phrase precludes action which is in anticipation of future aggressive conduct on the part of another State.[31] Bowett, on the other hand, argues that no State should be expected to wait for an actual attack to occur before it can take defensive measures, particularly when the state of armaments is such that an initial attack may well destroy the State's capacity for further resistance and so jeopardize its very existence.[32] Indeed, in his dissenting judgment in the *Nicaragua Case*, Judge Schwebel noted that article 51 does not say "if, and only if, an armed attack occurs".[33]

Which begs the question, *when does an armed attack begin to "occur"*?[34] There is, again, a divergence of views. The permissive view, known as the "cumulation of events" theory of self-defence, argues that a series of attacks should be viewed as a whole, so that action taken to prevent future attacks in the series can be seen as self-defence against a continuing attack, rather than as anticipatory self-defence. This theory has been advocated by the United Kingdom, Israel, the United States and South Africa in incidents such as the 1964 British bombing of Harib Fort in the

---

[30] "Guidelines of the Committee of Ministers of the Council of Europe on Human Rights and the Fight Against Terrorism, Appendix 3 to the Report of the 53rd Meeting of the Steering Committee for Human Rights (CDDH), Strasbourg, 25–28 June 2002, part XVI.

[31] Brownlie, I., *International Law and the Use of Force by States* (1963) 275; Henkin, L., *How Nations Behave* (1979) 141–142.

[32] Above, n 21, 192.

[33] Above, n, 12, 347. The Judge was alone in expressing a view on anticipatory self-defence in the *Nicaragua Case*. Indeed, the majority specifically refused to express a view on the issue because it had not been raised: para 194.

[34] As framed by Professor Harris: above, n 22, 851.

Yemen,[35] the 1968 Israeli raid on Beirut airport,[36] the 1986 US raid on Libya,[37] and numerous cross-border raids by South Africa into neighbouring African Sates to attack ANC bases.[38] The Security Council, however, has consistently rejected the cumulation of events theory.[39]

Does a Restrictive Approach Lead to an Absurd Result?

One of the already noted criticisms of a restrictive approach to self-defence is that no State should be expected to await an initial attack before it may take defensive measures. To paraphrase, a restrictive approach is absurd. It might be plausible, however, to respond by arguing that anticipatory self-defence is not a necessary vehicle through which UN member States can and should defend themselves. In the absence of an actual armed attack that activates article 51 of the Charter, the appropriate means of resolving imminent or perceived threats to the security of a State is through the United Nations Security Council. By providing the mechanisms under Chapter VII, the Charter effectively replaced the need for the former *Caroline Case* norms. By consenting to be bound by such mechanisms, member States limited themselves to acting only when authorized by the Security Council or within the narrow terms of article 51.

Support for such an approach can be found in the recent declaration on the use of force, by the Institut de Droit International, where it said:[40]

> Only the Security Council, or the General Assembly acting under the more limited framework of the "Uniting for Peace" Resolution of 1950, may, depending on the particular circumstances at hand, decide that a given situation constitutes a threat to international peace and security, without this necessarily meaning that the recourse to force is the only possible adequate response.

In other words, if an imminent threat exists, it is for the Security Council, not individual States, to determine whether the use of force is called for (by way of action under Chapter VII of the United Nations Charter).

The response to such an approach, and that advocated by various States including the United States, is that the process by which the Security

---

[35] Ibid, 870.

[36] Ibid.

[37] Ibid, 868.

[38] Ibid, 851, n 23.

[39] As noted by Bowett, D.W., "Reprisals Involving Recourse to Armed Force", (1972) *American Journal of International Law* 66.

[40] Institut de Droit International, Bruges Declaration on the Use of Force, 2 September 2003.

Council makes its decisions (the power of veto in particular) is insufficient to properly deal with such threats.[41] By way of example, the permanent members' power of veto plagued the Council with difficulties throughout the Cold War[42] and was the subject of much debate during the Iraq crisis of 2002/2003. Having said that, it should be noted that the Security Council and its Counter-Terrorism Committee have dedicated considerable time and resources to establishing an international regime to combat terrorism.[43] It might equally be argued, therefore, that the Security Council is cognizant of the issue of terrorist threats such that it will respond appropriately to any petition seeking measures against a particular threat of terrorist conduct.

Summary

To the writer's mind, the arguments in favour of a restrictive approach (one that excludes the existence of parallel customary norms permitting anticipatory self-defence) outweigh those in support of a broader approach. The adoption of the United Nations Charter saw the creation of a peremptory norm of customary international law, excluding the unilateral use of force except where a State is actually attacked, and establishing compensatory mechanisms through the UN Security Council to deal with imminent or other threats to the peace. Having said that, it must be acknowledged that alternative arguments exist. It would therefore be improper to entirely dismiss pre-emptive strikes, without further discussion. Consideration should be given to the scope of anticipatory self-defence, as it might exist, and whether the anti-terror pre-emptive strike policies fit within its parameters.

---

[41] See, for example, the statement of US Secretary of State Colin Powell concerning intervention in Iraq, in which he said that "if the UN does not act, then it would be necessary for the United States to act with a willing coalition": see News Release 16 March 2003, "Legal basis for use of force against Iraq", British High Commission in Canada News, URL <http://www.britainincanada.org/News/Release/2003/mar03/nr1617.htm> at 1 September 2003.

[42] From 1945 to 1992, by way of illustration, the use of the veto was as follows: Soviet Union 114; USA 69; UK 30; France 18; China 3: Murphy, S.D., "The Security Council Legitimacy, and the Concept of Collective Security After the Cold War", (1994) 31 *Columbia Journal of Transnational Law* 201.

[43] See Chapter 2, 23–29.

The Scope of Anticipatory Self-Defence

Proponents of anticipatory self-defence would argue that this is an aspect of inherent self-defence that has continued to lie alongside the codified Charter right of self-defence. If correct, it is then necessary to examine what the content of such law is. Proponents point to the existence, well before the United Nations Charter, of a customary rule of anticipatory self-defence as articulated in the *Caroline Case*[44] and later confirmed by the International Military Tribunal at Nuremberg.[45]

The *Caroline Case* arose out of the Canadian Rebellion of 1837. Rebel leaders secured assistance from a large number of American nationals (despite steps by US authorities to prevent assistance being given). The resulting rebel force established itself on Navy Island in Canadian waters and supplies were provided to it from America by an American ship, the *Caroline*. On the night of 29–30 December 1837, the *Caroline* was seized by the British in the American port of Schlosser, set alight and sent over the Niagara Falls. A British subject, McLeod, was arrested by United States authorities on charges of murder and arson following the death of two American nationals on board the *Caroline*. In correspondence between Great Britain and the United States, Mr Webster on behalf of the United States wrote:[46]

> It will be for ...[Her Majesty's] Government to show a necessity of self-defence, instant, overwhelming, leaving no choice of means, and no moment for deliberation. It will be for it to show, also, that the local authorities of Canada, even supposing the necessity of the moment authorised them to enter the territories of the United States at all, did nothing unreasonable or excessive; since the act, justified by the necessity of self-defence, must be limited by that necessity, and kept clearly within it. It must be shown that admonition or remonstrance to the person on board the *Caroline* was impracticable, or would have been unavailing; it must be shown that day-light could not be waited for; that there could be no attempt at discrimination between the innocent and the guilty; that it would not have been enough to seize and detain the vessel; but that there was a necessity, present and inevitable, for attacking her in the darkness of night, while moored to the shore...

---

[44] 29 British Forces and State Papers (BFSP) 1137–1138; 30 BFSP 195–196; see also Jennings (1938) 32 *American Journal of International Law* 82.

[45] (1947) 41 *American Journal of International Law* 204, where it had been argued that the German invasion of Norway in 1940 was an act of self-defence in the face of an imminent Allied landing there. The Tribunal said that preventive action in foreign territory is justified only in the circumstances cited by Mr Webster in the *Caroline Case*.

[46] Letter from Mr Webster to Mr Fox, 24 April 1841; see Harris, above, n 22, 848.

In his response to this, Lord Ashburton accepted that the applicable principles of international law were accurately reflected in Mr Webster's letter.[47] Throughout the pre-UN Charter period, scholars appear to have agreed that anticipatory self-defence could therefore be used if a State could demonstrate necessity (imminent engagement by another State in an armed attack) and proportionality (in the defensive measures employed).[48]

Preventive versus Pre-emptive Strikes

What must next be considered is whether any norm of "anticipatory" self-defence permits pre-emptive measures, or merely preventive ones.

The bombing of the Osirak atomic reactor, located in the vicinity of Baghdad, Iraq, by the Israeli Air Force warrants consideration. In lodging its article 51 notification with the Security Council,[49] Israel advised that the bombing was undertaken on the grounds that the reactor was designed to produce atomic bombs to be used against Israel and, on the basis that the reactor was expected to become operational within a short period of time, the Government of Israel has decided to act "to ensure its people's existence".[50] Israel was thus relying on the notion of pre-empting a threat to the life of the Israeli State by eliminating that threat. During subsequent Security Council deliberations, it argued that this was an exercise of self-defence as provided for under the Charter and as "understood in general international law".[51] To the contrary, Iraq argued that the attack was an unprovoked and illegal act of aggression.[52] In its Resolution 487, the Security Council provided that it:[53]

> 1. *Strongly condemns* the military attack by Israel in clear violation of the Charter of the United Nations and the norms of international conduct.

This might be seen as evidence of the rejection of the doctrine of anticipatory self-defence by the Security Council and, on the face of the Resolution that does appear to be a valid inference. Equally, however, the

---

[47] Letter from Lord Ashburton to Mr Webster, 28 July 1842; see Harris, above, n 22, 848.

[48] Arend, above, n 23, 91.

[49] This being a requirement of the exercise of action reliant upon article 51: see Chapter 3, 42–44.

[50] Letter from the Permanent Representative of Israel to the President of the United Nations Security Council dated 8 June 1981, S/14510.

[51] United Nations, *Repertory of Practice of United Nations Organs Supplement No 6*, Volume III (1979–1984) Article 51, para 32.

[52] Ibid, para 33.

[53] United Nations Security Council Resolution 487 of 19 June 1981, S/RES/487 (1981).

United Nations Repertory of Practice refers to the fact that in the deliberations leading up to the adoption of the Resolution, a number of Council members took the view that the bombing was unlawful because it constituted a "preventive", rather than "pre-emptive", action. In other words, they took the view that to *pre-empt* threats (by taking steps to avoid the threat arising) was not permitted at international law, whereas action could be justified as being in self-defence if the reason for it was "instant, overwhelming, leaving no choice of means and no moment for deliberation" (*preventing* the execution of the threat).[54]

Anticipatory Self-Defence in the War on Terror

The result of the above discussion is, regrettably, unclear. There are meritorious arguments for both the restrictive and broad approaches. What can be said is this: if the restrictive approach is correct, then self-defence is limited to conduct in response to an actual armed attack and in reliance upon article 51. Adoption of the restrictive approach rules out any pre-emptive action, and means that the Bush and Howard administrations' policies on the War on Terror do not comply with international law.[55]

If, on the other hand, one concludes that anticipatory self-defence remains alive under customary international law, and parallel to the UN Charter, the next step is to ask if the expressions of an anti-terror pre-emptive strike policy are consistent with those customary norms. Do the policies comply with the requirements of necessity and proportionality, as set out in the *Caroline Case*? One further question arises, not out of the *Caroline Case*, but through the particularities of the War on Terror: how does one deal with the fact that terrorist conduct is generally perpetrated by non-State actors?

Necessity and Proportionality

As discussed, anticipatory self-defence has been recognized as requiring necessity (through the imminent threat of engagement by another State in an armed attack) and proportionality (in the defensive measures employed). The latter requirement, proportionality, is a matter that falls for analysis on

---

[54] Above, n 51, para 33.

[55] Professor Tony Arend, of the Department of Government and School of Foreign Service at the University of Georgetown, accepts that the Bush Administration's approach to pre-emption is clearly unlawful under the UN Charter, although he argues that one must look beyond the Charter to the parallel customary international law norms: ibid, 91.

a case-by-case basis and cannot, therefore, be fairly assessed within this chapter. Consideration of whether the Bush and Howard policies might satisfy necessity can be considered.

The Bush Doctrine, as contained within his administration's National Security Strategy (NSS), urges that the United States "must adapt the concept of imminent threat to the capabilities and objectives of today's adversaries".[56] To do so, the NSS advises that:

> The greater the threat, the greater is the risk of inaction – and the more compelling the case for taking anticipatory action to defend ourselves, even if uncertainty remains as to the time and place of the enemy's attack.

It is here that an important distinction should be drawn between the policies of the United States and Australia. The Bush Doctrine seeks to go beyond the notion of imminent danger, and into the real of *pre-emptive* rather than *preventive* measures. As discussed, however, pre-emptive measures aimed at eliminating the emergence of a threat do not fall within the necessity requirement of the *Caroline Case*, and have been forcefully rebutted by the Security Council in its consideration of anticipatory self-defence measures.[57] In the case of Prime Minister Howard's statements, although imprecise, they might nevertheless be construed as taking a more restrictive and *preventive* approach, the Prime Minister referring to action where there is a belief "...that somebody was going to launch an attack against your country" and if "...there was no alternative other than to use that capacity [force]".[58]

Focusing on the Bush Doctrine, then, commentators such as McLain have criticized the National Security Strategy as far from falling within any accepted view of anticipatory self-defence.[59] That criticism is, in the author's view, valid and thereby fatal to the US anti-terror pre-emptive strike policy. The Strategy claims a right to pre-emptive self-defence where there is "uncertainty"[60] about the time or place of the attack. It therefore takes a step beyond the already controversial concept of anticipatory self-defence. In the *Caroline Case*, the United States required

---

[56] Above, n 6.

[57] See the discussion above concerning the bombing of the Osirak reactor.

[58] Ibid.

[59] McLain P., "Settling the Score with Saddam: Resolution 1441 and Parallel Justifications for the Use of Force Against Iraq" (2003) 13 *Duke Journal of Comparative and International Law* 233, 268. See also United Nations Foundation, "Chomsky Says Bush Doctrine Lowers the Bar for Aggression", *UN Wire*, <http://www.unwire.org/UNWire>, 4 February 2004.

[60] As stated within the quote above.

Britain to justify its conduct by showing that it acted out of "necessity of self-defence, instant, overwhelming, leaving no choice of means, and no moment for deliberation";[61] whereas the US now seeks to justify pre-emptive action "even if uncertainty remains".[62]

Furthermore, although the Bush Administration has characterized the War of Terror as a unique and unprecedented challenge, that is not in fact the case. The Security Council itself gave consideration to the notion of pre-emptive strikes in anticipation of terrorist acts in 1979, concerning the situation in Southern Lebanon. During the Security Council's consideration of the issue, the Permanent Representative of Israel argued that it, like every other State, had the right to take measures in order to half and foil terrorist activities emanating from across its boundaries in order to protect the lives and safety of its citizens.[63] Israel argued that the Lebanese Government had failed to prevent the use of its territory as the base from which the Palestine Liberation Organization (PLO) conducted terrorist attacks against Israel. Israel's response was characterized by Lebanon as retaliatory and unlawful, whereas Israel mooted that it acted within the bounds of the inherent right of self-defence.

The majority of the Security Council rejected this broad definition of inherent self-defence and emphasized that self-defence was permitted only against armed attacks and subject to the limits of necessity and proportionality.[64] Reprisals against terrorist attacks were considered unjustified under article 51 and contrary to General Assembly Resolution 2625.[65] The Council adopted Resolution 450, deploring the attacks by Israel and calling upon it to cease its retaliatory acts.[66]

Although this discussion helps to inform the issue at hand, it should be noted that a distinguishing feature between the subject matter then considered by the Security Council and the NSS is that the 1979 crisis involved retaliatory conduct.

---

[61] As expressed by Mr Webster in his letter of 24 April 1841, above, n 46.

[62] As expressed in the US National Security Strategy of September 2002, above, n 6.

[63] Above, n 51, para 16.

[64] Ibid, para 17.

[65] United Nations General Assembly Resolution 2626 (XXV) of 24 October 1970 (1883rd Plenary Meeting, during the Twenty-Fifth Session), the *Declaration on Principles of International Law Concerning Friendly Relations and Cooperation Among States in Accordance with the Charter of the United Nations*, A/RES/25/2625.

[66] United Nations Security Council Resolution 450 of 14 June 1979, S/RES/450 (1979), paras 1 and 2.

Attributing Responsibility to States

Much debate on the question of anticipatory self-defence arose during the Cold War, at a time when considerable tension existed between the USA and the USSR.[67] The fear then was that weapons of mass destruction (nuclear weapons in particular) might be deployed by one against another and the question was whether one State might – in anticipation of such an attack – launch a protective strike. Ultimately, and fortunately for all, the psychological threat of "mutually assured destruction" was great enough to prevent armed attacks and pre-emptive strikes by either side.[68]

What differs considerably between the Cold War and the War on Terror is the question of attribution of responsibility. During the Cold War it was clear who the parties to the conflict were and who held "responsibility" in terms of the threat of and the ability to use weapons of mass destruction. Thus, during the Cold War, the argument of anticipatory self-defence was clear: "Russia/America poses an imminent threat to use nuclear weapons against us, and we must – in anticipation of and to prevent such an attack – strike against Russia/America".

The question of attribution in the War on Terror is much more complex. While terrorist conduct often contains elements of warfare, politics and propaganda,[69] terrorist organizations (for security reasons and due to lack of popular support) are usually small, making detection and infiltration difficult. As recognized by the United Nations Office for Drug Control and Crime Prevention (ODCCP), although the goals of terrorists are sometimes shared by wider constituencies, their methods are generally abhorred.[70] It is proposed that it will be rare, if ever, that a State will accept responsibility for conduct of a terrorist organization.

This being the case, the anti-terror pre-emptive strike policy faces a considerable final hurdle in the analysis undertaken in this chapter: that of attributing responsibility for terrorist conduct to a State, in order to justify

---

[67] See, for example: Professor Edward McWhinney, *"Peaceful Coexistence" and Soviet-Western International Law*, Leyden, 1964; and Ronald Powaski, *The Cold War: The United States and the Soviet Union, 1917–1991*, Oxford University Press, 1998.

[68] Much has been written on the subject of mutually assured destruction: by way of example, contrast Stephen Del Rosso, "The Insecure State", *Daedalus*, Vol 124, 1995 with James Ewing, "The 1972 US-Soviet ABM Treaty: Conerstone of Stability or Relic of the Cold War?", *William and Mary Law Review*, Vol 43, Issue 2 (2001), p787.

[69] United Nations Office for Drug Control and Crime Prevention, "UN Action Against Terrorism", web site <www.odccp.org/terrorism.html>, at 19/06/02.

[70] Ibid.

pre-emptive action against the State.[71] There appear to be two ways in which responsibility might be attributed, each to be discussed.

The "but for" test. Although not formulated in these precise words, the attribution of responsibility for the September 11 bombings rests on the view that the terrorist attacks against America could not have occurred, but for the assistance of the Afghani State. Through various resolutions, the UN Security Council expressed the view that al-Qaida was responsible for the terrorist attacks of September 11, 2001 and that it could not have perpetrated those attacks but for the assistance of the Taliban regime in Afghanistan.[72]

Within Resolution 1378 of 14 November 2001, the Council attributed responsibility to the Taliban regime for allowing Afghanistan to be used as a base of operations by al-Qaida.[73] It later noted, within Resolution 1390,[74] that the Taliban had failed to comply with earlier resolutions of the Security Council, requiring it to stop providing sanctuary and training for international terrorists;[75] to turn over Usama bin Laden;[76] and to close all camps where terrorists were trained within the territory under the Taliban's control.[77] This attribution of responsibility finds similar support within the British report, "Responsibility for the Terrorist Atrocities in the United States", tabled before the English Parliament.[78]

Although some might criticize the attribution of responsibility to the Taliban on the particular facts of that case as lacking sufficiently cogent evidence, the writer is open to the view that a "but for" test in attributing responsibility for terrorist conduct may be appropriate. Even if it is, however, this does not further the argument in favour of the US anti-terror pre-emptive strike policy. A "but for" test, as applied against the Taliban, is reflective. The test involves consideration of conduct that has actually occurred. It therefore does not fall within the ambit of anticipatory self-defence, but rather within the restrictive notion of self-defence in response to an actual armed attack.

---

[71] Assuming, of course, that pre-emptive action is permissible under international law, as discussed already.

[72] This issue is discussed in more detail within Chapter 3, 46–51.

[73] United Nations Security Council Resolution 1378 (2001).

[74] Under United Nations Security Council Resolution 1390 (2002).

[75] See United Nations Security Council Resolutions 1214 (1998) and 1333 (2000).

[76] See United Nations Security Council Resolutions 1267 (1999) and 1333 (2000).

[77] See United Nations Security Council Resolution 1333 (2000).

[78] Her Majesty's Government, 4 October 2001.

Attributing a responsibility upon States to combat terrorism. The second means by which attribution might be made is by arguing that a State has breached, or is breaching, a common duty to combat terrorism within its borders. In this regard, consideration of three documents is called for.

1. *Declaration on Measures to Eliminate International Terrorism.* The first document from which a general responsibility to combat terrorism might be drawn is the General Assembly's Declaration on Measures to Eliminate International Terrorism.[79] The Declaration describes terrorism as a grave violation of the purposes and principles of the United Nations, which may pose a threat to international peace and security, and jeopardize friendly relations among States.[80] It expresses that States must refrain from organizing, instigating, assisting or participating in terrorist acts in territories of other States, or from acquiescing in or encouraging activities within their territories directed towards the commission of terrorist acts.[81] More particularly, it maintains that States have obligations under the UN Charter and other provisions of international law to combat international terrorism, in particular:[82]

> To refrain from organizing, instigating, facilitating, financing, encouraging or tolerating terrorist activities and to take appropriate practical measures to ensure that their respective territories are not used for terrorist installations or training camps, or for the preparation or organization of terrorist acts intended to be committed against other States or their citizens;
> To ensure the apprehension and prosecution or extradition of perpetrators of terrorist acts, in accordance with the relevant provisions of their national law;
> To endeavour to conclude special agreements to that effect on a bilateral, regional and multilateral basis, and to prepare, to that effect, model agreements on cooperation;
> To cooperate with one another in exchanging relevant information concerning the prevention and combating of terrorism;
> To take promptly all steps necessary to implement the existing international conventions on this subject to which they are parties, including the harmonization of their domestic legislation with those conventions;
> To take appropriate measures, before granting asylum, for the purpose of ensuring that the asylum seeker has not engaged in terrorist activities and, after

---

[79] Adopted under United Nations General Assembly Resolution 49/60, "Measures to Eliminate International Terrorism", A/RES/49/60, 84th Plenary Meeting of the UNGA, 9 December 1994.
[80] Ibid, para 2.
[81] Ibid, para 4.
[82] Ibid, para 5.

granting asylum, for the purpose of ensuring that the refugee status is not used in a manner contrary to the provisions set out in subparagraph (a) above;

These "obligations" (as they are referred to within the Declaration) might be argued to establish an attribution of responsibility upon States to combat terrorism, the breach of which could be used to justify pre-emptive strikes.[83] That position might hold merit, at face value, but fails in the author's view for two main reasons. Firstly, the Declaration does not define the ambit of "terrorism" or "terrorist activities". Indeed, there is no internationally agreed-upon definition of terrorism.[84]

Secondly, and more importantly, the Declaration is not law. Although compelling and strongly worded, the Measures to Eliminate International Terrorism is a Declaration only and therefore does not have the same weight as a treaty, nor does it have signatories that are bound by its content. Indeed, article 10 of the Charter specifically provides that resolutions and declarations of the United Nations General Assembly are recommendatory only. Accordingly, its provisions could not form the basis upon which to attribute responsibility upon a State for breach of its provisions.

2. *Security Council Resolution 1373.* In contrast to a resolution of the General Assembly, resolutions of the UN Security Council are binding upon members of the United Nations by application of article 25 of the Charter. Accordingly, the obligations pertaining to counter-terrorism set out within Security Council Resolution 1373[85] might form the basis for the attribution of responsibility.[86] As with the General Assembly's Declaration on Measures to Eliminate International Terrorism, the problem with relying upon Resolution 1373 is the failure of the Resolution to define the term "terrorism". Criticizing an earlier resolution of the Security Council pertaining to terrorism, the Executive Director of the International Policy Institute for Counter-Terrorism, Boaz Ganor, has emphasized the point that resolutions on counter-terrorism can only have an effective impact once all States agree upon what type of acts constitute terrorism and if the resolutions set out that definition.[87]

---

[83] Provided that any breach is of a specified "obligation" within paragraph 5 of the declaration, as quoted.

[84] On this point, see the discussion in Chapter 2, 11–20.

[85] United Nations Security Council Resolution 1373 of 28 September 2001, S/RES/1373 (2001), paras 1 and 2.

[86] For a discussion of those obligations, see Chapter 2, 23–25.

[87] Ganor B, "Security Council Resolution 1269: What it Leaves Out", 25 October 1999, website of the International Policy Institute for Counter-Terrorism, <www.ict.org.il/articles/articledet.cfm?articleid=93>, 01/06/02.

3. *The Draft Comprehensive Convention on International Terrorism.* A potential avenue for the attribution of responsibility in the future could rest with the proposed Comprehensive Convention on International Terrorism.[88] The draft does set out a definition of terrorism and contains various articles creating obligations upon States parties. As discussed in Chapter 2, however, the working party tasked with finalizing the Comprehensive Convention has been unable to agree upon a definition of the term and, for that reason, there is doubt that the Convention will come to fruition.

The writer therefore concludes that, unless responsibility can be attributed to a State by way of a "but for" or higher test (which is unlikely in any anticipatory action), any use of force would be unlawful.

Conclusion

What might be described as the "anti-terror pre-emptive strike" policies of the United States and Australia face many considerable hurdles on the track to justification under international law. First, it is debatable whether a doctrine of anticipatory self-defence has survived the advent of the United Nations Charter. The adoption of the Charter saw the creation of a peremptory norm of customary international law, excluding the use of force except where a State is attacked, and establishing compensatory mechanisms through the UN Security Council to deal with imminent threats to the peace.

Even if the doctrine of anticipatory self-defence did survive the Charter, it requires a State to demonstrate necessity and proportionality. While proportionality cannot be prospectively assessed, it can be said that the Bush Doctrine falls outside the requirement of necessity, the Security Council having rejected (at the very least) the concept of *pre-emptive* as opposed to *preventive* action. The US National Security Strategy claims a right to pre-emptive self-defence where there is "uncertainty" about the time or place of an attack and therefore takes a step beyond the already controversial concept of anticipatory self-defence. In contrast, Prime Minister Howard's statements, although imprecise, might be construed as taking a more restrictive approach, within the ambit of *Caroline* necessity.

Finally, the policies face the considerable problem of attributing responsibility upon States for conduct of terrorist, non-State, actors. While a "but for" test to attribute responsibility seems appropriate, it does not

---

[88] For a more detailed discussion of the draft convention, see Chapter 2, 18–20.

advance the argument in favour of the anti-terror pre-emptive strike policies. The test involves reflection upon conduct that has actually occurred, which is unlikely to assist in justifying any anticipatory action. Although strongly worded, neither the General Assembly's Declaration on Measures to Eliminate International Terrorism nor Security Council Resolution 1373 can be seen as adequate bases for attribution of responsibility upon States to justify pre-emptive strikes.

Chapter 6

Iraq, Kuwait and
Weapons of Mass Destruction

Introduction

The second major challenge to international security in the 21st century, and to the role of the United Nations in maintaining peace and security, has been the intervention in Iraq in 2003 under *Operation Iraqi Freedom*. It is not possible, however, to properly examine that intervention and the issues leading up to the intervention in isolation and without first having regard to the last decade and a half of conflict. Indeed, in considering whether or not the most recent intervention is legal, it is that period of armed and political conflict with Iraq that is partly determinative.[1]

This chapter focuses on two distinct periods, each of which are critical (as will be seen) to the evaluation of the legality of intervention in Iraq under *Operation Iraqi Freedom*. The first is the lead-up to *Operation Desert Storm* in 1991, the aim of which was to repel Iraqi forces from Kuwait after their invasion of that neighbouring territory. The second period is that between the expulsion of Iraqi forces from Kuwait in 1991 and up to *Operation Desert Fox* in 1998, involving consideration of action, and difficulties faced, by the United Nations Security Council and UN weapons inspectors.

Thematically, the examination of *Operations Desert Storm* and *Desert Fox* draws out three important issues concerning the means by which the United Nations discharges its role of maintaining peace and security. First, the lead-up to both operations involved trade sanctions which, while they certainly placed pressure upon the Iraqi regime, might equally be described as failures. Consideration is given to trade sanctions, their impact upon the targeted State as well as neighbouring States, and their effectiveness as tools for the maintenance of peace and security. Next, the authorization of the US-led coalition to undertake *Operation Desert Storm* stands as an example of "collective security", action undertaken with the express

---

[1] *Operation Iraqi Freedom*, and the legality or otherwise of the intervention, is examined in the following chapter.

authority of the Security Council for the restoration of peace and security, and the rectification of a breach of the peace. Finally, consideration of the legality of *Operation Desert Fox* brings to bear an examination of the concept of "automaticity". This is the idea, as argued by the US Administrations in justifying intervention in both *Operations Desert Fox* and *Iraqi Freedom*, that a series of Security Council resolutions can act together to implicitly authorize the use of force.

Operation Desert Storm

As neighbouring States, Iraq and Kuwait have experienced a long history of territorial conflict between them. It is not feasible, or relevant, to give full consideration to that history. A brief overview is, however, helpful to gain an understanding of the lead up to *Operation Desert Storm* and the Security Council resolutions that followed.[2]

In 1963, the State of Kuwait and the Republic of Iraq entered into a Treaty of Friendly Relations, under which they agreed upon a boundary between the two States.[3] Despite the Treaty, Iraq had long regarded Kuwait as part of its own territory. In March 1973, Iraq took hold of as-Samitah, a border post on the Kuwaiti border, in response to a refusal by Kuwait to allow Iraqi occupation of the Kuwaiti islands of Bubiyan and Warbah. The League of Arab States, Saudi Arabia in particular, successfully negotiated the peaceful withdrawal of Iraq from as-Samitah. A period of relative stability between Kuwait and Iraq followed, during which the States appeared to form a relatively strong alliance. Indeed, during the first Persian Gulf War between Iraq and Iran, Kuwaiti forces acted in support of Iraq. At the conclusion of the conflict with Iran, in which Iraqi forces were ultimately driven back by Iran after almost eight years of war, relations between Iraq and Kuwait deteriorated mainly, some say, due to a lack of gratitude from Saddam Hussein for Kuwait's support in the war.[4] Those tensions escalated during 1989 and 1990 and, together

---

[2] For a better understanding of the lead up to and conduct of *Operation Desert Storm*, see Matthews, K., *The Gulf Conflict and International Relations*, (1993) New York, USA, Routledge, and Hutchison, K.D., *Operation Desert Shield / Desert Storm*, (1995) Westport, USA, Greenwood Publishing Group.

[3] Iraq and Kuwait signed at Baghdad on 4 October 1963 a document entitled "Agreed Minutes between the State of Kuwait and the Republic of Iraq regarding the Restoration of Friendly Relations, Recognition and Related Matters" (commonly referred to as the Treaty of Friendly Relations).

[4] See *The Persian Gulf War (1990–1991)*, URL <http://www.historyguy.com/ GulfWar.html> at 7 May 2004.

with entrenched issues concerning territorial control and oil reserves straddling the Kuwait-Iraq border, Iraq invaded Kuwait on 2 August 1990.

Security Council Action Following the Invasion of Kuwait

The Iraqi attack against Kuwait resulted in the issuing of Resolution 660 on the same day, under which the Security Council condemned the invasion as a breach of international peace and security and demanded the immediate and unconditional withdrawal of Iraq from Kuwaiti territory.[5]   The Resolution also called upon Iraq and Kuwait to begin negotiations towards a resolution of disputes between them and encouraged assistance from the League of Arab States.[6] A series of further resolutions by the Council saw the imposition of trade sanctions upon, and further demands of, Iraq.[7]

Trade sanctions.   On 6 August 1990, the Security Council issued Resolution 661 following the continued advance of Iraq into Kuwaiti territory and despite expressions by the Kuwaiti Government of preparedness to undertake negotiations with Iraq.[8] Affirming the inherent right of individual and collective self-defence,[9] the Resolution imposed various trade sanctions against Iraq: prohibiting the importing of all commodities and products from Iraq and Kuwait; requiring members to prevent their nationals from assisting in the export of commodities and products from Iraq and Kuwait; prohibiting the sale by members or their individuals of commodities and products, including weapons, to Iraq or Kuwait, except medical supplies or foodstuffs in humanitarian circumstances; and prohibiting UN members and their individuals from making financial or economic resources available to Iraq and its occupying

---

[5] United Nations Security Council Resolution 660 of 2 August 1990, S/RES/660 (1990), para 2: see Appendix 6A herein. The Security Council meeting was prompted by letters from the Permanent Representative of Kuwait and the United States to the United Nations of 2 August 1990: S/21423 and S/21424 respectively in *Official Records of the Security Council, Forty-Fifth Year, Supplement for July, August and September 1990*. The Council invited representatives from Iraq and Kuwait to attend its meeting, without vote.
[6] Ibid, para 3.
[7] A total of 14 resolutions were made by the Security Council against Iraq during the five months between the invasion of Kuwait (2 August 1990) until the commencement of *Operation Desert Fox* (17 January 1991): two of which related to Iraq and Iran (Resolutions 671 and 676); with the rest concerning Iraq and Kuwait (Resolutions 660, 661, 662, 664, 665, 666, 667, 669, 670, 674, 677 and 678).
[8] United Nations Security Council Resolution 661 of 6 August 1990, S/RES/661 (1990) – Appendix 6B herein.
[9] See the final paragraph of the preamble to Resolution 661, ibid.

forces.[10] The Resolution also called upon members of the United Nations to take measures to protect the assets of the Kuwaiti Government and not to recognize any regime within Kuwait established by the Iraqi occupation.[11] The Council established a Sanctions Committee to monitor the implementation of the sanctions under Resolution 661 and to coordinate with member States to give best effect to the sanctions.[12]

Authority was given to member States in late August 1990 to halt inward and outward maritime shipping to and from Kuwait to enable the inspection and verification of cargoes for the purpose of enforcing the economic sanctions under Resolution 661.[13] Resolution 665 authorized member States to use "such measures commensurate to the specific circumstances as may be necessary" to achieve the halting and inspection of vessels.[14]

Sanctions prohibiting the trade in commodities and the provision of financial or economic assistance[15] later became the subject of concern by some States and non-governmental organisations in light of the adverse humanitarian effects of the war in Kuwait.[16] The prohibitions concerned were already drafted in a manner excluding the application of the sanctions to humanitarian crises. The prohibition on the trade in commodities was expressed not to include "supplies intended strictly for medical purposes, and, in humanitarian circumstances, foodstuffs".[17] Likewise, "payments exclusively for strictly medical or humanitarian purposes and, in humanitarian circumstances, foodstuffs"[18] were permitted under Resolution 661. In response to the concerns raised, the Security Council charged the Sanctions Committee with keeping the situation regarding foodstuffs in

---

[10] At paras 3 and 4.

[11] At para 9.

[12] The Committee was established under rule 28 of the *Provisional Rules of Procedure of the Security Council*, S/96/Rev.7 (this revision remains current), which allows the Security Council to appoint a commission, committee or a rapporteur for a specified question. The Committee consisted of representatives of all the members of the Security Council at that time: see Resolution 661, above, n 128, para 6.

[13] United Nations Security Council Resolution 665 of 25 August 1990, S/RES/665 (1990), para 1.

[14] Ibid.

[15] As contained within paras 3(c) and 4 of Resolution 661, above, n 8.

[16] As recognized within the preamble to United Nations Security Council Resolution 666 of 13 September 1990, S/RES/666 (1990). This was followed by a further perambulatory statement "*Emphasising* that it is for the Security Council, alone or acting through the Committee [the Sanctions Committee established under Resolution 661], to determine whether humanitarian circumstances have arisen".

[17] At para 3(c).

[18] At para 4.

Kuwait and Iraq under constant review[19] and established mechanisms by which the Committee could receive pertinent information.[20]

Not surprisingly, Iraq took the view that the sanctions imposed upon it were unjust and that the conduct of any States complying with the sanctions was arbitrary. The Revolutionary Command Council of Iraq consequently enacted Act No 57 of 16 September 1990.[21] Article 7 of the Act provided that:[22]

> All assets and funds, as well as the income accruing therefrom, which belong to Governments, institutions, companies and banks of States which have taken arbitrary decisions against Iraq shall be frozen.

The result of this, and Iraq's suspension of foreign debt repayments, was that by the end of September 1990, neighbouring States, including Jordan for example, were experiencing adverse consequences of the UN trade sanctions. Under article 50 of the UN Charter, those States requested the Security Council to consider a solution to those problems. That task was delegated to the Sanctions Committee, which was asked to examine the article 50 requests and make recommendations to the President of the Security Council.[23] The Security Council also expressed the relevant provisions of the Iraqi Act No 57 as being null and void, taking the view that this was aimed at undermining the effectiveness of trade sanctions, in violation of articles 25 and 48 of the Charter.[24] It made it clear that the trade sanctions applied to all means of transport, including aircraft, and required member States to deny permission for any aircraft destined to Iraq or Kuwait to take off from or overfly its territory unless authorized by the Sanctions Committee or unless the aircraft was first inspected to ensure

---

[19] Resolution 666, above, n 16, para 1.

[20] Ibid, paras 3 to 6.

[21] Enacted under Decree No 377 of the Revolutionary Command Council of Iraq, 16 September 1990.

[22] Official United Nations translation of Iraqi Act No 57: see United Nations Compensation Commission, *Report and Recommendations made by the Panel of Commissioners Concerning the Fourth Installment of "E2" Claims*, 22 March 2000, S/AC.26/2000/2, para 27.

[23] United Nations Security Council Resolution 669 of 24 September 1990, S/RES/669 (1990).

[24] United Nations Security Council Resolution 670 of 25 September 1990, S/RES/670 (1990), preamble. Article 25 of the United Nations Charter makes decisions of the United Nations Security Council binding upon members of the United Nations. Article 48 requires States to take action in compliance with any decision of the Security Council.

compliance with Resolution 661.[25] The Resolution also emphasized, and
expanded upon, the obligations of UN member States to comply with the
trade sanctions and went so far as to articulate that the Security Council
would consider measures against States that failed to comply with or evade
the obligations under Resolution 661.[26]

The annexation of Kuwait and the violation of diplomatic premises. Iraq,
undeterred by the economic sanctions imposed under Resolution 661,
issued a declaration of a "comprehensive and eternal merger" with Kuwait
on 8 August 1990. The declaration purported to annex Kuwait as the
nineteenth province of Iraq. The United Nations responded by pronouncing
that the annexation of Kuwait had no legal validity and by calling upon all
States, organizations and agencies not to recognize the annexation or do
anything that might be interpreted as an indirect recognition of the
annexation.[27] This approach is consistent with the post-1945 development
in international law concerning the use of force, whereby the acquisition of
territory by force was no longer recognized. Whereas conquest was a valid
method of acquiring territory up to the 20th century, the controls upon the
use of force between States through the League of Nations Covenant of
1919, the Paris Pact of 1928[28] and the United Nations Charter of 1945 saw
an end to such means of territorial acquisition. On 24 October 1970 the
United Nations General Assembly adopted what must be seen as one of the
most significant resolutions in its history, Resolution 2626(XXV), the
Declaration on Principles of International Law Concerning Friendly
Relations and Cooperation Among States in Accordance with the Charter
of the United Nations.[29] Of the various principles enunciated in the

---

[25] Or unless the aircraft was authorized by the United Nations as being solely for the
purposes of the United Nations Iran-Iraq Military Observer Group: see Resolution 670, ibid,
paras 3 and 4.

[26] At paras 5 to 12 inclusive.

[27] United Nations Security Council Resolution 662 of 9 August 1990, S/RES/662 (1990),
paras 1 and 2. The resolution also called upon Iraq to rescind its actions purporting to annex
Kuwait: para 3.

[28] The General Treaty for the Renunciation of War 1928, also known as the Kellogg-Briand
Pact.

[29] United Nations General Assembly Resolution 2626 (XXV) of 24 October 1970 (1883rd
Plenary Meeting, during the Twenty-Fifth Session), the *Declaration on Principles of
International Law Concerning Friendly Relations and Cooperation Among States in
Accordance with the Charter of the United Nations*, A/RES/25/2625. The resolution was
adopted upon a report of the Special Committee on Principles of International Law
concerning Friendly Relations and Co-operation among States, *Official Records of the
General Assembly, Twenty-fifth Session, Supplement no 18*, A/8018. The Special
Committee was a sub-committee of the General Assembly's Sixth Committee (Legal).

Declaration, the principle on the prohibition of the use of force contained the following provision:[30]

> The territory of a State shall not be the object of military occupation resulting from the use of force in contravention of the provisions of the Charter. The territory of a State shall not be the object of acquisition by another State resulting from the threat or use of force. No territorial acquisition resulting from the threat or use of force shall be recognised as legal.

The Security Council's express rejection of Iraq's annexation of Kuwait therefore comes as no surprise. The Council reaffirmed that position in Resolution 664, also calling upon Iraq to permit and facilitate the departure of third-State nationals from Kuwait and Iraq.[31]

The annexation of Kuwait was followed by the abduction of diplomats and foreign nationals within Kuwait and an order by Iraqi authorities to close diplomatic missions in Kuwait along with a withdrawal of the privileges and immunities of those missions. As recognized by the Security Council,[32] this amounted to clear violations of the Vienna Convention on Diplomatic Relations[33] and the Vienna Convention on Consular Relations.[34] Iraq's occupation of Kuwait also involved the destruction of Kuwaiti public records and public and private property, including hospital supplies and equipment, and the relocation or forced departure of Kuwait's population. Again, therefore, Iraq was perpetrating violations of unambiguous and well-known principles of international law, including the Geneva Convention on the Protection of Civilian Persons in Time of War.[35]

Despite these breaches the United Nations did no more than express alarm, condemn the conduct and demand the release and protection of those

---

[30] *The principle that States shall refrain in their international relations from the threat or use of force against the territorial integrity or political independence of any State, or in any other manner inconsistent with the purposes of the United Nations* is the first of seven principles set out within the declaration.

[31] United Nations Security Council Resolution 664 of 18 August 1990, S/RES/664 (1990), para 3 and 1 respectively.

[32] United Nations Security Council Resolution 667 of 16 September 1990, S/RES/667 (1990), preamble.

[33] *Vienna Convention on Diplomatic Relations*, opened for signature 14 April 1961, 500 UNTS 95 (entered into force 24 April 1964).

[34] *Vienna Convention on Consular Relations*, opened for signature 24 April 1963, 596 UNTS 262 (entered into force 19 March 1967).

[35] *Geneva Convention relative to the Protection of Civilian Persons in Time of War*, opened for signature 12 August 1949, 75 UNTS 287 (entered into force 21 October 1950, also referred to as the Fourth Geneva Convention.

abducted.[36] Having said this, there was little more that the Security Council could do, in light of the sanctions it had already imposed and the demands made of Iraq, other than authorize the use of force by its members. The question, then, is whether the Council should have acted to that effect. Was the United Nations too slow to respond to the aggressive conduct of the Iraqi regime and, as a consequence, was there an unnecessary loss of life or injury to people within Kuwait? The question is all too easy to ask in retrospect. On the one hand, emphasis could be placed on the fact that an authorization to use force does not have to amount to an open, unlimited authority to intervene. Just as Resolution 665 authorized the use of necessary means to interdict vessels to and from Kuwait for the enforcement of trade sanctions, the Security Council could have authorized member States concerned to conduct operations for the extraction of diplomatic staff from Kuwait.

Before judging the reluctance of the Council to authorize intervention, however, it should be remembered that the aim of the United Nations, and particularly the Security Council, is to maintain international peace and security primarily through the peaceful settlement of disputes rather than to an immediate recourse to force. Two of the preambular paragraphs of Resolution 674 illustrate the Security Council's thinking to that end:[37]

> *Reaffirming* the goal of the international community of maintaining international peace and security by seeking to resolve international disputes and conflicts by peaceful means,
> ...
> *Reaffirming* its determination to ensure compliance by Iraq with its resolutions by maximum use of political and diplomatic means,

This is also reflected within paragraph 12 of Resolution 674, through which the Security Council entrusted the UN Secretary-General to make available his "good offices" (conciliation or mediation) and to undertake diplomatic efforts to reach a peaceful solution to the crisis.

Operation Desert Storm

By late November 1990, Iraq had still failed to withdraw from Kuwait, despite the various measures taken by the United Nations and the political

---

[36] See Resolution 667, above, n 31, particularly paras 1 to 4; United Nations Security Council Resolution 674 of 29 October 1990, S/RES/674 (1990), particularly paras 1 to 10; and United Nations Security Council Resolution 677 of 28 November 1990, S/RES/677 (1990), para 1.
[37] Ibid.

pressures brought to bear against the Iraqi Government. The failure by Iraq to withdraw resulted in the Security Council issuing a further Resolution, 678, of 29 November 1990.[38] The Resolution expressed the following position of the Security Council:

1. *Demands* that Iraq comply fully with resolution 660 (1990) and all subsequent relevant resolutions, and decides, while maintaining all its decisions, to allow Iraq one final opportunity, as a pause of goodwill, to do so;

2. *Authorises* Member States co-operating with the Government of Kuwait, unless Iraq on or before 15 January 1991 fully implements, as set forth in paragraph 1 above, the above-mentioned resolutions, to use all necessary means to uphold and implement resolution 660 (1990) and all subsequent relevant resolutions and to restore international peace and security in the area;

Iraq's failure to withdraw from Kuwait by 15 January 1991 resulted in the commencement of *Operation Desert Storm* on 17 January 1991.[39] The Operation was commenced through significant and sustained air strikes over a period of weeks, followed by the entry of ground troops into Kuwait and Iraq on 23 February 1991. The US-led forces were ordered to cease fire by President George Bush (Snr) on 27 February 1991, in response to letters to the President of the Security Council and to the UN Secretary-General from the Deputy Prime Minister and Minister of Foreign Affairs of Iraq. Those letters expressed Iraq's agreement to comply with the earlier Security Council resolutions discussed and its intention to immediately release prisoners of war. With that in mind, the Security Council issued Resolution 686 on 2 March 1991, setting out the terms upon which the authorization to use force would expire.[40] Iraqi leaders formally accepted the terms of the Resolution on 3 March 1991.[41]

A significant point about *Operation Desert Storm* is that the authority to intervene, under Resolution 678, is a conventional example of "collective security". It illustrates a delegation of authority from the Security Council to a coalition of UN member States for the purpose of restoring peace and security, which has been unable to be achieved through peaceful means. This is a fundamental cornerstone of the United Nations system. It rests on the idea that collectively, through the mechanisms of the

---

[38] United Nations Security Council Resolution 678 of 29 November 1990, S/RES/678 (1990) – Appendix 6D herein

[39] Air raids commenced 17 January 1991 at 2:38 a.m. (local time) or January 16 at 6:38PM EST (due to an eight-hour time difference), with an Apache helicopter attack: see *Operation Desert Storm*, URL <http://www.desert-storm.com/War/chronology.html> at 7 May 2004.

[40] United Nations Security Council Resolution 686 of 2 March 1991, S/RES/686 (1991).

[41] Above, n 39.

United Nations, the international community can achieve peace and security and thereby avoid another world war, the second of which triggered the creation of the United Nations. That notion is reflected throughout the Charter and the structure of the institution. It is implicit in the very name "United Nations", an organization comprised of nations that have united for the purposes set out in the organization's constitutive treaty.[42]

For the sake of this discussion, consideration is not given to the means by which the operation was conducted and whether or not the laws of armed conflict were complied with. There is no doubt that the law of armed conflict, or international humanitarian law, and subsequent issues concerning the means by which any violations of that body of law was, or should have been, dealt with are all issues that concern the broader concern of "international security". However, the aim of this book is to focus upon international security through the United Nations (that is, through the Security Council and General Assembly), having particular regard to Afghanistan and Iraq. It is for that reason that issues concerning international humanitarian and criminal law are not considered.

Peace and Security in the Region

Despite the repulsion of Iraqi forces from Kuwait under *Operation Desert Storm*, Iraq remained belligerent. It threatened to use chemical and biological weapons against Kuwait. It did in fact fire ballistic missiles in unprovoked attacks against Kuwait, and US and UK intelligence sources reported that Iraq was attempting to acquire materials for a nuclear weapons programme. The result was that, exactly one month after the conclusion of *Desert Storm*,[43] the Security Council issued a further resolution against Iraq. Resolution 687 was adopted on 3 April 1991, again under Chapter VII of the UN Charter, with various distinct objectives.[44]

---

[42] In that regard, see Chapter 1, which considers the framework of the United Nations and the Charter pertaining to the maintenance of international peace and security.

[43] Iraqi leaders formally accepted the ceasefire of US-led forces under *Operation Desert Storm* on 3 March 1991.

[44] United Nations Security Council Resolution 687 of 3 April 1991, S/RES/687 (1991) – Appendix 6C herein.

The Demilitarized Zone Between Iraq and Kuwait

The first objective under Resolution 687 was to establish a ceasefire between Iraq and Kuwait, which is addressed within Parts A and B of the Resolution. Part A, through paragraphs 2 to 4 inclusive, demanded that Iraq respect the inviolability of the international boundary with Kuwait, as had been set out in the 1963 Treaty of Friendly Relations between the two States. It called upon the establishment of a demilitarized zone[45] and authorized the use of force to enforce the ceasefire. Paragraph 4, by which the latter authority was issued, was specific in its authority being limited to the enforcement of the ceasefire and for no other reason:

> 2. *Demands* that Iraq and Kuwait respect the inviolability of the international boundary and the allocation of islands set out in the "Agreed Minutes between the State of Kuwait and the Republic of Iraq regarding the restoration of friendly relations, recognition and the related matters", signed by them in the exercise of their sovereignty at Baghdad on 4 October 1963 and registered with the United Nations;
>
> 3. *Calls upon* the Secretary-General to lend his assistance to make arrangements with Iraq and Kuwait to demarcate the boundary between Iraq and Kuwait, drawing on appropriate material including the maps transmitted with the letter dated 28 March 1991 addressed to him by the Permanent Representative of the United Kingdom of Great Britain and Northern Ireland to the United Nations, and to report back to the Council within one month;
>
> 4. *Decides* to guarantee the inviolability of the abovementioned international boundary and to take, as appropriate, all necessary measures to that end in accordance with the Charter of the United Nations;

It should be noted at this stage that Resolution 687 contains no other provision authorizing the use of force. The relevance of this becomes clear in the examination of the United Kingdom's and United States's arguments of implied authority to use force under *Operation Iraqi Freedom*.[46]

---

[45] The demilitarized zone was specified in Part B of the resolution as being 10 km into Iraqi territory and 5 km into Kuwaiti territory from the international boundary under the 1963 Treaty of Friendship between Iraq and Kuwait (see para 5), as recommended in a letter dated 28 March 1991 from the Permanent Representative of the United Kingdom to the United Nations Secretary-General.

[46] The argument being, in part, that Resolution 687 was one of three resolutions of the Security Council from which there was implicit authority to use force against Iraq for failure to comply with United Nations Security Council Resolution 1441 of 8 November 2002, S/RES/1441 (2002) – Appendix 6H herein. See Chapter 7.

Part B of the Resolution set out the means by which the ceasefire was to operate and be monitored, including the establishment of a UN observer unit (the United Nations Iraq-Kuwait Observation Mission) and the implementation of the terms of surrender by Iraq as specified in Resolution 686.[47] The balance of Resolution 687 addressed the issue of weapons of mass destruction; the return or Kuwaiti property;[48] the liability of Iraq for its debts;[49] trade sanctions (including trade in arms and weapons-related materials);[50] and humanitarian assistance.[51]

Boundary demarcation. As part of the initiative to maintain peace and security between Kuwait and Iraq, the UN established the United Nations Iraq-Kuwait Demarcation Commission to undertake the technical task of determining, for the first time, the precise coordinates of the boundary that had been agreed upon under the 1963 Treaty of Friendly Relations.[52] Within Security Council Resolution 773, which considered the work of the Demarcation Commission, the Council reiterated its preparedness to enforce any violation of the cease fire in the demilitarized zone, stating at paragraph 4 that it:[53]

> *Underlines* its guarantee of the inviolability of the above-mentioned international boundary and its decision to take as appropriate all necessary measures to that end in accordance with the Charter, as provided for in paragraph 4 of resolution 687 (1991);

As indicated, the mandate of the Commission was not to reallocate a boundary between Iraq and Kuwait, but simply to define the geographic coordinates of the previously agreed-upon boundary. As a result of the

---

[47] The mandate, conduct and authority of the United Nations Iraq-Kuwait Observation Mission was subsequently addressed within United Nations Security Council Resolutions 689 of 9 April 1991, S/RES/689 (1991); and 806 of 5 February 1993, S/RES/806 (1993).

[48] The return of Kuwaiti property was addressed within Part D of Resolution 687.

[49] The liability of Iraq for its debts and obligations was addressed within Part E of Resolution 687; and subsequently within United Nations Security Council Resolutions 692 of 20 May 1991, S/RES/692 (1991); and 705 of 15 August 1991, S/RES705 (1991).

[50] The issue of trade sanctions was addressed within Part F of Resolution 687; and subsequently within United Nations Security Council Resolution 700 of 17 June 1991, S/RES/700 (1991).

[51] Humanitarian assistance was addressed within Part G of Resolution 687; and subsequently within United Nations Security Council Resolution 688 of 5 April 1991, S/RES/ 688 (1991), concerning the repression of Kurdish-populated areas within Iraq.

[52] See the report of the Secretary-General, *Report of the Secretary-General Regarding Paragraph 3 of Security Council Resolution 687 (1991)*, S/2258, 2 May 1991.

[53] United Nations Security Council Resolution 773 of 26 August 1992, S/RES/773 (1992).

work undertaken by the Commission, however, and perhaps not surprisingly, Iraq claimed that the Commission's report deprived it from land and water territories that it had possessed before its aggression against Kuwait in 1990.[54] The demilitarized zone was, following acceptance by the Security Council of the Commission's report, realigned accordingly.[55] Due to Iraq's dissatisfaction with the report, there were a series of early incidents at the realigned border, drawing the condemnation of the Security Council, affirmation of the finality of the decisions of the Commission, and reiteration of its position on the inviolability of the boundary.[56]

Further incidents. The only further incident drawing the comment of the Security Council concerning the demilitarized zone arose in 1994 where aggressive statements were made by the Revolution Command Council of Iraq and military deployments made in the direction of the border with Kuwait.[57] The Security Council demanded, in response, the immediate and complete withdrawal of all military units so deployed.[58] The Permanent Representative of Iraq had, just prior to this, advised of his Government's decision to withdraw those troops, and Iraq acted accordingly.[59] The demilitarized zone, and the security of the Iraq-Kuwait border, has not been a subject of Security Council resolutions since that time.

Oil for Food Programme

In the immediate aftermath of the Gulf War in 1991, the Secretary-General dispatched an inter-agency mission to assess the humanitarian needs arising in Iraq and Kuwait. The mission visited Iraq from 10 to 17 March 1991 and reported that "the Iraqi people may soon face a further imminent catastrophe, which could include epidemic and famine, if massive life-

---

[54] A useful consideration of Iraq's complaint on that subject was carried out by the Centre for Research and Studies on Kuwait, *The United Nations Iraq-Kuwait Demarcation Commission*, URL <http://www.crsk.org.un.htm> at 19 May 2004.

[55] As noted within United Nations Security Council Resolution 806 of 5 February 1993, S/RES/806 (1993), preambular para 3.

[56] Ibid, para 1. See also United Nations Security Council Resolution 833 of 27 May 1993, S/RES/833 (1993), paras 4 to 6.

[57] As brought to the attention of the Security Council by the letter from the Permanent Representative of Kuwait of 6 October 1994, S/1994/1137.

[58] United Nations Security Council Resolution 949 of 15 October 1994, S/RES/949 (1994), paras 2 to 4.

[59] Letter from the Permanent Representative of Iraq of 10 October 1994, S/1994/1149.

supporting needs are not rapidly met".[60] In July 1991, the Secretary-General submitted a further report to the Security Council outlining concerns about the serious nutritional and health situation of the Iraqi civilian population and the belief that the situation would further deteriorate.[61] The report concluded that the magnitude of the humanitarian needs in Iraq required funding that exceeded international aid and short-term palliatives, and could only be met from Iraq's own petroleum resources. The report recognized that trade sanctions imposed by the Security Council prevented Iraq from generating adequate revenue from those resources, but at the same time suggested the implementation of arrangements whereby Iraq could sell petroleum and request imports to meet humanitarian needs. The response of the Security Council was to offer Iraq an opportunity to sell limited quantities of oil to fund humanitarian needs.[62] The Government of Iraq declined the offers.

Although the Oil for Food Programme did not become established as an official programme of the United Nations until April 1995, steps towards this began through Security Council Resolutions 706 and 712, which established mechanisms for an exchange of trade in oil for food, authorized establishment of an escrow account, and set a goal of raising $1.6 billion from the sale of Iraqi oil during the first six months of the informal programme.[63] Indeed, the vast majority of resolutions adopted by the Security Council on Iraq from 1992 until the termination of the programme on 21 November 2003 were concerned with this subject.[64]

Weapons of Mass Destruction

The second major objective of Resolution 687 was to address the issue of weapons of mass destruction, in response to the threats made by Iraq

---

[60] *Report to the Secretary-General on humanitarian need in Kuwait and Iraq in the immediate post-crisis environment by a mission to the area led by Mr. Martii Ahtisaari, Under-Secretary-General for Administration and Management, dated 20 March 1991,* contained within the Secretary-General's letter of the same date to the Security Council, S/22366, 20 March 1991.

[61] *Report to the Secretary-General dated 15 July 1991 on humanitarian needs in Iraq prepared by a mission led by the Executive Delegate of the Secretary-General for humanitarian assistance in Iraq,* S/22799, 17 July 1991.

[62] See, in particular, United Nations Security Council Resolutions 706 of 15 August 1991, S/RES/ 706 (1991) and 712 of 19 September 1991, S/RES/712 (1991).

[63] United Nations Security Council Resolutions 706 of 15 August 1991, S/RES/706 (1991), and 712 of 19 September 1991, S/RES/712 (1991).

[64] The United Nations hosts a useful site on the Oil for Food Programme: see URL <http://www.un.org/Depts/oip>.

against Kuwait and due to the fear that Iraq was commencing a nuclear weapons programme.

Within the jurisdiction of the UN Weapons of Mass Destruction Branch, "weapons of mass destruction" are defined as nuclear, chemical and biological weapons, as well as ballistic missiles.[65] As highlighted within the Resolution, Iraq had obligations at that time under the Protocol for the Prohibition of the Use in War of Asphyxiating, Poisonous or Other Gases, and of Bacterial Methods of Warfare.[66] Iraq had also subscribed to the Final Declaration adopted by all States participating in the conference of States parties to the latter Protocol, that declaration establishing the objective of the universal elimination of chemical and biological weapons.[67] In 1972, it had signed the Convention on the Prohibition of the Development, Production and Stockpiling of Bacteriological (Biological) and Toxin Weapons and on Their Destruction (commonly referred to as the "Biological Weapons Convention", which augmented the 1925 Protocol.[68] Iraq had not, at the time of Resolution 687, ratified the Biological Weapons Convention. It had, however, signed and ratified the Convention on the Non-Proliferation of Nuclear Weapons (the "Non-Proliferation Treaty").[69] The Convention on the Prohibition of the Development, Production, Stockpiling and Use of Chemical Weapons and on Their Destruction (the Chemical Weapons Convention) had not been opened for signature at the time of Resolution 687.[70] On the issue of missiles there was then, and is still, no universally accepted norm or instrument specifically governing the

---

[65] The United Nations Weapons of Mass Destruction Branch is part of the organization's Department for Disarmament Affairs, governed by the General Assembly's First Committee on Disarmament and International Security.

[66] Signed at Geneva on 17 June 1925 and registered on 7 September 1929. Iraq became a party to the Protocol by accession on 8 September 1931.

[67] The *Conference of States Parties to the 1925 Geneva Protocol and Other Interested Parties* was held at Paris from 7 to 11 January 1989.

[68] The *Convention on the Prohibition of the Development, Production and Stockpiling of Bacteriological (Biological) and Toxin Weapons and on their Destruction*, opened for signature 10 April 1972, 1015 UNTS 168 (entered into force 26 March 1975). Iraq signed on 11 May 1972. It ultimately ratified, through pressure put upon it under Resolution 687, on 19 June 1991.

[69] The *Convention on the Non-Proliferation of Nuclear Weapons*, opened for signature 1 July 1968, 729 UNTS 169 (entered into force 5 March 1970). Iraq was an original signatory and ratified the treaty on 29 October 1969.

[70] The *Convention on the Prohibition of the Development, Production, Stockpiling and Use of Chemical Weapons and on Their Destruction*, opened for signature 13 January 1993, CD/CW/WP.400/Rev.1 (entered into force 29 April 1997). Iraq has, at June 2004, neither signed nor acceded to the Chemical Weapons Convention.

development, testing, production, acquisition, transfer, deployment or use of missiles.[71]

Despite the various legal and good faith obligations referred to, Iraq had previously used chemical weapons and was making threats to do use both chemical and biological weapons against Kuwait, notwithstanding its formal acceptance of a ceasefire as a consequence of *Operation Desert Storm*. It also launched unprovoked ballistic missile attacks against Kuwait. Against that background, and together with intelligence reports that Iraq was attempting to acquire materials for a nuclear weapons programme, it was imperative for the Security Council to properly address the issue of weapons of mass destruction and the threat posed by such weapons to peace and security in the region.

Weapons verification programme. Under Resolution 687, Iraq was required to destroy, remove, or render harmless all chemical and biological weapons and related systems and development facilities and all ballistic missiles with a range greater than 150 km.[72] It was also required to unconditionally undertake not to use, develop, construct or acquire nuclear weapons and related systems, components and development facilities.[73] Iraq was obliged to submit a formal adoption of Resolution 687, and invited to unconditionally reaffirm its commitment to the Treaty on the Non-Proliferation of Nuclear Weapons.[74] This second major objective of the Resolution is set out within Part C but, unlike Part A of the Resolution, is not accompanied with an authority to use force for the implementation of the provisions within that Part.[75]

As will be seen through the discussion of weapons inspectors below, Resolution 687 contains significant detail in terms of the obligations of Iraq concerning weapons of mass destruction and the various tasks to be undertaken by United Nations inspectors. Concerning the more general

---

[71] In November 2000, the General Assembly requested the Secretary-General, with the assistance of a Panel of Governmental Experts, to prepare a report for the consideration of the General Assembly at its 57th session on the issue of missiles in all its aspects: United Nations General Assembly Resolution 55/33A of 20 November 2000, *Missiles*, A/RES/55/33A (2002). The Panel, after holding three sessions in 2001 and 2002, adopted a report by consensus and submitted it to the General Assembly at its 57th session: Report of the Secretary-General, *The Issue of Missiles in All its Aspects*, A/57/229.

[72] At para 8.

[73] At para 12.

[74] See paras 9 and 11.

[75] There is one further set of provisions, within Part G of Resolution 687, mainly dealing with post-conflict humanitarian issues (paras 30, 31 and, to some extent, 33) and requiring Iraq to undertake not to resort to, or support, terrorism (para 32).

question of peace and security in the region, which becomes relevant in the examination of the legality of intervention under *Operation Iraqi Freedom*, is the following provision of the Resolution:

14. *Notes* that the actions to be taken by Iraq in paragraphs 8 to 13 [inspections and disarmament] represent steps towards the goal of establishing in the Middle East a zone free from weapons of mass destruction and all missiles for their delivery and the objective of a global ban on chemical weapons;

Security Council Resolution 687 also called for the establishment of a Special Commission of the Security Council to act in liaison with the International Atomic Energy Agency (IAEA). The tasks of the IAEA and the Special Commission reflected the following corresponding obligations upon Iraq under the Resolution:

- to permit immediate on-site inspections of Iraq's nuclear capabilities;[76]
- to permit on-site inspections of Iraq's biological, chemical and missile capabilities;[77]
- to yield possession to the Special Commission of all chemical and biological weapons and all stocks of agents and related subsystems and components and all related research, development, support and manufacturing facilities (for them to be destroyed, removed or rendered harmless);[78] and
- to destroy, under the supervision of the Special Commission, all of its missile capabilities (including launchers) with a range greater than 150 km.[79]

For the purpose of implementing those tasks, the Director-General of the IAEA, Hans Blix, established the Iraq Action Team on 15 April 1991. That team comprised of IAEA officials and experts (covering all areas of nuclear technology as well as supporting specialties such as radiation protection, explosive ordnance disposal, communications and field security), as well as personnel of the Special Commission, under the leadership of a Chief Inspector. On 16 May 1991, the Director-General submitted a report to the Security Council setting out a plan for implementation of the Iraq Action

---

[76] See paras 12 and 13.
[77] At para 9(b)(i).
[78] At para 9(b)(ii). See also para 8(a).
[79] At para 9(b)(ii). See also para 8(b).

Team Mandate.[80] In his report, he informed the Council that the first on-site inspection commenced on 15 May 1991. The Director-General's plan was approved by the Security Council under Resolution 699.[81]

Implementation of the Resolution 687 regime. Difficulties in the implementation of the weapons inspection plan arose as early as mid-1991. A high-level mission consisting of the Executive Chairman of the Special Commission, the Director-General of the IAEA and the UN Under-Secretary for Disarmament Affairs was, in response, held with the Government of Iraq.[82] The subsequent report of the mission pointed to non-compliance on the part of Iraq with its obligations under Part C of Resolution 687, including incomplete declarations and general non-cooperation with weapons inspectors.[83] The Security Council condemned this as a material breach of Resolution 687 and expressed compliance to be an essential condition to the restoration of peace and security in the region.[84] It reaffirmed Iraq's Part C obligations and set out various further obligations concerning weapons of mass destruction disarmament.[85]

From that time until mid-1996, the verification programme ran reasonably smoothly, at least smoothly enough not to invoke adverse comments from the Security Council. On 11 and 12 June 1996, access by a Special Commission inspection team to sites in Iraq, which had been designated by the Commission for inspection, was excluded by Iraqi authorities. The Security Council considered that this constituted a clear violation of the verification regimes under Resolutions 687, 707 and 715 and demanded that Iraq provide inspectors with "immediate, unconditional and unrestricted access to any and all areas, facilities, equipment, records and means of transportation which they wish to inspect".[86] Iraq complied with the Resolution.

---

[80] Contained within the report of the United Nations Secretary-General to the Security Council, *Plan Developed by the Director General of the International Atomic Energy Agency (IAEA) for the Destruction, Removal or Rendering Harmless of Nuclear-Weapons-Usable Materials in Iraq*, S/22615, 17 May 1991 – Appendix 7 herein.

[81] United Nations Security Council Resolution 699 of 17 June 1991, S/RES/699 (1991). The implementation plan was further amended and approved under Resolution 715 of 11 October 1991, S/RES/715 (1991).

[82] At the request of the Secretary-General on 28 June 1991.

[83] See the preambular statements within United Nations Security Council Resolution 707 of 15 August 1991, S/RES/707 (1991) – Appendix 6E herein.

[84] Ibid, para 1.

[85] Above, n 44, paras 3 to 5. See also United Nations Security Council Resolution 715 of 11 October 1991, S/RES/715 (1991) – Appendix 6F herein.

[86] United Nations Security Council Resolution 1060 of 12 June 1996, S/RES/1060 (1996), paras 1 and 2.

Similar incidents arose 12 months later, where access was denied to an inspection team to designated sites within Iraq on 10 and 12 June 1997. The response of the Council was to again demand immediate and unconditional compliance, and to also express that non-compliance would result in the imposition of additional measures, including travel bans on Iraqi officials involved in refusing to grant access.[87] Iraq this time maintained its position, continuing to deny access to weapons inspectors. The further condemnation of the Council and threat to impose sanctions under Resolution 1134 did not persuade Iraq to comply.[88] Tensions escalated, seeing the Deputy Prime Minister of Iraq advise the President of the Security Council that inspections would only be permitted on conditions suitable to Iraq, including the withdrawal of reconnaissance aircraft operating on behalf of the Special Commission.[89] In response to that advice, the International Atomic Energy Agency immediately suspended its monitoring activities.[90] The Special Commission attempted to carry on its work, but access continued to be denied. Travel bans were accordingly imposed upon all Iraqi officials and members of the Iraqi armed forces who were responsible for or participated in the instances of non-compliance.[91] Iraq remained defiant and all weapons inspectors and Special Commission staff withdrew from Iraq, with the Security Council issuing Resolution 1154 in March 1998.[92]

Operation Desert Fox

By Resolution 1154, the Security Council stressed upon Iraq that the provision of immediate and unrestricted access to IAEA weapons inspectors was necessary for the implementation of Resolution 687.[93] The

---

[87] United Nations Security Council Resolution 1115 of 21 June 1997, S/RES/1115 (1997), paras 2 and 3 (demands for compliance) and 6 (intention to impose measures in the event of non-compliance).

[88] United Nations Security Council Resolution 1134 of 23 October 1997, S/RES/1134 (1997), paras 1 to 4 (condemnation, expression of non-compliance being a violation of the verification regime and demands for immediate compliance) and para 6 (intention to impose measures in the event of non-compliance).

[89] Letter of 29 October 1997, S/1997/829.

[90] See the letter of the Director-General of the International Atomic Energy Agency, Hans Blix, to the United Nations Secretary-General of 31 October 1997, S/1997/833.

[91] United Nations Security Council Resolution 1137 of 12 November 1997, S/RES/1137 (1997), para 4.

[92] United Nations Security Council Resolution 1154 of 2 March 1998, S/RES/1154 (1998) – Appendix 6G.

[93] At para 3.

Resolution stated, in that context, that "any violation would have severest consequences for Iraq".[94] The failure by Iraq to permit the return of inspectors on those terms led to the UK/US-led coalition action under *Operation Desert Fox*. *Desert Fox* comprised a series of air strikes for four days and nights from 16 December 1998, with its expressed aims being the degrading of Iraq's capability to build and use weapons of mass destruction and diminishing the military threat posed by Iraq to its neighbours.[95]

Operation Desert Fox was immediately criticized by States from both within and outside the Security Council as being illegal at international law and pre-emptive of the authority of the Security Council, since there was no further resolution of the Council authorizing "all necessary means" to enforce Resolution 1154 or its predecessors. The position adopted by coalition States was that there was no need for any further resolution, the authority to use force being implied from the combination of Resolutions 678, 687 and the wording of Resolution 1154 notifying Iraq that non-compliance would result in the "severest consequences". This argument, which has come to be known as one of "automaticity", was also adopted by coalition States in the 2003 intervention in Iraq and is considered in detail in the next chapter.

Trade Sanctions in the Maintenance of Peace and Security

For the sake of simplicity, this chapter has only focused, in any detail, on the trade sanctions issued against Iraq leading up to *Operation Desert Storm*.

In the context of the refusals to grant access to weapons inspectors in 1996 and 1997, it has been discussed that the Security Council took the view that each incident constituted a violation of the weapons verification regime established under Resolution 687, 707 and 715. At face value, that is certainly a logical conclusion, since the regime required unconditional access to be granted to weapons inspectors. The counter-argument, and that adopted by Iraq, concerned the continuance of trade sanctions against Iraq. Although the argument could not displace the verification obligations upon Iraq (which were mandatory under article 25 of the UN Charter and which had not been lifted), the position advocated by the Iraqi Government was that there no longer remained any incentives for it to comply with the

---

[94] Ibid.

[95] See the United States Department of Defense website *DefenceLINK*, at URL <http://www.defenselink.mil/specials/desert_fox>.

verification regime. Specifically, Iraq pointed to the trade sanctions imposed under Resolution 661, and expanded upon under the subsequent resolutions discussed above, and the notion that the continued imposition of those sanctions was improper, given Iraq's compliance with the verification regime from the end of 1991 until mid-1996.

From this latter point, and issues discussed earlier within this chapter, there appear to be various lessons to be learnt about the manner in which trade sanctions are imposed for the furtherance of peace and security.

The targeting of sanctions. It is trite to say that non-military sanctions should function in such a manner as to target the regime in question, thus placing economic or other pressure upon a non-compliant State to adhere to relevant international law norms or resolutions of the Security Council. Equally, however, this has proven to be a difficult task for the Security Council to achieve. As seen in the case of sanctions imposed upon Iraq following the second Gulf War, under *Operation Desert Storm*, sanctions that were originally intended to put pressure upon the regime and turn the Iraqi people against the leadership indirectly led to concerns about the malnutrition and health of the Iraqi people. Because of the belligerent position adopted by the Iraqi regime, sanctions that were meant to last for a short time and compel the State instead became oppressive against the civilian population and ultimately led to the Oil for Food Programme.

In contrast, the article 41 measures imposed following the 1996 and 1997 refusals to grant site access to weapons inspectors were directly targeted against those personnel involved in non-compliance with the weapons verification regime.[96]

Sensible terms and maintenance of sanctions. The final issue concerns the maintenance of sanctions and the need to adopt an even-handed approach so that States against whom sanctions are imposed have achievable incentives for compliance with regimes and resolutions of the Security Council. As seen through the crises in 1996 and 1997, Iraq became disheartened with the fact that it had been complying with Resolution 687 and the verification regime but, despite this, saw no relaxing of the sanctions against it. It accordingly denied access to weapons inspectors. This is partly due to the conditions upon which the sanctions would be lifted: namely, the lifting of sanctions was made dependent upon the delivery of an inspection report to the Security Council stating that all that could be used in the production of nuclear, biological or chemical weapons

---

[96] Through the imposition of travel bans against such personnel.

had been found and destroyed and that there was nothing left anywhere in Iraq.[97]

The Transnational Foundation for Peace and Future Research identified a number of highly compelling questions that do not appear to have been properly considered in the imposition of the Resolution 661 sanctions:[98]

1. Will it at all be possible for inspectors to state that no amount of a substance pertaining to weapons of mass-destruction exists in a country that covers about half a million square kilometres and is not exactly eager to reveal everything about its military?

2. Is it wise to make the lifting of sanctions conditional upon such a declaration by inspectors, i.e. to use sanctions as leverage for the disarmament process?

3. What if the process takes a much longer time and inspectors will still be there in, say, 2003? If we want 100% compliance and a guarantee that Iraq is 100% clean, that will take time. Sanctions are known to have negative effects on citizens. So, isn't there a risk that, if we make slow progress, we will be made morally responsible for the increasingly destructive humanitarian consequences?

Lessons. These are all excellent questions and strike at the heart of concerns surrounding the use of economic and other non-military sanctions for the maintenance of peace and security. To the author's mind, the process by which non-military sanctions are imposed and maintained requires the establishment of a permanent sanctions committee of the Security Council, much along the lines of the situation-specific committees currently utilized under Rule 28 of the Rules of Procedure of the Security Council.[99] By establishing a permanent committee, rather than ones on an ad hoc basis, expertise can be accumulated on the appropriate terms of economic sanctions and the need to take into account humanitarian and other needs. It should be that committee which drafts the terms of sanctions, with the mandate to monitor how the sanctions are impacting upon citizens of the State in question, as well as its neighbours,[100] and make

---

[97] Resolution 687, above, n 44, Part F.

[98] Oberg, J. and Harleman, C., "Why the Security Council Will Never Lift the Sanctions on Iraq", Transnational Foundation for Peace and Future Research, URL <http://www.jacksonprogressive.com/issues/iraq2002/pressinfo176-031303.html> at 14 June 2004.

[99] The one established, for example, concerning Iraq: above, n 12.

[100] That issue has been the subject of detailed attention by the Special Committee on the Charter of the United Nations and on the Strengthening of the Role of the Organization,

recommendations for amendment of sanctions accordingly. In particular, care should be taken in setting the terms upon which sanctions are to be modified or lapse.

Conclusion

Iraq is a State which has been identified as the cause of much conflict and instability in the Middle East. Its unsuccessful battle with Iran during the First Persian Gulf War of 1980 to 1988 was soon followed by its invasion of Kuwait in 1990 after reigniting long-held disputes with Kuwait concerning the border between Kuwait and Iraq, the consequent ownership of oil fields and the independent status of Kuwait. Through refusals to withdraw from Kuwait, trade sanctions were imposed against Iraq and, ultimately, military sanctions were authorized by the Security Council under Resolution 678 in order to repel Iraqi forces from Kuwait. This Second Persian Gulf War, conducted under *Operation Desert Storm*, succeeded in its mandate but did not dissuade the Government of Iraq from making threats to use weapons of mass destruction, launching unprovoked missile attacks against Kuwait, and moving forces towards the international boundary with Kuwait. The United Nations response was threefold. First, the Security Council established a ceasefire under Resolution 687, with an authority to use force in the event of a breach of the ceasefire. Next, and in furtherance of resolving the dispute about territory, the UN established a Demarcation Commission to determine the geographic coordinates of the international boundary between Iraq and Kuwait. Next, and again under Resolution 687 (together with subsequent Resolutions 707 and 715), it imposed disarmament and non-proliferation obligations upon Iraq, coupled with a verification programme under the supervision of the United Nations Special Commission (UNSCOM) and the International Atomic Energy Agency (IAEA).

These events reveal the complex nature of the United Nations' role in the maintenance of peace and security and the ill-effects that can result from either reacting too slowly and without sufficient vigour, or too onerously and without proper reconsideration or incentives for compliance. Examples of tardy responses can be seen through a reluctance to authorize the use of force in response to the invasion of Kuwait in 1990 and the continuing advance of Iraqi troops despite non-military sanctions,

---

Report of the Special Committee on the Charter of the United Nations and on the Strengthening of the Role of the Organization, 22 May 2000, A/55/33, paras 16–97.

potentially contributing to the additional material damage and loss of life in Kuwait. On the other hand, economic sanctions have been identified by some as having been ineffectively targeted against the Government of Iraq, resulting in humanitarian crises for the people of Iraq and ultimately requiring action to be taken under the Oil for Food programme. Likewise, the sanctions have been criticized as lacking objectivity and a system of incremental incentives by which compliance with the weapons verification programme imposed against Iraq might be rewarded. The continued existence of sanctions was, in part, relied on by Iraq as the reason for its refusal to continue to cooperate with UNSCOM and the IAEA weapons inspectors, which ultimately led to their withdrawal from Iraq in 1997 and the US-led *Operation Desert Fox* in December 1998.

Chapter 7

Operation Iraqi Freedom

Introduction

The intervention in Iraq in 2003 has been a matter of considerable controversy, both prior to the commencement of operations and since the intervention in light of the failure of coalition forces to find weapons of mass destruction within the Iraqi territory, and allegations of faulty intelligence and misleading public statements by State officials. Many issues arise out of the war, including the basis upon which States may use force against one another; the effectiveness of the various international instruments governing the non-proliferation and disarmament of weapons of mass destruction; the conduct of military operations in the field; the role of the United Nations and others in post-war reconstruction; the accuracy or otherwise of military intelligence used by leaders to justify action against Iraq; and the role and relevance of international law in modern politics. All are important. All have an impact on the maintenance of international peace and security. The focus of this chapter, however, is a limited one and considers an important aspect of the overall theme of this text: the role of the Security Council in maintaining international peace and the exclusivity of that role.[1]

Of the various key issues arising from the 2003 intervention in Iraq, the basis upon which States may use force against one another has attracted significant attention. Various arguments might be employed in an attempt to validate the action against Iraq. It might be argued, for example, that intervention was permissible as an act of anticipatory self-defence, in the face of intelligence suggesting that Iraq was in a position to launch

---

[1] Regard will not be had to the United Nations post-conflict role in Iraq for two principal reasons: first, due to the still fast-developing nature of post-conflict operations in Iraq and, second, due to the fact that the United Nations' role in post-conflict reconstruction has already received considerable attention within Chapter 4. Likewise, regard will not be givento the United Nations action on disarmament and non-proliferation. While certainly an important aspect of the UN role in the maintenance of peace and security, this is an extensive subject. Some consideration, in the Iraqi context, has been given to this subject within Chapter 6 and this will be the extent of consideration of that subject, given the "case-study" nature of this text.

weapons of mass destruction at 45 minutes' notice. This would have to be tempered against the subsequent finding by the United Kingdom Parliamentary Foreign Affairs Committee on 7 July 2003 that a dossier on Iraq's weapons, relied upon by Prime Minister Blair in his address to Parliament on 18 March 2003, was incorrect. The contention would also need to reflect upon the legal arguments that neither the United Nations Charter, nor customary international law, permit anticipatory self-defence.[2] A more controversial position might also have been posited: that action was permissible by way of humanitarian intervention, due to the dreadful human rights record of the Saddam regime.[3]

Ultimately, however, it is only one argument that was used by all members of the coalition forces. As will be seen through the overview of the respective positions of coalition States, below, the intervention in Iraq was founded on the basis that there existed an implied authority from United Nations Security Council resolutions to use force against Iraq, and through Iraq's failure to comply with the UN-imposed weapons of mass destruction disarmament and verification programme established under those resolutions. This concept of implied authority has come to be known as one of "automaticity" and was also adopted by coalition States in the 1998 intervention in Iraq under *Operation Desert Fox*.[4]

Respective Positions on the Authority to Intervene in Iraq

As indicated, the common justification for intervention in Iraq employed by coalition forces has been the existence of an implied authority through Security Council resolutions. In an answer to a question raised in the United Kingdom Parliament, Attorney General Lord Goldsmith advised the House on 17 March 2003 that intervention in Iraq was justified:[5]

> Authority to use force against Iraq exists from the combined effect of resolutions 678, 687 and 1441. All of these resolutions were adopted under Chapter VII of the UN Charter which allows the use of force for the express purpose of restoring international peace and security.

---

[2] As considered within Chapter 5.

[3] "Humanitarian intervention" involves the notion that States may intervene by use of force against another State where the latter state is committing gross human rights violations and where immediate action is necessary to prevent further loss of life.

[4] See Chapter 6, 132.

[5] A full copy of the advice is available within the Report of a Committee of Privy Counsellors, *Review of Intelligence on Weapons of Mass Destruction*, ordered by the United Kingdom House of Commons to be printed 14 July 2004, Annex D – Appendix 8 herein.

The following day, Australian Prime Minister John Howard said this at a news conference:[6]

> The action that might be taken as a result of this decision [to commit Australian troops] has a sound legal basis in the resolutions of the Security Council that have already been passed. If you go back to Resolution 678, 687 and 1441, you find ample legal authority. That [advice] ... is almost identically the published view of the Attorney-General of the United Kingdom Government.

In a press release from the United States Department of State, Secretary of State Colin Powell took a much more robust approach. He too made reference to the existence of an implied authority to act, but went further to say:[7]

> If the UN does not act, then it would be necessary for the United States to act with a willing coalition.

Opposed to the latter positions, numerous States took the position that intervention in Iraq was not permissible without a further resolution of the Security Council providing an explicit authority to use all necessary means, including force, to enforce Resolution 1441 and its predecessors.[8] The question, then, is this: *did* the combination of the Security Council resolutions relied upon (Resolutions 678, 687 and 1441) act to trigger a right of UN members to use force for the enforcement of those Resolutions?[9] That is the argument of automaticity. Given that this position relies on the combined effect of Security Council Resolutions 678,

---

[6] Transcript available from ABC News Online, "Howard confirms Australian military commitment to Iraq war", URL <http://www.abc.net.au/public/s809462.htm>.

[7] US Department of State website, "Powell: Issue is Iraqi Compliance, Not More Inspectors", 9 February 2003, URL <http://usinfo.state.gov/regional/nea/iraq/text2003/0209pwl.htm>.

[8] Including France and Russia, both permanent members of the Security Council. French President Jacques Chirac and German Chancellor Gerhard Schroeder issued a joint declaration at a head-of-government summit meeting in Hanover on 8 September stating that they would not agree to take part in any armed intervention in Iraq without such explicit authority: see McWhinney, E., "The United Nations Charter and the Non-Use-of-Force: The *Chrétien Doctrine* and the Iraq Crisis", *Bulletin of the Canadian Council on International Law*, Vol 1, No 1, Winter/Spring 2003, URL <http://www.ccil-ccdi.ca/bulletin/mcwhinney.html> at 24 March 2004.

[9] In the situation of *Operation Desert Fox*, the argument was that authority to intervene flowed from the combined effect of United Nations Security Council Resolutions 678 of 29 November 1990, S/RES/678 (1990), 687 of 3 April 1991, S/RES/687 (1991) and 1154 of 2 March 1998, S/RES/1154 (1998) – Appendices 6C, 6D and 6G herein.

687 and 1441, it is important to place those Resolutions in perspective and examine their provisions and effect.

Before considering the particular Security Council resolutions in question and the meaning of them, it is important to have regard to the comments of the International Court of Justice on the interpretation of Security Council resolutions. In the *Namibia Advisory Opinion*, where the sole decision of the world court was sought concerning this question, the Court emphasized the need to give very careful consideration to both the words and context of resolutions:[10]

> The language of a resolution of the Security Council should be carefully analyzed ... having regard to the terms of the resolution to be interpreted, the discussions leading to it, the Charter provisions invoked and, in general, all circumstances that might assist in determining the legal consequences.

Security Council Resolutions 678 and 687

The background to, and provisions of, these first two resolutions has already been discussed in detail in the preceding chapter. Security Council Resolution 678 provided Iraq with a final opportunity to withdraw from Kuwait, following its act of aggression in August 1990, and authorized the use of all necessary means by coalition forces to uphold and implement the Resolution. Iraq's failure to comply resulted in *Operation Desert Storm* in 1991. Following the successful repulsion of Iraqi forces from Kuwait and due to Iraq's continued belligerence and intelligence concerning weapons of mass destruction within Iraq, Security Council Resolution 687 implemented a ceasefire regime between Kuwait and Iraq. It also required Iraq: to destroy, remove, or render harmless all chemical and biological weapons and related systems and development facilities and all ballistic missiles with a range greater than 150 km;[11] to unconditionally undertake not to use, develop, construct or acquire nuclear weapons and related systems;[12] and to provide immediate and unrestricted access to its territory by a Special Commission and the International Atomic Energy Agency to verify the latter obligations.[13]

---

[10] *Advisory Opinion on the Legal Consequences for States of the Continued Presence of South Africa in Namibia* (Namibia Advisory Opinion) 1971 ICJ Reports 15, 23.
[11] At para 8.
[12] At para 12.
[13] Part C.

Turning to Lord Goldsmith's position, what can be taken from Resolutions 678 and 687? His advice, in answer to the question of the legality of the intervention, contained the following references to the Resolutions at hand:

1. In resolution 678 the Security Council authorized force against Iraq, to eject it from Kuwait and to restore peace and security in the area.

3. A material breach of resolution 687 revives the authority to use force under resolution 678.

Each point warrants detailed attention.

What is the Extent of the Authority to Use Force under Resolution 678?

The legal advice given was premised, as stated by the Attorney General, on the fact that the Resolutions, including Resolution 678, were adopted under Chapter VII of the UN Charter, which allows the use of force for the express purpose of restoring international peace and security. To that extent, he is correct. The preamble to Resolution 678 expressed itself as an action under Chapter VII of the United Nations Charter and reaffirmed the Council's earlier determination under Resolution 660 that the invasion of Kuwait constituted a breach of peace; and Chapter VII does indeed permit the Security Council to authorize the use of force for the purpose of restoring peace and security. Resolution 678 specifically authorizes member States to use "all necessary means" to uphold and implement Resolution 660:

> 2. *Authorizes* Member States co-operating with the Government of Kuwait, unless Iraq on or before 15 January 1991 fully implements, as set forth in paragraph 1 above, the above-mentioned resolutions, to use all necessary means to uphold and implement resolution 660 (1990) and all subsequent relevant resolutions and to restore international peace and security in the area;

The Attorney General then makes the point is that the Resolution authorized force against Iraq for two purposes: (1) to eject Iraq from Kuwait, in respect of which there can be no argument; and (2) to restore peace and security in the area. Technically speaking, the latter position is also correct since paragraph 2 of the Resolution authorizes the use of all necessary means to uphold and implement Resolution 660 "and all subsequent relevant resolutions and to restore international peace and security in the area". The question becomes one of extent and, with all due respect to the Attorney General, Resolution 678 bears no relevance at all to the Iraqi crisis of 2002 and 2003.

The first point to make in that regard is that the use of force was authorized to uphold Resolution 660 "and all subsequent *relevant* resolutions". In other words, it was adopted by the Security Council to secure the withdrawal of Iraq from Kuwait. The modern crisis, and the resultant Security Council Resolution 1441, did not have anything to do with an Iraqi presence in Kuwait and cannot therefore be said to form part of "subsequent relevant resolutions" to activate the paragraph 2 authority. For the same reason, the modern crisis has nothing to do with the restoration of international peace and security within the terms of Resolution 678, since the concern about peace and security (within Resolution 678) was with the Iraqi presence in Kuwait. Examining the Resolution in its context, it gave an authority to use force *if* Iraq failed to withdraw from Kuwait by 15 January 1991 and for the purpose of restoring the democratic republic of Kuwait. It is an untenable stretch of the imagination to say that it was also intended to provide an infinite, or at least long-lasting, authority to use force against Iraq to maintain peace and security in the region. Furthermore, the specific wording of the authorizing paragraph supports this analysis. The defining portion of the paragraph, by which the use of force is authorized, provides as follows: "*Authorizes* Member States co-operating with the Government of Kuwait...". The authority thereby expressly limits itself to the situation of conflict that was then presented.

Does a Material Breach of Resolution 687 Revive the Authority to Use Force under Resolution 678?

Resolution 687 was adopted, again under Chapter VII, on 3 April 1991 with two principal and distinct objectives. The first was to establish a ceasefire between Iraq and Kuwait, which is addressed within Part A of the Resolution, through paragraphs 2 to 4 inclusive. Part A called upon the establishment of a demilitarized zone[14] and authorized the use of force to enforce the ceasefire. Paragraph 4, by which the latter authority was issued, was specific in its authority being limited to the enforcement of the ceasefire and for no other reason:

> *Decides* to guarantee the inviolability of the abovementioned international boundary and to take, as appropriate, all necessary measures to that end in

---

[14] See Chapter 6x, 123–125.

accordance with the Charter of the United Nations;

Resolution 687 contains no other provision authorizing the use of force. Once more, the cease-fire has no bearing on the 2002/2003 Iraqi crisis. The relevance of Resolution 687 is limited to the fact that it placed upon Iraq certain obligations pertaining to disarmament and non-proliferation of weapons of mass destruction under the second main objective of the Resolution. The question raised by Lord Goldsmith, then, is whether a breach of this disarmament and verification regime revives the use of force authority under Resolution 678. First, one has to recognize that Resolution 687 does not invoke Resolution 678, except in its preambular paragraphs to say that the Resolution is "recalled"[15] and as follows:[16]

> *Affirming* the commitment of all Member States to the sovereignty, territorial integrity and political independence of Kuwait and Iraq, and noting the intention expressed by the Member States cooperating with Kuwait under paragraph 2 of resolution 678 (1990) to bring their military presence in Iraq to an end as soon as possible consistent with paragraph 8 of resolution 686 (1991),

Again, the terms of the Resolution restrict themselves to the question of the security threat posed by Iraq to Kuwait. Despite this, the United Kingdom Foreign and Commonwealth Office issued advice that Resolution 678 was not repealed by Resolution 687 but that, to the contrary:[17]

> ...it confirmed that SCR 678 remained in force. The authorisation was suspended for so long as Iraq complied with the conditions of the ceasefire.

As just discussed, however, reference to Resolution 678 is limited to the preambular paragraphs of Resolution 687. Resolution 687 makes no mention at all to suspension or reactivation of Resolution 678. There is no basis upon which a breach of the disarmament provisions of Resolution 687 can revive the Resolution 678 authority to use force.

Subsequent Resolutions

A further point should be made about the manner in which the Security Council has subsequently dealt with the Iraq-Kuwait ceasefire as opposed to the weapons verification regime.

---

[15] Preambular para 1.

[16] Preambular para 3.

[17] Above, n 5, para 5 of the Foreign and Commonwealth Office summary.

Threats by Iraq to Kuwait's sovereignty, either verbal or through the movement of troops, were addressed by the Security Council in its Resolutions 687, 773, 806 and 833. On each occasion, the Council reiterated the inviolability of the international boundary between Iraq and Kuwait, and expressed a willingness to take all necessary measures as appropriate to guarantee that inviolability.[18] The preparedness to use force was explicitly addressed and notified through the Security Council's resolutions.

In marked contrast, resolutions concerned with the weapons verification programme made no mention of such measures. Resolutions 707, 1060, 1115, 1134 and 1137 all condemned Iraq for material breaches of the programme, but did no more than demand the immediate and unconditional compliance of Iraq and, at best, threatened measures against those State officials refusing to allow access to Iraqi sites by weapons inspectors.[19]

The Security Council has therefore treated the issues as being quite separate from one another, calling for different responses on its part.

Summary

Addressing the two propositions of the UK Attorney General: first, Resolution 678 is limited, in its authorization of the use of force, to the maintenance of the sovereign independence of Kuwait and the exclusion of Iraqi forces from Kuwait; and, second, a material breach of the disarmament provisions of Resolution 687 does not revive the authority to use force under Resolution 678.

Security Council Resolution 1154

In the context of *Operation Desert Fox*, it is also of note that Resolution 687 led to the establishment of an Iraq Action Team and that difficulties arose with weapons inspections during 1996 and 1997, ultimately resulting

---

[18] United Nations Security Council Resolutions 687 of 4 April 1991, S/RES/687, para 4; 773 of 26 August 1992, S/RES/773 (1992), para 4; 806 of 5 February 1993, S/RES/806 (1993), para 1; and 833 of 27 May 1993, S/RES/833 (1993), para 6.
[19] United Nations Security Council Resolutions 707 of 15 August 1991, S/RES/707 (1991), para 1; 1060 of 12 June 1996, S/RES/1060 (1996), paras 1 and 2; 1115 of 21 June 1997, S/RES/1115 (1997), paras 2, 3 and 6; 1134 of 23 October 1997, S/RES/1134, paras 1 to 4 and 6; and 1137 of 12 November 1997, S/RES/1137 (1997), para 4.

in the withdrawal of the Action Team in 1998.[20] By Resolution 1154 of 2 March the same year, the Security Council therefore stressed upon Iraq that the provision of immediate and unrestricted access to the IAEA weapons inspectors was necessary for the implementation of Resolution 687.[21] Resolution 1154 stated, in that context, that "any violation would have severest consequences for Iraq".[22] The failure by Iraq to permit the return of inspectors on those terms led to the UK/US-led coalition action under *Operation Desert Fox*, a series of air strikes for four days and nights from 16 December 1998. In line with this century's position on the Iraqi intervention, the United Kingdom and United States then argued, in the debates of the Security Council on 16 December 1998, that this conduct was impliedly authorized through the combined effect of Resolutions 687 and 1154. The majority of the Council disagreed with that view, a matter for later discussion within this chapter.

Security Council Resolution 1441

At the instigation of the Bush Administration, the United Nations Security Council adopted Resolution 1441 on 8 November 2002, following the continued refusal by Iraq to comply with its obligations to provide UN weapons inspectors with unrestricted access to its facilities, and in view of growing concern that Iraq had re-established a weapons of mass destruction programme.[23] The Resolution begins by reiterating that Iraq remained in breach of Resolution 687.[24] It does not state which part of Resolution 687 it refers to, but it can only refer (by logic) to those parts of the Resolution pertaining to weapons of mass destruction. Part A of Resolution 687, in which the sole authority to use force is contained, relates to the ceasefire with Kuwait. As discussed, this portion of the 1991 Resolution does not hold any relevance to the concerns of the Bush and Blair Administrations. Furthermore, paragraph 1 of Resolution 1441 is limited in its reference to Iraq's breaches relating to its failure to cooperate with United Nations inspectors and to complete the actions under paragraphs 8 to 13 of Resolution 687.

---

[20] See Chapter 6, 128–131.

[21] At para 3.

[22] Ibid.

[23] United Nations Security Council Resolution 1441 of 8 November 2002, S/RES/1441 (2002) – Appendix 6H herein.

[24] At para 1.

Under paragraph 3, Iraq was required, as a first step towards compliance with its disarmament obligations, to submit a declaration concerning all aspects of its programmes to develop chemical, biological and nuclear weapons, ballistic missiles and other delivery systems. The Resolution expressly provided Iraq with "a final opportunity to comply with its disarmament obligations"[25] and in the penultimate paragraph:[26]

> *Recalls*, in that context, that the Council has repeatedly warned Iraq that it *will face serious consequences* as a result of its continued violations of its obligations; [emphasis added]

Subsequent to the adoption of Resolution 1441, Iraq lodged with the United Nations Secretary-General the declaration required of it under paragraph 3.[27] The United Nations Monitoring, Verification and Inspection Commission (UNMOVIC),[28] again under the leadership of Dr Hans Blix, carried out inspections of various facilities in Iraq, albeit that this was preceded by various stall tactics and initial difficulties in the conduct of inspections. The United States and United Kingdom complained that Iraq was in violation of Resolution 1441 through an alleged failure by Iraq to provide a full and accurate declaration as required under paragraph 3.[29] Interestingly, however, members of the Security Council were not united on the question of whether the allegations made against Iraq constituted a material breach of Resolution 1441.

On 6 March 2003, UNMOVIC lodged a report with the Security Council,[30] presented with an accompanying oral report from Hans Blix.[31] Dr Blix acknowledged some initial difficulties, but stated that UNMOVIC

---

[25] At para 2.

[26] At para 13.

[27] Lodged on 7 December 2002.

[28] UNMOVIC was established under United Nations Security Council Resolution 1284 (17 December 1999) to undertake the responsibilities of the former United Nations Special Commission (UNSCOM), which was charged with monitoring the elimination of weapons of mass destruction in Iraq.

[29] The address of US Secretary of State Colin Powell to the United Nations General Assembly on 5 February 2003 referred, for example, to: intercepted conversations within Iraqi military suggesting that evidence of weapons programmes was being destroyed; the finding by United Nations weapons inspectors of missile warheads capable of delivering chemical weapons; suspicion of mobile biological agent development facilities; and the existence of aluminium tubes capable of use for uranium enrichment.

[30] UNMOVIC Report, *Unresolved Disarmament Issues. Iraq's Proscribed Weapons Programmes*, 6 March 2003 (173 pages in length).

[31] The oral report was presented on 7 March 2003, a transcript of which is available online at URL <http://www.caabu.org/press/documents/blix-report-7march.html>.

had overall faced relatively few difficulties. He did not suggest that the inspection process had been easy, but he did acknowledge that UNMOVIC was able at that time to conduct professional no-notice inspections all over Iraq. In the final paragraph of his oral report, he said:

> How much time would it take to resolve the key remaining disarmament tasks? While cooperation can and is to be immediate, disarmament and at any rate the verification of it cannot be instant. Even with a proactive Iraqi attitude, induced by continued outside pressure, it would still take some time to verify sites and items, analyse documents, interview relevant persons, and draw conclusions. It would not take years, nor weeks, but months. Neither governments nor inspectors would want disarmament inspection to go on forever. However, it must be remembered that in accordance with the governing resolutions, a sustained inspection and monitoring system is to remain in place after verified disarmament to give confidence and to strike an alarm, if signs were seen of the revival of any proscribed weapons programmes.

Notwithstanding the calls for further inspectors and time for inspections, the US/UK-led coalition commenced military action against Iraq on 19 March 2003.

"All Necessary Means to Maintain Peace and Security"

Having already disposed of some of the issues in Lord Goldsmith's advice concerning the relevance of Security Council Resolutions 678 and 687, one further, vital, question remains. Did Resolutions 1154 and 1441 implicitly authorize the use of force against Iraq? Were the phrases "severest consequences for Iraq" and "it [Iraq] will face serious consequences" sufficient to trigger an authority for coalition forces to intervene in Iraq?

The starting point in this analysis is to have regard to the Security Council debates of 16 December 1998, the day *Operation Desert Fox* was commenced.[32] Within those debates, Sweden emphasized that responsibility for international peace and security was with the United Nations Security Council and that this responsibility, as laid down in the UN Charter, could not be circumvented.[33] Russia, China and France all

---

[32] The transcript of these debates are available online at URL <http://www.un.org/News/ Press/docs/1998/19981216.sc6611.html>.

[33] As summarized by Blokker, N., "Is the Authorization Authorized? Powers and Practice of the UN Security Council to Authorize the Use of Force by 'Coalitions of the Able and Willing'", 11 (2000) *European Journal of International Law*, 541.

voiced strong opposition to the intervention. The President of the Russian Federation, Boris Yeltzen, articulated that the resolutions existing at that time, 660, 678, 687 and 1154, (1) did not authorize members of the United Nations to act independently on behalf of the United Nations; and (2) did not, by themselves, authorize the use of force against Iraq but in fact required the adoption by the Security Council of a further and more specific resolution.[34] The first of these positions finds clear support within the jurisprudence of the International Court. The Court has held that the United Nations is an institution possessing international personality, a feature of which involves a distinction, in terms of legal powers and purposes, between the organization and its members.[35] It has further decided that this distinction is one whereby individual members of such an institution cannot assert a separate self-contained right over and above the organization's collective institutional activity.[36] The point was reaffirmed by the Insitut de Droit International in its *Bruges Declaration on the Use of Force*:[37]

> Only the Security Council, or the General Assembly acting under the more limited framework for the "Uniting for Peace" Resolution of 1950, may, depending on the particular circumstances at hand, decide that a given situation constitutes a threat to international peace and security, without this necessarily meaning that recourse to force is the only possible adequate response.

The second of the arguments posited by Russia and others requires further attention, in the absence of any judicial guidance in the matter. It goes to the heart of the issue at hand. Did the wording of Resolution 1441, and its similar predecessor 1154, trigger an implied authority to act, notwithstanding the general principle that a member of the United Nations cannot act independently of it?[38] In what way has the Security Council

---

[34] Lawyers Against the War, *The Use of Force by the United States Against Iraq: Legal Issues*, 30 September 2002, URL <http://www.lawyersagainstthewar.org>.

[35] *Reparations Case for Injuries Suffered in the Service of the United Nations* [1949] ICJ Rep 174.

[36] *South West Africa Cases 2nd Phase (Ethiopia v South Africa; Liberia v South Africa)* [1966] ICJ Rep 6.

[37] Insitut de Droit International, *Bruges Declaration on the Use of Force*, 2 September 2003, para 4.

[38] This was the issue dominating the meeting of the Security Council in adopting resolution 1154. The view of the United States and United Kingdom was that the resolution provided "automaticity": an automatic right by United Nations members to use force in the case of a violation of the requirements of the resolution: see Blokker, N., above, n 34. No agreement

authorized the use of force by its members in the past? Are there particular words required? What follows is an examination of various conflicts in which the Security Council has, under Chapter VII of the Charter, authorized the use of force.

Express Security Council Authorizations to Use Force

There have been various instances where the Council has provided its members with an express authority to use force against States. It is useful to briefly consider a number of these instances in their context. What will be seen is an emergence of a clear pattern, whereby the relevant resolutions express an ability to use *all necessary means or measures* to enforce the resolution, combined with a delegation of that authority to United Nations members.

North Korea, 1950. Following a report of the United Nations Commission on Korea,[39] the Security Council expressed grave concern about the armed attack on the Republic of Korea by forces from North Korea and determined that this action constituted a breach of the peace within the terms of Chapter VII of the United Nations Charter.[40] Under Resolution 82 it called upon the immediate cessation of hostilities and withdrawal of North Korean forces. The failure by North Korea to do so resulted in the adoption of Resolution 83 on 27 June 1950, in which the Security Council noted that urgent military measures were required to restore international peace and security and recommended:[41]

> ...that the Members of the United Nations furnish such assistance to the Republic of Korea as may be necessary to repel the armed attack and to restore international peace and security in the area.

Rhodesia, 1966. Towards the end of 1965, the Security Council imposed trade sanctions against Southern Rhodesia, calling on all United Nations members to do their utmost to break off economic relations with the country, including an embargo on oil and petroleum products.[42] The

---

on that point was reached prior to the adoption of the resolution, but the US and UK did not receive support for their view.

[39] Document S/1469.

[40] United Nations Security Council Resolution 82 (25 June 1950).

[41] United Nations Security Council Resolution 83 (27 June 1950), final paragraph in an un-numbered series of paragraphs.

[42] United Nations Security Council Resolutions 216 (12 November 1965) and 217 (20 November 1965).

United Nations received reports that substantial supplies of oil were to reach Southern Rhodesia as a result of an oil tanker having arrived at Beira and the approach of a further tanker. This, coupled with concern that Southern Rhodesia would be capable of resuming oil pumping through the Companhia do Pipepeline with the acquiescence of the Portuguese authorities, led to Resolution 221. The Security Council considered that oil supplies would afford great assistance and encouragement to the illegal regime in Southern Rhodesia and called upon the Portuguese Government not to permit oil to be pumped through the pipeline from Beira to Southern Rhodesia. The Resolution also called on the United Kingdom to prevent the arrival at Beira of vessels reasonably believed to be carrying oil destined for Southern Rhodesia "by the use of force if necessary".[43]

Iraq, 1990–1993. Following the invasion of Kuwait by Iraq in 1990, a series of preliminary resolutions were issued by the United Nations Security Council, demanding the withdrawal of Iraqi forces and imposing oil trade sanctions upon Iraq.[44] In breach of the economic sanctions under Resolution 661, Iraq continued to export oil using Iraqi flag vessels. In order to ensure Iraqi compliance with the economic sanctions, the Security Council authorized the use of "such measures commensurate to the specific circumstances as may be necessary ... to halt all inward and outward maritime shipping" under Resolution 665 (1990).

By the end of November 1990, Iraq had still refused to comply with the Security Council's demands for it to withdraw from Kuwait. The Security Council had made the demand for Iraq to withdraw on 2 August 1990, the day of the Iraqi invasion of Kuwait.[45] Acting under Chapter VII of the United Nations Charter, the Security Council set out the following demands and authorisations under Resolution 678:[46]

> *Demands* that Iraq comply fully with resolution 660 (1990) and all subsequent relevant resolutions, and decides, while maintaining all its decisions, to allow Iraq one final opportunity, as a pause of goodwill, to do so;
> *Authorizes* Member States co-operating with the Government of Kuwait, unless Iraq on or before 15 January 1991 fully implements, as set forth in paragraph 1 above, the above-mentioned resolutions, to use all necessary

---

[43] United Nations Security Council Resolution 221 (9 April 1966), final paragraph in an unnumbered series of paragraphs.
[44] United Nations Security Council Resolutions 660 (2 August 1990), 661 (6 August 1990), 662 (9 August 1990) and 664 (18 August 1990).
[45] United Nations Security Council Resolution 660 (2 August 1990).
[46] United Nations Security Council Resolution 678 (29 November 1990), paras 1 and 2.

means to uphold and implement resolution 660 (1990) and all subsequent relevant resolutions and to restore international peace and security in the area;

As already indicated, Iraq failed to comply with this "one final" opportunity set out within Resolution 678, which thereby authorized the use of all necessary means by United Nations members to ensure the withdrawal of Iraqi forces from Kuwait. The result was *Operation Desert Storm*, which commenced with a series of air strikes on 16 January 1991 and ultimately led to Iraq formally accepting ceasefire terms between it and Kuwait on 3 March 1991.[47]

The Security Council subsequently reiterated its preparedness to enforce any violation of the ceasefire in the demilitarized zone, stating at paragraph 4 of Resolution 773 that it:[48]

Underlines its guarantee of the inviolability of the above-mentioned international boundary and its decision to take as appropriate all necessary measures to that end in accordance with the Charter, as provided for in paragraph 4 of resolution 687 (1991);

This position was repeated, again referring to "all necessary measures", within Resolutions 806 and 833.[49]

Somalia, 1992. Although initially very slow to act in response to the internal conflict within Somalia, the Security Council ultimately decided to authorize the use of force through Resolution 794 of 3 December 1992. Mass genocide was occurring within Somalia, exacerbated by obstacles in the distribution of humanitarian aid, and recognized as constituting a threat to international peace and security.[50] Following an offer by the United States to establish and lead an operation for the creation of a secure environment in Somalia,[51] the Security Council authorized the Secretary-General and UN members to implement that offer and, in doing so, authorized those states "to use all necessary means to establish as soon as

---

[47] Such acceptance being in response to United Nations Security Council Resolution 686 (2 March 1991), paras 3 and 7.

[48] United Nations Security Council Resolution 773 of 26 August 1992, S/RES/773 (1992).

[49] United Nations Security Council Resolutions 806 of 5 February 1993, S/RES/806 (1993) and 833 of 27 May 1993, S/RES/833 (1993).

[50] United Nations Security Council Resolution 794 (3 December 1992), perambulatory paragraphs.

[51] As recognized in the report of the United Nations Secretary-General in his report to the United Nations Security Council of 29 November 1992 (S/24868) and within Resolution 794 (para 8).

possible a secure environment for humanitarian relief operations in Somalia".[52]

Republic of Bosnia and Herzegovina, 1993–1995. In response to the internal conflict within the former Yugoslavia, which had commenced in 1991, various measures were implemented by the United Nations, including the establishment of the United Nations Protection Force (UNPROFOR) and the imposition of no-fly zones.[53] Despite the establishment of these no-fly zones, the ban on military flights in the airspace of Bosnia and Herzegovina was repeatedly violated. Against that background, the Security Council allowed a further seven-day period for compliance, following which member states were authorized to use "all necessary measures", proportionate to the specific circumstances, to ensure compliance with the ban.[54]

The continued fighting within the former Yugoslavia and attacks on ethnic groups prompted the Security Council to establish safe areas within the Republic.[55] Notwithstanding this, the Council was later faced with military attacks on these safe areas and therefore decided to extend the mandate of UNPROFOR to enable it to deter attacks against the safe areas.[56] It authorized UNPROFOR:[57]

> ...acting in self-defence, to take the necessary measures, including the use of force, in reply to bombardments against the safe areas by any of the parties or to armed incursion into them...

At the end of 1995, the Republic of Bosnia and Herzegovina, the Republic of Croatia and the Federal Republic of Yugoslavia signed a peace agreement.[58] To ensure the proper implementation of that agreement, the Security Council authorized the establishment of a multinational implementation force (IFOR).[59] IFOR was authorized to use "all necessary measures" to ensure implementation of the peace agreement.[60]

---

[52] United Nations Security Council Resolution 794, para 10.
[53] United Nations Security Council Resolutions 781 (9 October 1992) and 786 (10 November 1992)
[54] United Nations Security Council Resolution 816 (31 March 1993), para 4.
[55] United Nations Security Council Resolutions 819 (16 April 1993) and 824 (6 May 1993).
[56] United Nations Security Council Resolution 836 (4 June 1993), para 5.
[57] Resolution 836, para 9.
[58] The *General Framework Agreement for Peace in Bosnia and Herzegovina*, signed at the Paris Peace Conference on 14 December 1995 (S/1995/999).
[59] United Nations Security Council Resolution 1031 (15 December 1995), para 14.
[60] Ibid, paras 15 to 17.

Rwanda, 1994. Following a failed attempt by the United Nations Assistance Mission in Rwanda (UNAMIR) to establish a meaningful ceasefire agreement in Kigali and outlying areas of Rwanda,[61] the Security Council authorized the establishment of a multinational force in Rwanda to maintain a presence in Rwanda until an expanded UNAMIR was deployed.[62] Under Resolution 929 of 22 June 1994, the United Nations Security Council authorized the multinational force to contribute to the security and protection of persons at risk in Rwanda, using "all necessary means".[63]

Haiti, 1994. In July 1993, the Governors Island Agreement was signed between the President of the Republic of Haiti and the Commander-in-Chief of the Armed Forces of Haiti, under which the United Nations was requested to provide assistance for modernizing the armed forces of Haiti and establishing a new police force.[64] As a result, the United Nations dispatched the UN Mission in Haiti (UNMIH).[65] The Mission, however, encountered obstruction from the Haitian military and were not even able to land on the island. The Security Council in due course determined that the regime in Haiti was an illegal de facto regime and that it had failed to comply with the Governors Island Agreement and was in breach of its obligations under the relevant United Nations Security Council resolutions.[66] In July 1994 it authorized the establishment of a multinational force:[67]

> ...to use all necessary means to facilitate the departure from Haiti of the military leadership, consistent with the Governors Island Agreement, the prompt return of the legitimately elected President and establish and maintain a secure environment...

East Timor, 1999. In the wake of pro-Indonesian riots following the East Timorese vote in favour of independence, and the widespread massacres of

---

[61] As recommended by the United Nations Secretary-General in his report to the Security Council of 20 April 1994 (S/1994/470) and authorized under United Nations Security Council Resolution 912 (21 April 1994), paragraph 8(c).

[62] As recommended by the Permanent Representative of France to the United Nations, Mr Jean-Bernard Merinee (S/1994/734), and accepted by the Security Council in its Resolution 929 (22 June 1994), paragraph 2.

[63] United Nations Security Council Resolution 929 (22 June 1994), paragraph 3.

[64] Governors Island Agreement, 3 July 1993, S/26063, paragraph 5.

[65] United Nations Security Council Resolution 867 (23 September 1993).

[66] United Nations Security Council Resolution 940 (31 July 1994), paragraph 3.

[67] Resolution 940, paragraph 4.

East Timorese people, the United Nations established the United Nations Transitional Authority in East Timor (UNTAET) and authorized UNTAET to take all necessary measures to fulfil its mandate.[68]

Summary. By way of summary, the Security Council has made the following express delegations of authority since 1950:

1. *North Korea, 1950*, in response to a breach of the peace by North Korea's military invasion of the Republic of Korea, an authorization was made to furnish "such assistance … as may be necessary".

2. *Rhodesia, 1966*, in the implementation of trade sanctions, the United Kingdom was called upon to act "by the use of force if necessary".

3. *Iraq, 1990–1993*, to implement trade sanctions and in response to the invasion of Kuwait, members were authorize to use "such measures … as may be necessary" (Resolution 665), "all necessary means" (Resolution 678) and "all necessary measures" (Resolutions 773, 806 and 833).

4. *Somalia, 1992*, "all necessary means" were authorized to assist the delivery of humanitarian aid.

5. *Republic of Bosnia and Herzegovina, 1993–1995*, "all necessary measures" were authorized to enforce a no-fly zone; "necessary measures, including the use of force" were permitted in response to the bombing of safe havens; and "all necessary measures" to enforce the 1995 peace agreement.

6. *Rwanda, 1994*, "all necessary means" were authorized to assist humanitarian relief.

7. *Haiti, 1994*, in the restoration of the democratic government, the multinational force was authorized to use "all necessary means".

8. *East Timor, 1999*, UNTAET was authorized to use "all necessary measures" to implement its peacekeeping mandate.

A clear pattern can be seen through the resolutions providing United Nations members with the authority to use force. The early resolutions, pertaining to North Korea and Southern Rhodesia, authorized assistance or the use of force if "necessary". In the 1990 to 1993 conflict in Iraq, the word "necessary" was repeated and the language "measures" (665, 773,

---

[68] United Nations Security Council Resolution 1272 (25 October 1999), para 4.

806 and 833) and "means" (678) introduced. From that point on, all resolutions in which United Nations members have been expressly authorized to use force have sanctioned "all necessary..." "...means" or "...measures".

Having regard to article 31(3)(b) of the Vienna Convention on the Law of Treaties,[69] this fact is significant:

SECTION 3: INTERPRETATION OF TREATIES
Article 31 General Rules of Interpretation
3. There shall be taken into account, together with the context:
b. Any subsequent practice in the application of the treaty which establishes the agreement of the parties regarding its interpretation;

The issue that consequently arises is whether the practice of the United Nations Security Council, in using the term "all necessary means/measures" in authorizing the use of force under Chapter VII of the United Nations Charter, is a practice in the application of the Charter that establishes the agreement of the parties regarding the interpretation of resolutions made under Chapter VII. Given the consistency in the manner by which the Security Council has expressed authorizations to use force, there is a strong argument in favour of such a view.

Implied Authority to Use Force

There is one further matter to consider, however, concerning instances where the Council has clearly adopted provisions within its resolutions with an *implicit*, rather than express, authority to use force. Two such instances illustrate this point.

Albania, 1997. In early 1997, the United Nations authorized the establishment of a multinational peacekeeping force in Albania and:[70]

...further authorizes these Member States to ensure the security and freedom of movement of the personnel of the said multinational protection force;

In order to facilitate the delivery of humanitarian aid, the Security Council later gave an identical authority under Resolution 1114.[71]

---

[69] Opened for signature 23 May 1969, 1155 UNTS 331 (entered into force 27 January 1980).
[70] United Nations Security Council Resolution 1101 (28 March 1997), paragraph 4.
[71] United Nations Security Council Resolution 1114 (19 June 1997), paragraph 4.

Central African Republic, 1997. In response to militia action in the Central African Republic, the Inter-African Mission to Monitor the Implementation of the Bangui Agreements (MISAB) was created. Under Resolutions 1125 and 1136, the Security Council authorized participating States to ensure the security and freedom of movement of their personnel".[72]

Nowhere in these Resolutions is there any expression permitting the use of force or the use of necessary or reasonable means or measures to achieve certain ends. However, the common feature of the Resolutions is that there is a clear authority to member States to ensure the security and freedom of movement of their personnel, in the execution of a mandate provided to them by the Security Council. The Resolutions authorize members to do something within the territory of another State, from which it can be implied that force may be necessary to protect their own nationals in the execution of that task. The authority to use force in these contexts is ancillary to the United Nations sanctioned mandates.

Did Resolutions 1154 or 1441 Authorize the Use of Force?

Against the background of past Security Council authorizations, and article 31(3)(b) of the Vienna Convention, it is concluded that a member of the United Nations may be authorized under Chapter VII of the Charter to use force within another State in two situations only. The first is where authorized through the expression "all necessary means/measures". The second is where a member is provided with a mandate to conduct operations within another State, and it is implicit from the terms of the mandate that the member is able to use force for the protection of its personnel.

Neither of those situations apply to Resolutions 1154 or 1441. The Resolutions do not provide any member of the United Nations, or any coalition of members, with a mandate to conduct operations within Iraq from which it might be implied that the use of force was necessary. Nor does their wording refer to or permit the use of "all necessary means/measures". Rather, they warn of "severest/serious consequences".[73]

---

[72] United Nations Security Council Resolution 1125 (6 August 1997), para 3, and Resolution 1136 (6 November 1997), para 4.
[73] Resolution 1154 at para 3, and Resolution 1441 at para 13.

"One final opportunity". A further potential argument is that an authority to use force arose not just from the expression "serious consequences", but from the combined effect of that expression with the provision in paragraph 2 of Resolution 1441 (that Iraq was being provided with "one final opportunity" to comply with its disarmament obligations under Resolution 687). Why else would the Security Council express that Iraq had one final opportunity to comply, if it did not envisage the use of force would follow within the "serious consequences" referred to?

At first blush, that position might hold some appeal. Again, however, it can be dispelled by looking at the prior practice of the Security Council. In Resolution 678, to which Lord Goldsmith referred, Iraq was also given "one final opportunity" to comply with demands of the Security Council. That expression was immediately followed, however, by a time limitation for the exercise of that opportunity and with the express provision that a failure to exercise that opportunity within the time stated would result in the use of all necessary means:

> *Authorizes* Member States co-operating with the Government of Kuwait, unless Iraq on or before 15 January 1991 fully implements, as set forth in paragraph 1 above, the above-mentioned resolutions, to use all necessary means to uphold and implement resolution 660 (1990) and all subsequent relevant resolutions and to restore international peace and security in the area;

The time limitation and authorization to use *all necessary means* distinguish Resolution 678 from both Resolutions 1154 and 1441.

Wording of Resolution 1441. Finally, the words of Resolution 1441, present and absent, should be reflected upon. First, paragraph 12 provides as follows:

> *Decides* to convene immediately upon receipt of a report in accordance with paragraphs 4 or 11 above, in order to consider the situation and the need for full compliance with all of the relevant Council resolutions in order to secure peace and security;

That wording undoubtedly anticipates that Resolution 1441 was not a final step in the process. Rather, any adverse report made by the Executive Chairman of UNMOVIC under paragraphs 4 or 11 (pertaining to weapons inspections) were to be further considered by the Council. If any authority to use force was to be given, this provision makes it clear that it would not be before the convening of such a meeting and the issuing of a further resolution.

The second point to be made about the words of Resolution 1441 is that the absence of an authorization to use "all necessary means/measures" is no accident. The draft Resolution, first circulated at the United Nations at the beginning of October 2002, contained the following paragraph:[74]

> Decides that false statements or omissions in the declaration submitted by Iraq to the Council and the failure by Iraq at any time to comply and cooperate fully in accordance with the provisions laid out in this resolution, shall constitute a further material breach of Iraq's obligations, *and that such breach authorises member states to use all necessary means to restore international peace and security in the area*; [emphasis added]

This paragraph was highly controversial and was opposed by two of the five permanent members of the Security Council, Russia and France. It was as a result of that opposition that the United Kingdom and United States presented a modified draft resolution which removed any reference to an authorization to use "all necessary means". The Council, knowing that such a phrase authorizes the use of force, consciously excluded the phrase prior to the adoption of the resolution. In addition, paragraph 12 (just mentioned) was also inserted.

Conclusion

The principal basis relied upon by coalition forces to legitimize the intervention in Iraq has been an authority arising out of the combined effect of Security Council Resolutions 678, 687 and 1441. Such a position, however, is fundamentally flawed. Resolution 678 had no bearing on the conflict at hand since it related exclusively to the military intervention by Iraq against Kuwait, and peace in the region within the context of the conflict between those two States. Similarly, while Resolution 687 is relevant to the extent that it imposed various obligations upon Iraq regarding weapons of mass destruction, it does not contain any authorization to use force in enforcement of those obligations. The sole authority to use force within that Resolution related to the ceasefire agreement between Iraq and Kuwait, following Iraq's repulsion from Kuwait in 1991.

---

[74] Singh, R., QC, and Kilroy, C., *Opinion in the Matter of the Potential Use of Armed Force by the UK Against Iraq and in the Matter of Reliance for that Use of Force on United Nations Security Council Resolution 1441*, 15 November 2002, para 7.

Resolutions 1154 and 1441 required Iraq to implement its obligations under Resolution 687 regarding weapons of mass destruction. They did not, however, express the ability to use all necessary means or measures to enforce their provisions, nor did they issue a mandate to United Nations members from which such an authority might be implied.

Regardless of one's views on the merits or otherwise of the removal of the Hussein regime in Iraq, the use of force against Iraq was unjustifiable at international law. The United Nations Security Council did not authorize intervention, nor are there any clear grounds from which an implied authority might be drawn. As emphasized by Sweden in the debates that followed *Operation Desert Fox*, it is the United Nations Security Council that bears the responsibility for maintaining international peace and security, as laid down in the UN Charter, and it is not open for individual member States to circumvent that authority by acting without the express command of the Council.

Chapter 8

Security Council Reform and Accountability

Introduction

The question of United Nations reform has been continuously raised since the adoption of the Charter of the United Nations and often as a result of particular crises experienced by the organization. As a result of various issues arising from the interventions in Afghanistan, and more so in Iraq, renewed calls for reform have been made. This chapter considers two areas in which reform has been suggested throughout various stages in the life of the United Nations: membership of the Security Council; and the power of veto held by permanent members of the Council. It also considers the issue of Security Council accountability in the context of the judicial review of Council decisions.

Amendment of the Charter of the United Nations

Before considering each of the issues identified, it is important to understand the mechanisms by which the UN Charter may be amended and the political limitations resulting from those mechanisms. The provisions of articles 108 and 109 of the Charter govern the issue:

Article 108
Amendments to the present Charter shall come into force for all Members of the United Nations when they have been adopted by a vote of two thirds of the members of the General Assembly and ratified in accordance with their respective constitutional processes by two thirds of the Members of the United Nations, including all the permanent members of the Security Council.

Article 109
1. A General Conference of the Members of the United Nations for the purpose of reviewing the present Charter may be held at a date and place to be fixed by a two-thirds vote of the members of the General Assembly and by a vote of any nine members of the Security Council. Each Member of the United Nations shall have one vote in the conference.

2.   Any alteration of the present Charter recommended by a two-thirds vote of the conference shall take effect when ratified in accordance with their respective constitutional processes by two thirds of the Members of the United Nations including all the permanent members of the Security Council.

3.   If such a conference has not been held before the tenth annual session of the General Assembly following the coming into force of the present Charter, the proposal to call such a conference shall be placed on the agenda of that session of the General Assembly, and the conference shall be held if so decided by a majority vote of the members of the General Assembly and by a vote of any seven members of the Security Council.

Proposals for amendment of the Charter can therefore be brought either by direct submission of a reform proposal under article 108, or by the calling of a General Conference under article 109.

General Review Conferences

General Conferences for the review of the Charter must be proposed under article 109(1) and will then be held if there is an affirmative vote of at least two-thirds of the General Assembly including any nine members of the Security Council. The power of veto is not exercisable on the question of calling such a conference, nor is the unanimous consent of the permanent members required. Where a Conference has not been held for ten years, the annual agenda of the General Assembly will automatically require the Assembly to give consideration to whether a Conference should be convened pursuant to article 109(3), thus prompting United Nations members to give thought to the issue on a periodic basis.

A proposal to convene a General Conference was triggered under article 109(3) during the tenth session of the General Assembly in 1955. It was decided to convene such a Conference under General Assembly Resolution 992(X) and Security Council Resolution 110.[1] During debates on 3 June 1957 in the Committee tasked to arrange the General Conference, it was decided that fixing a time and place for the Conference should be deferred for not more than two years.[2] In 1963, the Committee reported that while the holding of a General Conference was in principle meritorious, "there was general agreement that international circumstances at the present time were still not propitious for the holding of a General

---

[1] United Nations General Assembly Resolution 992(X) of 21 November 1955, A/RES/992(X) (1955), and United Nations Security Council Resolution 110 of 16 December 1955, S/RES/110 (1955).

[2] See *Repertory of Practice of United Nations Organs Supplement No 2*, Volume III (1955–1959) Articles 108 and 109, para 17.

Conference".[3]   The circumstances to which the Committee referred concerned the East-West tension of the Cold War and the rapidly increasing membership of the United Nations through decolonization. Bearing those factors in mind, the Committee was most likely correct in its assessment, since reform would neither have been achievable,[4] nor appropriate.[5]

Under General Assembly Resolution 2285(XXII), the holding of the General Conference was again postponed in 1967.[6] In 1970, however, the Sixth (Legal) Committee of the General Assembly was tasked with consideration of the issue and the Secretary-General asked to invite member States to communicate their views on the review of the Charter.[7] The response of members was mixed, some in favour of a general review, others suggesting that caution was necessary, and others strongly opposed to any review of the Charter.[8]

This mixed response saw the General Assembly establish an Ad Hoc Committee on Charter reform, consisting of 42 members of the United Nations, to consider the responses provided to the Secretary-General and any further proposals for amendment.[9] The Committee first met in 1975 and was subsequently reconvened as the Special Committee on the Charter of the United Nations and on the Strengthening of the Role of the Organization.[10] Although the Committee did not make any specific recommendations concerning the amendment of the Charter, it did prepare a draft text (ultimately adopted by the General Assembly) on the peaceful

---

[3] See *Repertory of Practice of United Nations Organs Supplement No 3*, Volume IV (1959–1966) Articles 108 and 109, para 53.

[4] Through a high likelihood of different approaches being taken within the Council and, thus, through the probable exercise of the "veto" under article 109(2). See the discussion below concerning Security Council consent to amendment of the Charter under articles 108 and 109(2).

[5] In light of the growing membership of the United Nations caused by the emergence of new independent States through decolonization, it was argued that any reform should wait for the process of decolonization to be completed, or at least stabilize, thus ensuring the participation of all potential member States of the United Nations in the issue of reform of its Charter.

[6] United Nations General Assembly Resolution 2285(XXII) of 5 December 1967, A/RES/2285(XXII).

[7] See United Nations General Assembly Resolution 2552(XXIV) of 12 December 1969, A/RES/2252(XXIV), 2697(XXV) of 11 December 1970, A/RES/2697(XXV), and 2698(XXVII) of 14 December 1970, A/RES/2698(XXVII).

[8] United Nations, *Repertory of Practice of United Nations Organs Supplement No 5*, Volume V (1970–1978) Articles 108 and 109, para 14.

[9] Ibid, para 19. See also United Nations General Assembly Resolution 3349(XXIX) of 17 December 1974, A/RES/3349(XXIX).

[10] United Nations General Assembly Resolution 3499(XXX) of 15 December 1975, A/RES/3499(XXX).

settlement of international disputes, known as the Manila Declaration.[11]
The Special Committee still operated and has been responsible for the
negotiation of various other texts, including the Declaration on the
Prevention and Removal of Disputes and Situations Which May Threaten
International Peace and Security and the Role of the United Nations in this
Field,[12] the Declaration on Fact-finding by the United Nations in the Field
of the Maintenance of Peace and Security[13] and the Resolution on the
Prevention and Peaceful Settlement of Disputes.[14]

During the fortieth anniversary of the United Nations in 1985, the issue
of Charter review was again raised within the General Assembly, although
not through explicit invocation of article 109. Again, various views were
advanced, with an interesting position recorded within the Repertory of
Practice:[15]

> The prevailing view, however, was that … the lack of effectiveness of the
> United Nations was not due to imperfections of the Charter but the lack of its
> respect by the Member States. Member States who held such view called for a
> recommitment to the Charter by all Member States, to make the United
> Nations a more effective Organization.

The observation might equally apply to an analysis of the interventions in
Afghanistan and Iraq in answer to criticisms that the United Nations failed
to maintain and protect peace and security.

Article 108 Proposals

Article 108 of the Charter anticipates the submission of specific proposals
for change by members of the UN, rather than through the holding of a
General Conference. Up to the end of the 20th century, numerous
proposals for amendment were submitted under this provision, concerning:
the membership of the Security Council (article 23); the power of veto
(article 27(3)); the use of regional organization by the Security Council

---

[11] The Manila Declaration on the Peaceful Settlement of International Disputes, adopted by
the General Assembly under United Nations General Assembly 37/10 of 15 November
1982, A/RES/37/10.

[12] Adopted under United Nations General Assembly Resolution 43/51 of 5 December 1988,
A/RES/43/51.

[13] Adopted under United Nations General Assembly Resolution 46/59 of 9 December 1991,
A/RES/49/59.

[14] Adopted under United Nations General Assembly Resolution 57/26 of 19 November
2002, A/RES/57/26.

[15] United Nations, *Repertory of Practice of United Nations Organs Supplement No 7*,
Volume VI (1985–1988) Articles 108 and 109, para 19.

(articles 53 and 107); the composition of the Economic and Social Council (article 61); the role and continuance of the Trusteeship Council (article 77 and Chapter XIII); the review mechanisms for the Charter (article 109); the Seat of the International Court of Justice, its jurisdiction and the number of Judges of the Court (articles 22, 69 and 96 of the Statute of the International Court of Justice).[16]

Adopting Reforms

The important thing to note about Charter reform is the significant hurdle posed by articles 108 and 109(2). The requirement for a two-thirds majority of the members of the General Assembly (in other words, two-thirds of UN member States) is not so problematic. Many constitutional documents provide for partial entrenchment of this kind, aiming to preserve the integrity of a constitution and protect it against perpetual change, thus limiting amendment to important issues in a manner consistent with the wishes of the greater majority. In a very significant document such as the Charter of the United Nations, those protections are both necessary and desirable.

What is more problematic is the special status afforded to the five permanent members of the Security Council, requiring any amendment of

---

[16] United Nations, *Repertory of Practice of United Nations Organs*, Volume V (1945–1954) Articles 108 and 109, paras 15–19 (concerning articles 27(3) and 61); *Repertory of Practice of United Nations Organs Supplement No 1*, Volume II (1954–1955) Articles 108 and 109, para 6 (concerning articles 23, 27 and 61 of the Charter, and article 69 of the Statute of the International Court of Justice); *Repertory of Practice of United Nations Organs Supplement No 2*, Volume III (1955–1959) Articles 108 and 109, paras 12–16 (concerning articles 23 and 61 of the Charter and article 69 of the Statute of the International Court of Justice); *Repertory of Practice of United Nations Organs Supplement No 3*, Volume IV (1959–1966) Articles 108 and 109, para 4 (concerning articles 23 and 61 of the Charter and article 69 of the Statute of the International Court of Justice); *Repertory of Practice of United Nations Organs Supplement No 4*, Volume II (1966–1969) Articles 108 and 109, para 17 (concerning article 22 of the Statute of the International Court of Justice); *Repertory of Practice of United Nations Organs Supplement No 5*, Volume V (1970–1978) Articles 108 and 109, paras 6–15 (concerning article 61 of the Charter and article 22 of the Statute of the International Court of Justice); *Repertory of Practice of United Nations Organs Supplement No 6*, Volume VI (1979–1984) Articles 108 and 109, paras 6–23 (concerning articles 23, 27 and 61); *Repertory of Practice of United Nations Organs Supplement No 7*, Volume VI (1985–1988) Articles 108 and 109, paras 8–18 (concerning articles 23, 27 and 109); *Repertory of Practice of United Nations Organs Supplement No 8*, Volume VI (1989–1994) Articles 108 and 109, paras 5–16 (concerning articles 23, 27, 53, 61, 77, 107 and 109); and *Repertory of Practice of United Nations Organs Supplement No 9*, Volume VI (1995–1999) Articles 108 and 109, paras 7–32 (concerning articles 23, 27, 53, 61, 77, 107 and 109 of the Charter and article 96 of the Statute of the International Court of Justice).

the Charter to also be with the consent of all five members. This is seen as being problematic because of the inevitable tendency of the permanent members to seek to protect their particular interests, just as any member would wish to do. It is likely, therefore, that any move to amend the Charter in a manner that adversely affects one of the permanent members, including the reduction in power of those members, will tend to be opposed. By that analysis, it seems highly unlikely that any attempt to remove the permanent members' power of veto under article 27(3) of the Charter would obtain the consent of those members and thus fail to satisfy article 108 and/or 109(2). As optimistic as the author would like to be about States adopting a disinterested stance on matters of reform that might, according to at least two-thirds of UN members, be for the betterment of the United Nations organization, realism must dictate that this would be very unlikely.

That does not mean, however, that the question of veto reform does not warrant consideration. The veto under article 27(3) has been characterized as anachronistic and morally indefensible, and it has been anticipated by some that an overwhelming majority of United Nations members would support the abolishment of it.[17] Despite the unlikely success of a move to abolish the power of veto, the merits of such a suggestion will be discussed and assessed within this chapter.

Reform of the Security Council

The composition and accountability of the Security Council and its members has been an issue of contention since the drafting of the Charter of the United Nations and a topic of concern throughout the life of the organization. As will be seen, Security Council reform was advocated during the first session of the UN General Assembly in 1946. The question has, however, been the subject of continuous deferral. While this is a cause of frustration for many member States, it is one born out of necessity. Given the limitations upon reform under articles 108 and 109(2), and the power struggle amongst permanent members of the Council during the Cold War, the deferral of Security Council reform is not overly surprising.

To complement the work of the Special Committee on the Charter of the United Nations and on the Strengthening of the Role of the Organization, and to focus on the particularities of the Security Council, the

---

[17] Schwartzberg, J.E., *Revitalising the United Nations. Reform Through Weighted Voting*, Institute for Global Policy World Federalist Movement (2004), 47.

General Assembly established a special Working Group in 1993.[18] In his 2002 report on the Strengthening of the United Nations, the Secretary-General encouraged the labour of the Working Group, noting that its deliberation had indeed resulted in improvement in the practices of the Security Council.[19] He pointed to a greater level of transparency through the invitation of non-Council members to participate in its work and an increased number of open meetings. One year later, in November 2003, the Secretary-General established a High-Level Panel on Threats, Challenges and Change, its Terms of Reference calling on the Panel:[20]

> To recommend clear and practical measures for ensuring effective collective action, based upon a rigorous analysis of future threats to peace and security, an appraisal of the contribution that collective action can make, and a thorough assessment of existing approaches, instruments and mechanisms, including the principal organs of the United Nations.

On the question of pursuing reform, and in anticipation of the 60th anniversary of the United Nations in 2005, Former Japanese Ambassador to the UN, Yukio Sato, said this:[21]

> To give up Security Council reform is tantamount to accepting an unacceptable consequence: that the Council will continue to be dominated by the victors of World War II.

Operation of the Security Council

In considering membership and voting reform, it is useful to first conduct an overview of the means by which the Security Council operates and the meaning and application of extant provisions of the Charter, particularly the question of voting. Matters of procedure are governed by articles 28 to 32 of the Charter and by the Rules of Procedure for the Security Council

---

[18] The Open-ended Working Group on the Question of Equitable Representation on and Increase in the Membership of the Security Council and Other Matters related to the Security Council, established under United Nations General Assembly Resolution 48/26 of 3 December 1993, A/RES/48/26.

[19] Report of the Secretary-General, *Strengthening of the United Nations: an Agenda for Further Change*, A/57/387, 9 September 2002, paras 20-22.

[20] United Nations Press Release, "Secretary-General Names High-Level Panel to Study Global Security Threats, and Recommend Necessary Changes", SG/A/857, 4 November 2003.

[21] United Nations Foundation, "UK to Press for UN Reform", *UN Wire*, <http://www.unwire.org/UNWire>, 3 February 2004.

(adopted under article 30).[22] Membership and voting are dictated by articles 23 and 27 respectively:

Article 23

1.   The Security Council shall consist of fifteen Members of the United Nations. The Republic of China, France, the Union of Soviet Socialist Republics, the United Kingdom of Great Britain and Northern Ireland, and the United States of America shall be permanent members of the Security Council. The General Assembly shall elect ten other Members of the United Nations to be non-permanent members of the Security Council, due regard being specially paid, in the first instance to the contribution of Members of the United Nations to the maintenance of international peace and security and to the other purposes of the Organization, and also to equitable geographical distribution.

2.   The non-permanent members of the Security Council shall be elected for a term of two years. In the first election of the non-permanent members after the increase of the membership of the Security Council from eleven to fifteen, two of the four additional members shall be chosen for a term of one year. A retiring member shall not be eligible for immediate re-election.

3.   Each member of the Security Council shall have one representative.

Article 27

1.   Each member of the Security Council shall have one vote.

2.   Decisions of the Security Council on procedural matters shall be made by an affirmative vote of nine members.

3.   Decisions of the Security Council on all other matters shall be made by an affirmative vote of nine members including the concurring votes of the permanent members; provided that, in decisions under Chapter VI, and under paragraph 3 of Article 52, a party to a dispute shall abstain from voting.

Voting – matters of procedure versus substance. The first point to note about the application of article 27 is the distinction made between procedural matters (paragraph 2) and non-procedural ones (paragraph 3). Whereas the power of veto may be exercised in respect of non-procedural matters, a simple vote of nine in favour of procedural issues is sufficient for adoption of a procedural resolution. Usefully, the Security Council has adopted a practice of normally indicating within the text of a resolution (or by footnote) whether that resolution is considered by the Council to be a question of procedure.[23] The preliminary question of *how* the Council

---

[22] *Provisional Rules of Procedure of the Security Council*, S/96/Rev.7 (this revision remains current).

[23] United Nations, *Repertory of Practice of United Nations*, Volume II (1945–1954) Article 27, paras 14–15. The Repertory illustrates that this approach has been adopted concerning the inclusion of items in an agenda, the order of agenda items, adjournment of meetings, the

determines whether a matter is procedural or substantive is one that ultimately rests with the President of the Council.[24]

Voting – operation of the veto under article 27(3). For a resolution to be adopted on a matter that is not procedural, nine affirmative votes are required, including "the concurring votes of the permanent members". Two questions arise in that regard: what if a permanent member is silent; and what if a permanent member is absent when a decision is taken by the Council? The clear and early practice of the Council has been to adopt resolutions even where a permanent member has abstained from voting. During the first eight years of its operation, 64 non-procedural decisions were adopted by the Security Council by a vote in which one or more of the permanent members abstained.[25]

Situations where a permanent member has been *absent* have caused more controversy. The first occurrence of this was in 1946 when the representative of the USSR absented himself from the meetings of the Council and, in his absence, resolutions were adopted concerning the presence of Soviet troops in Iran.[26] In part, this was justified on the basis that the decisions were procedural, simply allowing time for Soviet troops to withdraw and rescheduling consideration of the substantive issue. The Council also took the view that the absence of the USSR was equivalent to an abstention from voting, since article 27 did not mandate a quorum.[27] Substantive decisions of the Security Council were adopted in 1950 concerning the aggression by North Korea against the Republic of Korea, with the representative of the USSR again refusing to participate in deliberations of the Council.[28] The Soviet Union subsequently challenged the legality of the decisions, claiming that they were not made in conformity with article 27(3). Again, however, the Council took the view that absence of a member was not equivalent to a negative vote.[29] The

---

conduct of business and the removal of an item from the list of matters to be considered by the Council.

[24] Ibid, para 29.

[25] Ibid, para 46.

[26] United Nations Security Council Resolution 2 of 30 January 1946, S/RES/2 (1946), 3 of 4 April 1946, S/RES/3 (1946), and 5 of 8 May 1946, S/RES/5 (1946).

[27] Above, n 23, para 49.

[28] United Nations Security Council Resolutions 82 of 25 June 1950, S/RES/82 (1950), 83 of 27 June 1050, S/RES/83 (1950), 84 of 7 July 1950, S/RES/84 (1950), and 85 of 31 July 1950, S/RES/85 (1950).

[29] Above, n 23, para 52.

subsequent practice of the Council has been consistent with that approach.[30] Furthermore, the International Court of Justice has indicated that this is a proper approach.[31]

Membership of the Council

The composition of the Security Council has been a matter of debate not just because of the dynamics caused by the existence of permanent and non-permanent members, but also due to its limited membership of fifteen. At the time of adopting the Charter, when fifty States became parties to the treaty, a membership of fifteen was sensible. As the number of member States to the United Nations has increased, however, calls have been made for adjustment of the Council membership and structure.[32] Whereas the composition of the General Assembly automatically reflects the membership of the organization (with all members being entitled to one vote and five seats in the Assembly), neither the Economic and Social Council nor the Security Council have provision for adjustment of their membership to reflect overall UN membership.

Proposals put to the Working Group on Security Council reform have generally all called for an enlargement of the Council's membership, although discrepancy has existed concerning the particular means of expansion. The proposal apparently favoured by the Secretary-General's High-Level Panel would see the Security Council expand from its present two-tiered, fifteen-member structure to a three-tiered, twenty-four-member Council.[33] The proposal would see the current five permanent members remain and retain their permanent status. A second tier of seven or eight semi-permanent members would be elected on a regional basis and hold office for a renewable term of four or five years. The third tier would retain the current non-renewable two-year membership (also elected

---

[30] See, for example, United Nations, *Repertory of Practice of United Nations Supplement No 6*, Volume III (1979–1984) Article 27, para 11.

[31] See the comments of the Court concerning this practice in *Legal Consequences for States of the Continued Presence of South Africa in Namibia (South-West Africa) notwithstanding Security Council Resolution 276 (1990)*, (1970–1971), Advisory Opinion of the International Court of Justice of 21 June 1971, paras 19–41.

[32] The initial membership of the United Nations, as original States parties to the Charter, was fifty. The Democratic Republic of Timor-Leste (formerly known as East Timor and under Indonesian rule) became the 191st member of the organization, admitted under United Nations General Assembly Resolution 57/3 of 27 September 2002, A/RES/57/3.

[33] Global Policy Forum, "High Level Panel Nears Agreement on Security Council Makeup and Humanitarian Intervention", 28 July 2004, URL <http://www.globalpolicy.org/security/reform/cluster1/2004/0728threetier.htm>.

regionally). While this proposal would indeed see an increased membership in the Council, some criticize the proposal as being artificial and creating little effective change due to the continued advantage of the permanent members.[34]

The Power of Veto

At the time of its drafting, a number of provisions within the United Nations Charter were contentious, the power of veto being one. Member States ultimately, although many say reluctantly, agreed that given the circumstances just after the Second World War and the desire to include the major power-brokers of the international community, the permanent members should be accorded a special status through the veto power under article 27(3) and the similar power under articles 108 and 109(2) of the Charter. Ultimately, however, it has been the power of veto that has prevented the adoption of a number of resolutions by the Security Council. From 1945 to 1992, which reflects the gestation and life of the Cold War, the use of the power of veto was significant: it was exercised by the Soviet Union 114 times; by the United States 69 times; the United Kingdom 30 times; France 18 times; and China on three occasions.[35] The Security Council was thus rendered ineffective during the Cold War.

Within the context of the issues examined within this text, the veto has also been identified as being the root cause of the unwillingness or inability of the Council to decide on matters adversely affecting one or more of the permanent members. Examples discussed have included: the potential impact upon the authority and responsibility of the Council to monitor the conduct of operations under article 51 of the Charter;[36] the actual impact on the Council preventing it ruling on the status of Soviet troops in Afghanistan through exercise of the power of veto by the USSR;[37] the argued inappropriateness of the Security Council to deal with political and economic reconstruction issues;[38] concerns about leaving issues of imminent threats to the Council as opposed to permitting unilateral anticipatory conduct;[39] and the refusal by France and Russia to adopt the

---

[34] See, for example, the comments of Schwartzberg, ibid.

[35] Murphy, S.D., "The Security Council Legitimacy, and the Concept of Collective Security After the Cold War", (1994) 31 *Columbia Journal of Transnational Law* 201.

[36] Chapter 3, 68.

[37] Chapter 3, 69, and Chapter 4, 77. See also United Nations, *Repertory of Practice of United Nations Organs Supplement No 6*, Volume III (1979–1984) Article 51, para 28.

[38] Chapter 4, 91.

[39] Chapter 5, 101-102.

first draft of Resolution 1441 concerning Iraq (which had, under the draft, provided for an express authorization to use force).[40]

All of the matters identified in the preceding two paragraphs are significant to the issue of the maintenance of international peace, and impact upon the Security Council's responsibility under article 24 of the Charter. The question is whether the veto has acted, and is intended to act, as a safety mechanism to prevent the Council from adopting inappropriate resolutions. That argument might be applied, for example, to the position adopted by France and the Russian Federation concerning the terms of draft Resolution 1441.[41] The counter-argument is that the veto, while it may have been intended to secure the involvement of major powers at the end of the Second World War and reflected the political environment at that time, is no longer valid and is in fact a fetter upon the proper conduct of the Security Council. The inability of the Council to make decisions during the Cold War, due to the East-West political division between the permanent members, is an example of this. Without a power of veto, or potentially with a modified version of the veto power, its adverse impact on these matters of peace and security would not be felt.

Amendment of the power of veto was proposed during the very first session of the United Nations General Assembly, illustrating that this issue has been a matter of contention for decades and one that even predated the adoption of the Charter in 1945.[42] This first proposal sought to amend article 27(3) by changing the number of overall votes required for the adoption of a Security Council resolution and by reducing the number of required concurring votes of the permanent members:[43]

> Decisions of the Security Council on all other matters shall be made by an affirmative vote of seven members, including the concurring votes of at least three permanent members; provided that, in decisions under Chapter VI, and under paragraph 3 of Article 52, a party to a dispute shall abstain from voting.

During the 37th session of the Sixth (Legal) Committee of the General Assembly in 1982, the Committee considered a draft resolution sponsored by Benin, the Islamic Republic of Iran, Libya, Mali and Mauritiana.[44] The

---

[40] Chapter 7, 160.

[41] Ibid.

[42] See Schwartzberg, above, n 17.

[43] The first proposal to amend article 27(3) was made during the second part of the first session of the United Nations General Assembly by the representative of the Philippines: see United Nations, *Repertory of Practice of United Nations Organs*, Volume V (1945–1954) Articles 108 and 109, para 16.

[44] A/C.6/37/L.5/Rev.1.

draft General Assembly resolution sought to require the Special Committee on the Charter of the United Nations and on the Strengthening of the Role of the Organization to:[45]

> ...examine the possibility of eliminating the adverse effects for the maintenance of international peace and security arising out of the abuse of the rule of unanimity, taking into account ... the need to ensure that the rule of unanimity is not resorted to on matters relating to the inalienable rights of peoples struggling for self-determination, against colonialism, apartheid, foreign domination, intervention, aggression and occupation.

Proposed reforms of the power of veto, including those just mentioned, have taken various approaches:

- complete elimination of the power of veto;[46]
- reducing the number of overall votes required from nine to seven and the number of concurring permanent member votes from five to three;[47]
- limiting the exercise of the veto power to certain factual issues/situations;[48]
- curtailing the exercise of the veto by requiring any exercise of the power to be accompanied by a written explanation of the reasons for it;[49] and/or
- requiring the exercise of a veto to be subject to General Assembly action (much as might occur in the event of the President's exercise of veto under the United States Constitution).[50]

Complete elimination of the power of veto, while sensible in the author's view, is not a proposal that will result in any level of genuine consideration. While it is certainly true that the veto power reflects circumstances that

---

[45] Ibid, draft para 3(a). The resolution was not put to vote in the General Assembly, following a motion by Australia: see above, n 30, n 13.

[46] Above, n 17, 47.

[47] United Nations, *Repertory of Practice of United Nations Organs*, Volume V (1945–1954) Articles 108 and 109, para 16. See also the Report of the Open-ended Working Group on the Question of Equitable Representation on and Increase in the Membership of the Security Council and Other Matters related to the Security Council, Official Records, Fifty-seventh Session, Supplement No 47, A/57/47, Annex VI(II)(A)(2)(b)(4) and VI(II)(B).

[48] Above, n 44.

[49] Report of the Open-ended Working Group on the Question of Equitable Representation on and Increase in the Membership of the Security Council and Other Matters related to the Security Council, Official Records, Fifty-seventh Session, Supplement No 47, A/57/47, Annex VI(II)(A)(1)(b).

[50] Ibid, Annex VI(II)(A)(2)(b)(5).

existed at the close of the Second World War and that no longer reflect pressing or relevant concerns,[51] the reality is that the permanent members would never surrender the significant power and protection that comes with the veto. Even with a sustained level of external political pressure brought to bear, the power brokered by the permanent members, and the hegemonic approach taken by the United States in particular,[52] is unlikely to be sufficient to bring about this level of change. For the same reasons, it is not anticipated that a move to subject the exercise of the veto to General Assembly action would be successful.

Limiting the exercise of the veto power to certain areas seems problematic, in the author's view, certainly in the terms advocated by the draft resolution put to the Legal Committee.[53] It is clear that, appropriately or not, the Council sees a very broad range of issues as falling within the ambit of matters impacting upon the maintenance and promotion of peace and security.[54] It therefore seems doubtful that any proposal to this effect would meet with the concurring vote of the permanent members.

A proposal which may, on the other hand, engender the support of the permanent members while at the same time not removing the power of the veto, is that which requires any exercise of the power to be accompanied by a written explanation of the reasons for it. The Council has, as recognized by the Secretary-General, moved towards more transparent proceedings[55] and might therefore be quite willing to adopt such a proposal with a view to further improving transparency.

The proposal that appears to hold the most potential is that reducing the number of concurring permanent member votes from five to three, or even from five to four. The attraction of such a proposal is that it does not involve the abolishment of the power of veto but, instead, the restructuring of the rights of the permanent members to avoid one member alone preventing the adoption of a resolution. While retaining the power and protection of article 27(3), such an amendment should remove what many have come to refer to as the "abuse of the veto right".[56] Taking a pessimistic view, however, one might argue that *any* reduction in the protection afforded to the permanent members will be resisted by those

---

[51] As recently advocated by Japanese Ambassador Yukio Sato, above, n 21.

[52] See Joyner, C.C., "Gulliver Unbound: US Foreign Policy and its Implications for International Law", 1 (2004) *New Zealand Yearbook of International Law*, 9.

[53] Above n 45.

[54] See Chapter 4, 90-91.

[55] Above, n 19.

[56] See, for example, Simmer, B. (ed.), *The Charter of the United Nations. A Commentary*, 2nd edition, Oxford University Press, 2002, 514.

members. Although that is certainly a valid observation, this proposal may nevertheless be one in respect of which external political pressure by the balance of United Nations members can achieve results.

Reviewing Security Council Action

Prior to determining what measures might be called for under Chapter VII of the Charter, the Security Council must decide whether there exists a breach of, or a threat to, peace and security:

Article 39
The Security Council shall determine the existence of any threat to the peace, breach of the peace, or act of aggression and shall make recommendations, or decide what measures shall be taken in accordance with Articles 41 and 42, to maintain or restore international peace and security.

The question that arises is whether any determination under article 39, and subsequent measures imposed under articles 40 to 42 of the Charter, should be subject to judicial review by the International Court of Justice.

The issue arose in the *Lockerbie Cases*,[57] brought by Libya against the United Kingdom and the United States under the Montreal Convention for the Suppression of Unlawful Acts Against the Safety of Civil Aviation.[58] The cases concerned the explosion of a bomb bringing down Pan Am flight 103 over Lockerbie, Scotland, and the requests of a number of States (including the United States and United Kingdom) for Libya to surrender two suspects allegedly responsible for the bombing. Libya refused to extradite the suspects. The Security Council subsequently issued Resolutions 731, 748 and 883, in which it demanded that the Libyan Government surrender the suspects or render a full and effective response to the requests for extradition, and issued non-military sanctions against Libya.[59] In its claim before the World Court, Libya argued that the

---

[57] *Case Concerning Questions of Interpretation and Application of the 1971 Montreal Convention Arising from the Aerial Incident at Lockerbie (Libyan Arab Jamahiriya v United Kingdom and Libyan Arab Jamahiriya v United States of America)*, International Court of Justice, judgment of 27 February 1998.

[58] The Convention for the Suppression of Unlawful Acts Against the Safety of Civil Aviation 1971, opened for signature 23 September 1971, 974 UNTS 177 (entered into force 26 January 1073).

[59] United Nations Security Council Resolutions 731 of 21 January 1992, S/RES/731 (1992), para 3; 748 of 31 March 1992, S/RES/748 (1992), para 1; and 883 of 11 November 1993, S/RES/883 (1993), para 1. The latter two Resolutions were adopted *after* the issuing of proceedings before the International Court of Justice.

Montreal Convention was applicable to the dispute and that, having fully complied with its obligations under the Convention, Libya was not bound by the Security Council resolutions in question since they sought to reverse the legal effect of the Convention.[60]

The US and UK objected to the Court's jurisdiction, contending (in part) that Security Council Resolutions 748 and 883 created legal obligations upon Libya that rendered Libya's claim redundant, so that the ICJ could not proceed to a judgment on the merits. Their argument was based on the premise that: (1) Libya was obligated to comply with the Resolutions by virtue of article 25; and (2) in assessing any conflict between Libya's article 25 Charter obligations and the Montevideo Convention, article 103 of the Charter dictated that the Charter obligations were to prevail:[61]

Article 25
The Members of the United Nations agree to accept and carry out the decisions of the Security Council in accordance with the present Charter.

Article 103
In the event of a conflict between the obligations of the Members of the United Nations under the present Charter and their obligations under any other international agreement, their obligations under the present Charter shall prevail.

By twelve votes to four, the Court rejected the objection to admissibility. Ultimately, however, the *Lockerbie Cases* were removed from the Court's list at the joint request of the parties and a decision on the merits has therefore not been made.[62] Problematically, the decision on jurisdiction does not give a clear indication of whether the Court sees itself able to review decisions of the Council. A broad interpretation of the judgment would hold that the Court is willing to consider and rule on the relationship between Security Council resolutions and a potentially inconsistent treaty. A narrow view would posit that the judgment only opened the door for the Court to consider the meaning and application of the Montreal Convention.[63] Ultimately, the Court did not directly address the question of

---

[60] In particular, articles 5, 7, 8 and 11 of the Montreal Convention, above, n 58.

[61] Above, n 57, paras 37 and 41.

[62] International Court of Justice, "Cases Removed from the Court's List at the Joint Request of the Parties", Press Release 2003/29, 10 September 2003.

[63] For more detailed discussion of the potential interpretations of the decision see: Paulus, A.L., "Jurisprudence of the International Court of Justice. *Lockerbie* Cases: Preliminary Objections", 9 (1998) *European Journal of International Law* 550; and Alvarez, J.E., "Judging the Security Council", 90 (1996) *American Journal of International Law* 1.

whether it could and, if so, how to judicially review Security Council resolutions.

Is Judicial Review Possible?

The position of the United Kingdom in the *Lockerbie Cases* was certainly arguable, since article 103 of the Charter does indeed place any obligation upon member States above those under any other international agreement. The question, however, is whether the obligation under article 25 has been properly triggered. That is, although article 25 renders decisions of the Security Council binding upon UN members, it does not itself legitimize the Council's decisions. It in fact qualifies itself by stating that compliance is necessary with "decisions of the Security Council in accordance with the present Charter". It is therefore quite proper and permissible, in the author's view, to ask the question: *is the decision legitimate in the first place, as one properly made "in accordance with the present Charter"?* As such, the author concludes that decisions of the Security Council can be subject to judicial review by the International Court of Justice.

The question then becomes *how* the Court reviews decisions of the Security Council. This, in turn, brings into play two particular issues. The first requires consideration of article 39 of the Charter, concerning the Security Council determination of whether there exists a breach of, or threat to, international peace and security. The International Court should, to guard against clearly unmeritorious decisions, apply the well-known principles of review against unreasonableness or irrationality. However, it would no doubt also seek to limit the extent to which it interferes with this preliminary issue. Determination of whether a factual scenario constitutes a breach of, or threat to, peace and security is the sole charge of the Security Council under the Charter as a specialized body entrusted to deal with its maintenance. Just a municipal courts tend to show a level of deference to executive decision-makers, it is anticipated that any review of Security Council decisions would illustrate the same level of regard.

The second issue arises from the wording of article 25 and concerns whether the decision is otherwise made "in accordance with the present Charter". It is posited that this requires Security Council decisions to be taken in a manner that does not counter the rights of UN members under the Charter, unless expressly authorized.[64] It also requires decisions to be made within the authority of the Security Council, as provided within Chapter V (concerning functions and powers, voting and procedure).

---

[64] See, for example, article 2(7), discussed below.

The Merits of Judicial Review

Having concluded that the Security Council is indeed able to be subject to the judicial review of its decisions, it must be acknowledged that this is a relatively academic argument. As observed by Alvarez:[65]

> Far from being paradigmatic, the *Marbury*-style challenges to the Council suggested by the initial pleadings in the *Lockerbie* and *Bosnia* cases are aberrational and will likely remain so. If the debate over judicial review necessarily involves instances in which the Council takes such controversial action that a state is emboldened to mount a confrontational case in the World Court *and* manages to find a jurisdictional basis for doing so, one suspects that the issue, however doctrinally interesting to scholars, will have limited real-world consequences.

At the same time, however, there are some instances where the Security Council has purported, within the terms of its resolutions, to suspend other legal rights and norms. Within the context of this work, the following examples are relevant:

- Within its action against terrorism the Security Council called upon States, under Resolution 1456, to become a party to all counter-terrorist conventions and protocols, thus potentially impacting upon what is normally within the sole purview of domestic executives (to determine whether or not to become party to international conventions).[66]
- Similar to the *Lockerbie Cases*, the Security Council had in 1999 demanded that the Taliban regime in Afghanistan turn over Usama bin Laden, who had by that time been indicted for the 1998 bombings of the United States embassies in Nairobi, Kenya and Tanzania and for conspiring to kill American nationals outside the United States.[67] Those demands were reiterated in 2000[68] and again, following the terrorist attacks on September 11, in 2001.[69]

---

[65] Above, n 63, 7.

[66] United Nations Security Council Resolution 1456 of 20 January 2003, S/RES/1456 (2003), para 2(a) – Appendix 2H herein. For further discussion of the effect of this provision, see Chapter 2, 26–28.

[67] United Nations Security Council Resolution 1267 of 15 October 1999, S/RES/1267 (1999), para 2.

[68] United Nations Security Council Resolution 1333 of 19 December 200, S/RES/1333 (2000), para 2.

[69] United Nations Security Council Resolution 1378 of 14 November 2001, S/RES/1378 (2001), Preambular para 4.

- In the context of trade sanctions imposed against Iraq following its invasion of Kuwait in 1990, the Security Council required States to comply with those sanctions irrespective of any contrary contractual obligations with Iraq.[70]

Is the Security Council in a position to suspend such legal rights and duties? It might be argued that such action is contrary to the non-intervention norm articulated within article 2(7) of the Charter, by interfering with matters that are essentially within the domestic jurisdiction of States, and thus *not* "in accordance with the present Charter". The immediate counter to that argument is the express qualification within article 2(7), which excludes application of the principle to measures adopted under Chapter VII of the Charter:

> 7. Nothing contained in the present Charter shall authorize the United Nations to intervene in matters which are essentially within the domestic jurisdiction of any state or shall require the Members to submit such matters to settlement under the present Charter; but this principle shall not prejudice the application of enforcement measures under Chapter VII.

Would the same approach be taken to any purported suspension of international law? What if, for example, the Security Council purported to suspend the application of particular human rights when imposing counter-terrorist obligations? Surely that is an issue with real-world consequence and one in respect of which the World Court would be willing to act. To do otherwise would be to allow a body of limited membership to reverse decades of human rights jurisprudence and normative development. It would also go against the stated principle within the Charter to promote and encourage respect for human rights and for fundamental freedoms for all.[71]

Alternatives to Reform

As evident throughout this book, the parameters of the law prohibiting the use of force, and the issues involved in application of that law to factual scenarios, are complex. They are made more difficult in their application due to the differing positions adopted by members of the United Nations, particularly permanent members of the Security Council. If reform of the

---

[70] United Nations Security Council Resolution 661 of 6 August 1990, S/RES/661 (1990), para 5.
[71] Article 1(3).

Council is not achievable in a manner that assists resolution of these very significant issues, are there other means by which harmonization might be achieved? Three potential avenues appear to exist: obtaining an Advisory Opinion from the International Court of Justice; adoption by the General Assembly of clear guidelines on the subject of the use of force; or adoption of a treaty on the subject of the use of force (to act as a supplement to the UN Charter).

Advisory Opinion of the World Court

The most beneficial option, it seems, would be for the General Assembly or Security Council to invoke article 96 of the UN Charter and request the International Court of Justice for an Advisory Opinion on the legal parameters of the relevant non-use of force provisions of the Charter. Although Advisory Opinions are just that, *advisory*, they have in practice been of significant value and influence. To take two examples, the Court's advisory opinions in the *Reparations Case* and the *Reservations to the Genocide Convention Case* have each stood as the foundation of international law norms concerning the personality of international organizations and the ability to make, and the effect of, reservations to international treaties.[72] A ruling of the World Court on the parameters of articles 2(4), 51 and Chapter VII of the Charter would stand as a weighty reference point for the future conduct of States in matters concerning the use of force.

A call for such an opinion was in fact made by the Russian Federation and Belarus in 1999 following *Operation Desert Fox* and in response to the invocation by the coalition forces of the argument of automaticity.[73] In a proposal submitted to the Special Committee on the Charter of the United Nations, it was recommended that an Advisory Opinion be sought from the International Court as to the legal consequences of the resort to the use of force by States either without the prior authorization of the Security Council or outside the context of self-defence.[74] The most recent report of the Special Committee notes that this proposal was not adopted, due to an absence of the consensus necessary for the adoption of a recommendation

---

[72] *Reparation for Injuries Suffered in the Service of the United Nations* (1979) ICJ Reports 174 and *Reservations to the Convention on the Prevention and Punishment of the Crime of Genocide* (1951) ICJ Reports 15.
[73] See Chapter 6, 133-134, and Chapter 7.
[74] A/AC.182/L.104/Rev.1.

by the Committee.[75] Perhaps now, however, against the background of such controversy over the interventions in Afghanistan and Iraq, the General Assembly would be minded to seek an advisory opinion?

General Assembly Resolution

The second alternative proffered is by way of General Assembly resolution. Just as the General Assembly adopted its influential Resolution 2625(XXV) on the Principles of Friendly Relations,[76] it might also be able to draw together a set of clear and agreed-upon principles concerning the various contentious issues discussed within this work. Such a resolution, if combined with the requisite State practice, might become the basis upon which future customary international law is formed. The difficulty envisaged with this alternative is two-fold: first, the likely protracted process that would need to be undertaken to achieve consensus on such issues; and, second, the difficulty presented by inconsistent State practice (which might undermine the intent and beneficial value of a resolution of this kind).

Treaty on the Non-Use of Force

The final option falling short of UN reform would be that advocated by the Union of Soviet Socialist Republics in 1976 when it submitted a draft World Treaty on the Non-Use of Force in International Relations to the General Assembly.[77] The Assembly, through its Resolution 31/9, invited members of the United Nations to examine the draft treaty and communicate their views on this to the UN Secretary-General.[78] Despite repeated calls for completion of the treaty, and continued reaffirmations by the General Assembly of "the need for effectiveness in the universal application of the principle of the non-use of force in international

---

[75] Special Committee on the Charter of the United Nations and on the Strengthening of the Role of the Organization, *Report of the Special Committee on the Charter of the United Nations and on the Strengthening of the Role of the Organization*, 17 April 2002, A/58/33, para 166.

[76] United Nations General Assembly Resolution 2626 (XXV) of 24 October 1970 (1883rd Plenary Meeting, during the Twenty-Fifth Session), the *Declaration on Principles of International Law Concerning Friendly Relations and Cooperation Among States in Accordance with the Charter of the United Nations*, A/RES/25/2625.

[77] (Draft) World Treaty on the Non-Use of Force in International Relations, *Official Records of the General Assembly, Thirty-first Session, Annexes*, agenda item 124, document A/31/243, annex.

[78] United Nations General Assembly Resolution 31/9 of 8 November 1976, A/RES/31/9.

relations",[79] work on the draft text was abandoned in 1987 due to a lack of consensus on its provisions.[80]

Conclusion

Although pressing, and called for since the first session of the United Nations General Assembly, Charter reform is an issue that engenders divided views and has been plagued by constant review, reconsideration and deferral. Despite specific proposals on amendment having been submitted since the first session of the General Assembly, there have been no substantive amendments to the Charter since its adoption in 1945. Likewise, although there was agreement in 1955 by both the General Assembly and Security Council that a General Conference on Charter reform should be held, subsequent events have seen that process delayed. The Special Committee tasked with arranging the General Conference still operates and has undertaken significant work on the clarification of certain principles pertaining to the maintenance and promotion of peace and security, but the motivation to convene a General Conference appears to have lapsed until recent calls for Charter reform following the intervention in Iraq and Afghanistan. At the root of the problem lies the need to obtain the consent of all five permanent members of the Security Council to any amendment of the Charter, as required by articles 108 and 109(2).

Given the focus of this text upon peace and security, this chapter has focused upon the question of the reform and accountability of the Security Council. The 1993 Working Group has achieved some practical improvements in the operation of the Security Council, not through reform of the Charter but instead through the adoption by the Council of certain procedural habits which have resulted in greater transparency in the conduct of the Council. The question of membership and voting is currently under consideration by the Secretary-General's High-Level Panel on Threats, Challenges and Change. The Panel seems set to recommend the increased membership of the Security Council, although the manner in

---

[79] This being the phrase commonly used within the Preambular paragraphs of General Assembly resolutions considering the reports of the Special Committee on Enhancing the Effectiveness of the Principle of Non-Use of Force in International Relations.

[80] The last resolution of the General Assembly dealing with the subject was United Nations General Assembly Resolution 41/76 of 3 December 1986. Paragraph 8 of the Resolution recorded the General Assembly's decision to include the topic within the provisional agenda of its forty-second session in 1997. No subsequent reports of the Special Committee were lodged or considered by the Assembly.

which this is to be recommended has been criticized as failing to address the privileged position of the permanent members. On the question of voting, various means of amending the veto power have been proposed, from abolition to subtle and more strong modification.

The question of review of Security Council action is one that remains uncertain, the International Court of Justice not having provided any clear guidance or indication in the matter. It seems likely, though, that judicial review of Council decisions is possible, tempered against an anticipated level of judicial deference. Clearly, however, the relevant authorizing provisions of the Charter call for the Security Council to act in accordance with the Charter, and the World Court should therefore be disposed to measure that limitation.

Several alternatives to reform have also been considered. Of those, it appears that a request to the World Court for an Advisory Opinion on the parameters of the non-use of force provisions of the Charter would be the most effective in terms of both time and effect.

Chapter 9

Conclusion

The first half of the twentieth century was plagued with inhumanity and war on a scale never seen before in the history of humankind. Those events prompted the international community to adopt and implement a regime under the Charter of the United Nations based upon an absolute prohibition against the use of force, save in the event of special circumstances legitimizing self-defence or enforcement action by the Security Council to maintain or restore the peace.

The first five years of this century have already seen two major international conflicts, through the interventions in Afghanistan and Iraq, which have posed significant challenges to the United Nations and the international community. Has the interlude between the creation of the United Nations and the beginning of this century, a period during which there has been relative peace, been an aberration? Is intolerance and the waging of war in pursuit of religious, ideological, political and economic motives an inevitable feature of humanity? Are the events of the First and Second World Wars so distant in memory that we are no longer motivated to save succeeding generations from the scourge of war (as first stated in the preamble to the UN Charter)?

These are questions the international community should be cognizant of. International law plays a vital role in shaping the character of international society and the decision-making process concerning the security policies of international actors. It clearly prohibits the use of force between States and promotes the peaceful settlement of disputes. Like all laws this legal framework is subject to breaches of the law. Two significant differences exist, however, concerning the consequences of the breach of domestic law and that of the international law prohibiting the use of force. In most instances, an infringement of municipal law does not involve, at least not on a wide scale, the killing of human beings or the creation of humanitarian crises. In contrast, action in violation of the prohibition on the use of force involves a decision to go to war. It is a decision to compel a State to do, or to refrain from doing, something by selecting targets for destruction. Whether legitimate or not, that targeting involves the killing of human beings and, inevitably, a collateral killing of innocent men, women and children. As recently seen in both Afghanistan and Iraq, it involves the destruction of infrastructure, the collapse of an economy and a political regime, and has long-term consequences for the stability and internal security of the State being attacked and the welfare of the citizens within the State. Breaches of the international law on the non-use of force, even conduct that is legitimate within the special exceptions under Chapter VII and article 51 of the Charter, have an enormous cost. The cost goes well beyond the financial expenditure of States participating in a military conflict, and beyond the normally short life of such conflicts. It is against that background that the international community so long ago outlawed the use of force as a legitimate tool of international relations through the League of Nations Covenant of 1919, the Kellogg-Briand Pact of 1928 and the 1945 Charter of the United Nations.

The second distinction between breaches of domestic law and the international legal framework under the United Nations concerns the issue of accountability. While municipal frameworks have clear processes for the prosecution and punishment or rehabilitation of offenders, the international framework is subject to considerable voids. States offending against the prohibition against the use of force might be called to account before the International Court of Justice and ordered to make reparations. However, although most States have lodged declarations of compulsory jurisdiction with the World Court,[1] three permanent members of the Security Council and nine other States do not have extant declarations and remain largely outside the jurisdiction of the Court.[2] Equally, despite the existence of the Hague and Geneva Conventions and the Statute of the International Criminal Court, a number of States have determined to remain outside the framework of the International Criminal Court.

For some States, then, there are few, if any, disincentives for failing to comply with the international legal order should compliance go against their interests. This is particularly true of the permanent members of the Security Council who hold the power of veto as a means of precluding the adoption of decisions that might negatively impact upon them. This, coupled with the political and economic might of some States, renders the international legal framework largely impotent against such States.

Where to, then, for international law, the United Nations and the peaceful settlement of disputes? Was the second half of the last century indeed an aberration? Is the twenty-first century to see the end of the

---

[1] See article 36(2) of the Statute of the International Court of Justice.

[2] Bolivia, Brazil, China, El Salvador, France, Guatemala, Iran, Israel, South Africa, Thailand, Turkey and the United States of America.

United Nations? Has it failed? As elucidated within the prevailing view of the General Assembly during the fortieth anniversary of the United Nations, the lack of effectiveness of the UN is not due to imperfections of the Charter but the lack of its respect by member States. Whether a realist or optimist, one must hope that the international community has matured so that it does continue to aspire to the motives set out in the preamble to the Charter and towards the peaceful settlement of disputes. The alternative, in the age of weapons of mass destruction, is too abhorrent to consider. It must also be borne in mind that, despite the challenges to the United Nations and international law posed by the interventions in Afghanistan and Iraq, the UN framework has faced serious challenges throughout its life, including those during the Cuban Missile Crisis and the Cold War in general. Although the strengthening of the UN Charter does remain an issue that requires urgent attention, the United Nations can, and should, be the vehicle through which the world community can continue to improve itself.

Appendix 1

Charter of the United Nations[*]

WE THE PEOPLES OF THE UNITED NATIONS DETERMINED

to save succeeding generations from the scourge of war, which twice in our lifetime has brought untold sorrow to mankind, and

to reaffirm faith in fundamental human rights, in the dignity and worth of the human person, in the equal rights of men and women and of nations large and small, and

to establish conditions under which justice and respect for the obligations arising from treaties and other sources of international law can be maintained, and

to promote social progress and better standards of life in larger freedom,

AND FOR THESE ENDS

to practice tolerance and live together in peace with one another as good neighbours, and

to unite our strength to maintain international peace and security, and

to ensure, by the acceptance of principles and the institution of methods, that armed force shall not be used, save in the common interest, and

to employ international machinery for the promotion of the economic and social advancement of all peoples,

HAVE RESOLVED TO COMBINE OUR EFFORTS TO ACCOMPLISH THESE AIMS

Accordingly, our respective Governments, through representatives assembled in the city of San Francisco, who have exhibited their full powers found to be in good and due form, have agreed to the present Charter of the United Nations and do hereby establish an international organization to be known as the United Nations.

---

[*] Done at San Francisco on 26 June 1945.

CHAPTER I. PURPOSES AND PRINCIPLES

Article 1
The Purposes of the United Nations are:
1.   To maintain international peace and security, and to that end: to take effective collective measures for the prevention and removal of threats to the peace, and for the suppression of acts of aggression or other breaches of the peace, and to bring about by peaceful means, and in conformity with the principles of justice and international law, adjustment or settlement of international disputes or situations which might lead to a breach of the peace;
2.   To develop friendly relations among nations based on respect for the principle of equal rights and self-determination of peoples, and to take other appropriate measures to strengthen universal peace;
3.   To achieve international co-operation in solving international problems of an economic, social, cultural, or humanitarian character, and in promoting and encouraging respect for human rights and for fundamental freedoms for all without distinction as to race, sex, language, or religion; and
4.   To be a centre for harmonizing the actions of nations in the attainment of these common ends.

Article 2
The Organization and its Members, in pursuit of the Purposes stated in Article 1, shall act in accordance with the following Principles.
1.   The Organization is based on the principle of the sovereign equality of all its Members.
2.   All Members, in order to ensure to all of them the rights and benefits resulting from membership, shall fulfil in good faith the obligations assumed by them in accordance with the present Charter.
3.   All Members shall settle their international disputes by peaceful means in such a manner that international peace and security, and justice, are not endangered.
4.   All Members shall refrain in their international relations from the threat or use of force against the territorial integrity or political independence of any state, or in any other manner inconsistent with the Purposes of the United Nations.
5.   All Members shall give the United Nations every assistance in any action it takes in accordance with the present Charter, and shall refrain from giving assistance to any state against which the United Nations is taking preventive or enforcement action.
6.   The Organization shall ensure that states which are not Members of the United Nations act in accordance with these Principles so far as may be necessary for the maintenance of international peace and security.
7.   Nothing contained in the present Charter shall authorize the United Nations to intervene in matters which are essentially within the domestic jurisdiction of any state or shall require the Members to submit such matters to settlement under the present Charter; but this principle shall not prejudice the application of enforcement measures under Chapter VII.

CHAPTER II. MEMBERSHIP

Article 3
The original Members of the United Nations shall be the states which, having participated in the United Nations Conference on International Organization at San Francisco, or having previously signed the Declaration by United Nations of 1 January 1942, sign the present Charter and ratify it in accordance with Article 110.

Article 4
1.   Membership in the United Nations is open to all other peace-loving states which accept the obligations contained in the present Charter and, in the judgment of the Organization, are able and willing to carry out these obligations.
2.   The admission of any such state to membership in the United Nations will be effected by a decision of the General Assembly upon the recommendation of the Security Council.

Article 5
A Member of the United Nations against which preventive or enforcement action has been taken by the Security Council may be suspended from the exercise of the rights and privileges of membership by the General Assembly upon the recommendation of the Security Council. The exercise of these rights and privileges may be restored by the Security Council.

Article 6
A Member of the United Nations which has persistently violated the Principles contained in the present Charter may be expelled from the Organization by the General Assembly upon the recommendation of the Security Council.

CHAPTER III. ORGANS

Article 7
1.   There are established as the principal organs of the United Nations: a General Assembly, a Security Council, an Economic and Social Council, a Trusteeship Council, an International Court of Justice, and a Secretariat.
2.   Such subsidiary organs as may be found necessary may be established in accordance with the present Charter.

Article 8
The United Nations shall place no restrictions on the eligibility of men and women to participate in any capacity and under conditions of equality in its principal and subsidiary organs.

CHAPTER IV. THE GENERAL ASSEMBLY

COMPOSITION

Article 9
The General Assembly shall consist of all the Members of the United Nations. Each Member shall have not more than five representatives in the General Assembly.

FUNCTIONS and POWERS

Article 10
The General Assembly may discuss any questions or any matters within the scope of the present Charter or relating to the powers and functions of any organs provided for in the present Charter, and, except as provided in Article 12, may make recommendations to the Members of the United Nations or to the Security Council or to both on any such questions or matters.

Article 11
1.   The General Assembly may consider the general principles of co-operation in the maintenance of international peace and security, including the principles governing disarmament and the regulation of armaments, and may make recommendations with regard to such principles to the Members or to the Security Council or to both.
2.   The General Assembly may discuss any questions relating to the maintenance of international peace and security brought before it by any Member of the United Nations, or by the Security Council, or by a state which is not a Member of the United Nations in accordance with Article 35, paragraph 2, and, except as provided in Article 12, may make recommendations with regard to any such questions to the state or states concerned or to the Security Council or to both. Any such question on which action is necessary shall be referred to the Security Council by the General Assembly either before or after discussion.
3.   The General Assembly may call the attention of the Security Council to situations which are likely to endanger international peace and security.
4.   The powers of the General Assembly set forth in this Article shall not limit the general scope of Article 10.

Article 12
1.   While the Security Council is exercising in respect of any dispute or situation the functions assigned to it in the present Charter, the General Assembly shall not make any recommendation with regard to that dispute or situation unless the Security Council so requests.
2.   The Secretary-General, with the consent of the Security Council, shall notify the General Assembly at each session of any matters relative to the maintenance of international peace and security which are being dealt with by the Security Council and shall similarly notify the General Assembly, or the Members of the United

Nations if the General Assembly is not in session, immediately the Security Council ceases to deal with such matters.

Article 13
1.   The General Assembly shall initiate studies and make recommendations for the purpose of:
(a) promoting international co-operation in the political field and encouraging the progressive development of international law and its codification;
(b) promoting international co-operation in the economic, social, cultural, educational, and health fields, and assisting in the realization of human rights and fundamental freedoms for all without distinction as to race, sex, language, or religion.
2.   The further responsibilities, functions and powers of the General Assembly with respect to matters mentioned in paragraph 1 (b) above are set forth in Chapters IX and X.

Article 14
Subject to the provisions of Article 12, the General Assembly may recommend measures for the peaceful adjustment of any situation, regardless of origin, which it deems likely to impair the general welfare or friendly relations among nations, including situations resulting from a violation of the provisions of the present Charter setting forth the Purposes and Principles of the United Nations.

Article 15
1.   The General Assembly shall receive and consider annual and special reports from the Security Council; these reports shall include an account of the measures that the Security Council has decided upon or taken to maintain international peace and security.
2.   The General Assembly shall receive and consider reports from the other organs of the United Nations.

Article 16
The General Assembly shall perform such functions with respect to the international trusteeship system as are assigned to it under Chapters XII and XIII, including the approval of the trusteeship agreements for areas not designated as strategic.

Article 17
1.   The General Assembly shall consider and approve the budget of the Organization.
2.   The expenses of the Organization shall be borne by the Members as apportioned by the General Assembly.
3.   The General Assembly shall consider and approve any financial and budgetary arrangements with specialized agencies referred to in Article 57 and shall examine

the administrative budgets of such specialized agencies with a view to making recommendations to the agencies concerned.

VOTING

Article 18
1.   Each member of the General Assembly shall have one vote.
2.   Decisions of the General Assembly on important questions shall be made by a two-thirds majority of the members present and voting. These questions shall include: recommendations with respect to the maintenance of international peace and security, the election of the non-permanent members of the Security Council, the election of the members of the Economic and Social Council, the election of members of the Trusteeship Council in accordance with paragraph 1 (c) of Article 86, the admission of new Members to the United Nations, the suspension of the rights and privileges of membership, the expulsion of Members, questions relating to the operation of the trusteeship system, and budgetary questions.
3.   Decisions on other questions, including the determination of additional categories of questions to be decided by a two-thirds majority, shall be made by a majority of the members present and voting.

Article 19
A Member of the United Nations which is in arrears in the payment of its financial contributions to the Organization shall have no vote in the General Assembly if the amount of its arrears equals or exceeds the amount of the contributions due from it for the preceding two full years. The General Assembly may, nevertheless, permit such a Member to vote if it is satisfied that the failure to pay is due to conditions beyond the control of the Member.

PROCEDURE

Article 20
The General Assembly shall meet in regular annual sessions and in such special sessions as occasion may require. Special sessions shall be convoked by the Secretary-General at the request of the Security Council or of a majority of the Members of the United Nations.

Article 21
The General Assembly shall adopt its own rules of procedure. It shall elect its President for each session.

Article 22
The General Assembly may establish such subsidiary organs as it deems necessary for the performance of its functions.

CHAPTER V. THE SECURITY COUNCIL

COMPOSITION

Article 23
1.   The Security Council shall consist of fifteen Members of the United Nations. The Republic of China, France, the Union of Soviet Socialist Republics, the United Kingdom of Great Britain and Northern Ireland, and the United States of America shall be permanent members of the Security Council. The General Assembly shall elect ten other Members of the United Nations to be non-permanent members of the Security Council, due regard being specially paid, in the first instance to the contribution of Members of the United Nations to the maintenance of international peace and security and to the other purposes of the Organization, and also to equitable geographical distribution.
2.   The non-permanent members of the Security Council shall be elected for a term of two years. In the first election of the non-permanent members after the increase of the membership of the Security Council from eleven to fifteen, two of the four additional members shall be chosen for a term of one year. A retiring member shall not be eligible for immediate re-election.
3.   Each member of the Security Council shall have one representative.

FUNCTIONS and POWERS

Article 24
1.   In order to ensure prompt and effective action by the United Nations, its Members confer on the Security Council primary responsibility for the maintenance of international peace and security, and agree that in carrying out its duties under this responsibility the Security Council acts on their behalf.
2.   In discharging these duties the Security Council shall act in accordance with the Purposes and Principles of the United Nations. The specific powers granted to the Security Council for the discharge of these duties are laid down in Chapters VI, VII, VIII, and XII.
3.   The Security Council shall submit annual and, when necessary, special reports to the General Assembly for its consideration.

Article 25
The Members of the United Nations agree to accept and carry out the decisions of the Security Council in accordance with the present Charter.

Article 26
In order to promote the establishment and maintenance of international peace and security with the least diversion for armaments of the world's human and economic resources, the Security Council shall be responsible for formulating, with the assistance of the Military Staff Committee referred to in Article 47, plans to be submitted to the Members of the United Nations for the establishment of a system for the regulation of armaments.

VOTING

Article 27

1. Each member of the Security Council shall have one vote.
2. Decisions of the Security Council on procedural matters shall be made by an affirmative vote of nine members.
3. Decisions of the Security Council on all other matters shall be made by an affirmative vote of nine members including the concurring votes of the permanent members; provided that, in decisions under Chapter VI, and under paragraph 3 of Article 52, a party to a dispute shall abstain from voting.

PROCEDURE

Article 28

1. The Security Council shall be so organized as to be able to function continuously. Each member of the Security Council shall for this purpose be represented at all times at the seat of the Organization.
2. The Security Council shall hold periodic meetings at which each of its members may, if it so desires, be represented by a member of the government or by some other specially designated representative.
3. The Security Council may hold meetings at such places other than the seat of the Organization as in its judgment will best facilitate its work.

Article 29

The Security Council may establish such subsidiary organs as it deems necessary for the performance of its functions.

Article 30

The Security Council shall adopt its own rules of procedure, including the method of selecting its President.

Article 31

Any Member of the United Nations which is not a member of the Security Council may participate, without vote, in the discussion of any question brought before the Security Council whenever the latter considers that the interests of that Member are specially affected.

Article 32

Any Member of the United Nations which is not a member of the Security Council or any state which is not a Member of the United Nations, if it is a party to a dispute under consideration by the Security Council, shall be invited to participate, without vote, in the discussion relating to the dispute. The Security Council shall lay down such conditions as it deems just for the participation of a state which is not a Member of the United Nations.

CHAPTER VI. PACIFIC SETTLEMENT OF DISPUTES

Article 33
1.   The parties to any dispute, the continuance of which is likely to endanger the maintenance of international peace and security, shall, first of all, seek a solution by negotiation, enquiry, mediation, conciliation, arbitration, judicial settlement, resort to regional agencies or arrangements, or other peaceful means of their own choice.
2.   The Security Council shall, when it deems necessary, call upon the parties to settle their dispute by such means.

Article 34
The Security Council may investigate any dispute, or any situation which might lead to international friction or give rise to a dispute, in order to determine whether the continuance of the dispute or situation is likely to endanger the maintenance of international peace and security.

Article 35
1.   Any Member of the United Nations may bring any dispute, or any situation of the nature referred to in Article 34, to the attention of the Security Council or of the General Assembly.
2.   A state which is not a Member of the United Nations may bring to the attention of the Security Council or of the General Assembly any dispute to which it is a party if it accepts in advance, for the purposes of the dispute, the obligations of pacific settlement provided in the present Charter.
3.   The proceedings of the General Assembly in respect of matters brought to its attention under this Article will be subject to the provisions of Articles 11 and 12.

Article 36
1.   The Security Council may, at any stage of a dispute of the nature referred to in Article 33 or of a situation of like nature, recommend appropriate procedures or methods of adjustment.
2.   The Security Council should take into consideration any procedures for the settlement of the dispute which have already been adopted by the parties.
3.   In making recommendations under this Article the Security Council should also take into consideration that legal disputes should as a general rule be referred by the parties to the International Court of Justice in accordance with the provisions of the Statute of the Court.

Article 37
1.   Should the parties to a dispute of the nature referred to in Article 33 fail to settle it by the means indicated in that Article, they shall refer it to the Security Council.
2.   If the Security Council deems that the continuance of the dispute is in fact likely to endanger the maintenance of international peace and security, it shall

decide whether to take action under Article 36 or to recommend such terms of settlement as it may consider appropriate.

Article 38
Without prejudice to the provisions of Articles 33 to 37, the Security Council may, if all the parties to any dispute so request, make recommendations to the parties with a view to a pacific settlement of the dispute.

CHAPTER VII. ACTION WITH RESPECT TO THREATS TO THE PEACE, BREACHES OF THE PEACE, AND ACTS OF AGGRESSION

Article 39
The Security Council shall determine the existence of any threat to the peace, breach of the peace, or act of aggression and shall make recommendations, or decide what measures shall be taken in accordance with Articles 41 and 42, to maintain or restore international peace and security.

Article 40
In order to prevent an aggravation of the situation, the Security Council may, before making the recommendations or deciding upon the measures provided for in Article 39, call upon the parties concerned to comply with such provisional measures as it deems necessary or desirable. Such provisional measures shall be without prejudice to the rights, claims, or position of the parties concerned. The Security Council shall duly take account of failure to comply with such provisional measures.

Article 41
The Security Council may decide what measures not involving the use of armed force are to be employed to give effect to its decisions, and it may call upon the Members of the United Nations to apply such measures. These may include complete or partial interruption of economic relations and of rail, sea, air, postal, telegraphic, radio, and other means of communication, and the severance of diplomatic relations.

Article 42
Should the Security Council consider that measures provided for in Article 41 would be inadequate or have proved to be inadequate, it may take such action by air, sea, or land forces as may be necessary to maintain or restore international peace and security. Such action may include demonstrations, blockade, and other operations by air, sea, or land forces of Members of the United Nations.

Article 43
1. All Members of the United Nations, in order to contribute to the maintenance of international peace and security, undertake to make available to the Security Council, on its call and in accordance with a special agreement or agreements,

armed forces, assistance, and facilities, including rights of passage, necessary for the purpose of maintaining international peace and security.

2. Such agreement or agreements shall govern the numbers and types of forces, their degree of readiness and general location, and the nature of the facilities and assistance to be provided.

3. The agreement or agreements shall be negotiated as soon as possible on the initiative of the Security Council. They shall be concluded between the Security Council and Members or between the Security Council and groups of Members and shall be subject to ratification by the signatory states in accordance with their respective constitutional processes.

Article 44

When the Security Council has decided to use force it shall, before calling upon a Member not represented on it to provide armed forces in fulfilment of the obligations assumed under Article 43, invite that Member, if the Member so desires, to participate in the decisions of the Security Council concerning the employment of contingents of that Member's armed forces.

Article 45

In order to enable the United Nations to take urgent military measures, Members shall hold immediately available national air-force contingents for combined international enforcement action. The strength and degree of readiness of these contingents and plans for their combined action shall be determined within the limits laid down in the special agreement or agreements referred to in Article 43, by the Security Council with the assistance of the Military Staff Committee.

Article 46

Plans for the application of armed force shall be made by the Security Council with the assistance of the Military Staff Committee.

Article 47

1. There shall be established a Military Staff Committee to advise and assist the Security Council on all questions relating to the Security Council's military requirements for the maintenance of international peace and security, the employment and command of forces placed at its disposal, the regulation of armaments, and possible disarmament.

2. The Military Staff Committee shall consist of the Chiefs of Staff of the permanent members of the Security Council or their representatives. Any Member of the United Nations not permanently represented on the Committee shall be invited by the Committee to be associated with it when the efficient discharge of the Committee's responsibilities requires the participation of that Member in its work.

3. The Military Staff Committee shall be responsible under the Security Council for the strategic direction of any armed forces placed at the disposal of the Security

Council. Questions relating to the command of such forces shall be worked out subsequently.

4. The Military Staff Committee, with the authorization of the Security Council and after consultation with appropriate regional agencies, may establish regional sub-committees.

Article 48

1. The action required to carry out the decisions of the Security Council for the maintenance of international peace and security shall be taken by all the Members of the United Nations or by some of them, as the Security Council may determine.

2. Such decisions shall be carried out by the Members of the United Nations directly and through their action in the appropriate international agencies of which they are members.

Article 49

The Members of the United Nations shall join in affording mutual assistance in carrying out the measures decided upon by the Security Council.

Article 50

If preventive or enforcement measures against any state are taken by the Security Council, any other state, whether a Member of the United Nations or not, which finds itself confronted with special economic problems arising from the carrying out of those measures shall have the right to consult the Security Council with regard to a solution of those problems.

Article 51

Nothing in the present Charter shall impair the inherent right of individual or collective self-defence if an armed attack occurs against a Member of the United Nations, until the Security Council has taken measures necessary to maintain international peace and security. Measures taken by Members in the exercise of this right of self-defence shall be immediately reported to the Security Council and shall not in any way affect the authority and responsibility of the Security Council under the present Charter to take at any time such action as it deems necessary in order to maintain or restore international peace and security.

CHAPTER VIII. REGIONAL ARRANGEMENTS

Article 52

1. Nothing in the present Charter precludes the existence of regional arrangements or agencies for dealing with such matters relating to the maintenance of international peace and security as are appropriate for regional action provided that such arrangements or agencies and their activities are consistent with the Purposes and Principles of the United Nations.

2. The Members of the United Nations entering into such arrangements or constituting such agencies shall make every effort to achieve pacific settlement of

local disputes through such regional arrangements or by such regional agencies before referring them to the Security Council.

3. The Security Council shall encourage the development of pacific settlement of local disputes through such regional arrangements or by such regional agencies either on the initiative of the states concerned or by reference from the Security Council.

4. This Article in no way impairs the application of Articles 34 and 35.

Article 53

1. The Security Council shall, where appropriate, utilize such regional arrangements or agencies for enforcement action under its authority. But no enforcement action shall be taken under regional arrangements or by regional agencies without the authorization of the Security Council, with the exception of measures against any enemy state, as defined in paragraph 2 of this Article, provided for pursuant to Article 107 or in regional arrangements directed against renewal of aggressive policy on the part of any such state, until such time as the Organization may, on request of the Governments concerned, be charged with the responsibility for preventing further aggression by such a state.

2. The term enemy state as used in paragraph 1 of this Article applies to any state which during the Second World War has been an enemy of any signatory of the present Charter.

Article 54

The Security Council shall at all times be kept fully informed of activities undertaken or in contemplation under regional arrangements or by regional agencies for the maintenance of international peace and security.

CHAPTER IX. INTERNATIONAL ECONOMIC AND SOCIAL CO-OPERATION

Article 55

With a view to the creation of conditions of stability and well-being which are necessary for peaceful and friendly relations among nations based on respect for the principle of equal rights and self-determination of peoples, the United Nations shall promote:

(a) higher standards of living, full employment, and conditions of economic and social progress and development;

(b) solutions of international economic, social, health, and related problems; and international cultural and educational co-operation; and

(c) universal respect for, and observance of, human rights and fundamental freedoms for all without distinction as to race, sex, language, or religion.

Article 56

All Members pledge themselves to take joint and separate action in co-operation with the Organization for the achievement of the purposes set forth in Article 55.

Article 57

1.   The various specialized agencies, established by intergovernmental agreement and having wide international responsibilities, as defined in their basic instruments, in economic, social, cultural, educational, health, and related fields, shall be brought into relationship with the United Nations in accordance with the provisions of Article 63.

2.   Such agencies thus brought into relationship with the United Nations are hereinafter referred to as specialized agencies.

Article 58

The Organization shall make recommendations for the co-ordination of the policies and activities of the specialized agencies.

Article 59

The Organization shall, where appropriate, initiate negotiations among the states concerned for the creation of any new specialized agencies required for the accomplishment of the purposes set forth in Article 55.

Article 60

Responsibility for the discharge of the functions of the Organization set forth in this Chapter shall be vested in the General Assembly and, under the authority of the General Assembly, in the Economic and Social Council, which shall have for this purpose the powers set forth in Chapter X.

CHAPTER X. THE ECONOMIC AND SOCIAL COUNCIL

COMPOSITION

Article 61

1.   The Economic and Social Council shall consist of fifty-four Members of the United Nations elected by the General Assembly.

2.   Subject to the provisions of paragraph 3, eighteen members of the Economic and Social Council shall be elected each year for a term of three years. A retiring member shall be eligible for immediate re-election.

3.   At the first election after the increase in the membership of the Economic and Social Council from twenty-seven to fifty-four members, in addition to the members elected in place of the nine members whose term of office expires at the end of that year, twenty-seven additional members shall be elected. Of these twenty-seven additional members, the term of office of nine members so elected shall expire at the end of one year, and of nine other members at the end of two years, in accordance with arrangements made by the General Assembly.

4.   Each member of the Economic and Social Council shall have one representative.

FUNCTIONS and POWERS

Article 62

1. The Economic and Social Council may make or initiate studies and reports with respect to international economic, social, cultural, educational, health, and related matters and may make recommendations with respect to any such matters to the General Assembly to the Members of the United Nations, and to the specialized agencies concerned.

2. It may make recommendations for the purpose of promoting respect for, and observance of, human rights and fundamental freedoms for all.

3. It may prepare draft conventions for submission to the General Assembly, with respect to matters falling within its competence.

4. It may call, in accordance with the rules prescribed by the United Nations, international conferences on matters falling within its competence.

Article 63

1. The Economic and Social Council may enter into agreements with any of the agencies referred to in Article 57, defining the terms on which the agency concerned shall be brought into relationship with the United Nations. Such agreements shall be subject to approval by the General Assembly.

2. It may co-ordinate the activities of the specialized agencies through consultation with and recommendations to such agencies and through recommendations to the General Assembly and to the Members of the United Nations.

Article 64

1. The Economic and Social Council may take appropriate steps to obtain regular reports from the specialized agencies. It may make arrangements with the Members of the United Nations and with the specialized agencies to obtain reports on the steps taken to give effect to its own recommendations and to recommendations on matters falling within its competence made by the General Assembly.

2. It may communicate its observations on these reports to the General Assembly.

Article 65

The Economic and Social Council may furnish information to the Security Council and shall assist the Security Council upon its request.

Article 66

1. The Economic and Social Council shall perform such functions as fall within its competence in connexion with the carrying out of the recommendations of the General Assembly.

2. It may, with the approval of the General Assembly, perform services at the request of Members of the United Nations and at the request of specialized agencies.

3. It shall perform such other functions as are specified elsewhere in the present Charter or as may be assigned to it by the General Assembly.

VOTING

Article 67
1. Each member of the Economic and Social Council shall have one vote.
2. Decisions of the Economic and Social Council shall be made by a majority of the members present and voting.

PROCEDURE

Article 68
The Economic and Social Council shall set up commissions in economic and social fields and for the promotion of human rights, and such other commissions as may be required for the performance of its functions.

Article 69
The Economic and Social Council shall invite any Member of the United Nations to participate, without vote, in its deliberations on any matter of particular concern to that Member.

Article 70
The Economic and Social Council may make arrangements for representatives of the specialized agencies to participate, without vote, in its deliberations and in those of the commissions established by it, and for its representatives to participate in the deliberations of the specialized agencies.

Article 71
The Economic and Social Council may make suitable arrangements for consultation with non-governmental organizations which are concerned with matters within its competence. Such arrangements may be made with international organizations and, where appropriate, with national organizations after consultation with the Member of the United Nations concerned.

Article 72
1. The Economic and Social Council shall adopt its own rules of procedure, including the method of selecting its President.
2. The Economic and Social Council shall meet as required in accordance with its rules, which shall include provision for the convening of meetings on the request of a majority of its members.

CHAPTER XI. DECLARATION REGARDING NON-SELF-GOVERNING TERRITORIES

Article 73

Members of the United Nations which have or assume responsibilities for the administration of territories whose peoples have not yet attained a full measure of self-government recognize the principle that the interests of the inhabitants of these territories are paramount, and accept as a sacred trust the obligation to promote to the utmost, within the system of international peace and security established by the present Charter, the well-being of the inhabitants of these territories, and, to this end:

(a) to ensure, with due respect for the culture of the peoples concerned, their political, economic, social, and educational advancement, their just treatment, and their protection against abuses;

(b) to develop self-government, to take due account of the political aspirations of the peoples, and to assist them in the progressive development of their free political institutions, according to the particular circumstances of each territory and its peoples and their varying stages of advancement;

(c) to further international peace and security;

(d) to promote constructive measures of development, to encourage research, and to co-operate with one another and, when and where appropriate, with specialized international bodies with a view to the practical achievement of the social, economic, and scientific purposes set forth in this Article; and

(e) to transmit regularly to the Secretary-General for information purposes, subject to such limitation as security and constitutional considerations may require, statistical and other information of a technical nature relating to economic, social, and educational conditions in the territories for which they are respectively responsible other than those territories to which Chapters XII and XIII apply.

Article 74

Members of the United Nations also agree that their policy in respect of the territories to which this Chapter applies, no less than in respect of their metropolitan areas, must be based on the general principle of good-neighbourliness, due account being taken of the interests and well-being of the rest of the world, in social, economic, and commercial matters.

CHAPTER XII. INTERNATIONAL TRUSTEESHIP SYSTEM

Article 75

The United Nations shall establish under its authority an international trusteeship system for the administration and supervision of such territories as may be placed thereunder by subsequent individual agreements. These territories are hereinafter referred to as trust territories.

Article 76
The basic objectives of the trusteeship system, in accordance with the Purposes of the United Nations laid down in Article 1 of the present Charter, shall be:
(a) to further international peace and security;
(b) to promote the political, economic, social, and educational advancement of the inhabitants of the trust territories, and their progressive development towards self-government or independence as may be appropriate to the particular circumstances of each territory and its peoples and the freely expressed wishes of the peoples concerned, and as may be provided by the terms of each trusteeship agreement;
(c) to encourage respect for human rights and for fundamental freedoms for all without distinction as to race, sex, language, or religion, and to encourage recognition of the interdependence of the peoples of the world; and
(d) to ensure equal treatment in social, economic, and commercial matters for all Members of the United Nations and their nationals, and also equal treatment for the latter in the administration of justice, without prejudice to the attainment of the foregoing objectives and subject to the provisions of Article 80.

Article 77
1. The trusteeship system shall apply to such territories in the following categories as may be placed thereunder by means of trusteeship agreements:
(a) territories now held under mandate;
(b) territories which may be detached from enemy states as a result of the Second World War; and
(c) territories voluntarily placed under the system by states responsible for their administration.
2. It will be a matter for subsequent agreement as to which territories in the foregoing categories will be brought under the trusteeship system and upon what terms.

Article 78
The trusteeship system shall not apply to territories which have become Members of the United Nations, relationship among which shall be based on respect for the principle of sovereign equality.

Article 79
The terms of trusteeship for each territory to be placed under the trusteeship system, including any alteration or amendment, shall be agreed upon by the states directly concerned, including the mandatory power in the case of territories held under mandate by a Member of the United Nations, and shall be approved as provided for in Articles 83 and 85.

Article 80

1. Except as may be agreed upon in individual trusteeship agreements, made under Articles 77, 79, and 81, placing each territory under the trusteeship system, and until such agreements have been concluded, nothing in this Chapter shall be construed in or of itself to alter in any manner the rights whatsoever of any states or any peoples or the terms of existing international instruments to which Members of the United Nations may respectively be parties.

2. Paragraph 1 of this Article shall not be interpreted as giving grounds for delay or postponement of the negotiation and conclusion of agreements for placing mandated and other territories under the trusteeship system as provided for in Article 77.

Article 81

The trusteeship agreement shall in each case include the terms under which the trust territory will be administered and designate the authority which will exercise the administration of the trust territory. Such authority, hereinafter called the administering authority, may be one or more states or the Organization itself.

Article 82

There may be designated, in any trusteeship agreement, a strategic area or areas which may include part or all of the trust territory to which the agreement applies, without prejudice to any special agreement or agreements made under Article 43.

Article 83

1. All functions of the United Nations relating to strategic areas, including the approval of the terms of the trusteeship agreements and of their alteration or amendment, shall be exercised by the Security Council.

2. The basic objectives set forth in Article 76 shall be applicable to the people of each strategic area.

3. The Security Council shall, subject to the provisions of the trusteeship agreements and without prejudice to security considerations, avail itself of the assistance of the Trusteeship Council to perform those functions of the United Nations under the trusteeship system relating to political, economic, social, and educational matters in the strategic areas.

Article 84

It shall be the duty of the administering authority to ensure that the trust territory shall play its part in the maintenance of international peace and security. To this end the administering authority may make use of volunteer forces, facilities, and assistance from the trust territory in carrying out the obligations towards the Security Council undertaken in this regard by the administering authority, as well as for local defence and the maintenance of law and order within the trust territory.

Article 85
1.   The functions of the United Nations with regard to trusteeship agreements for all areas not designated as strategic, including the approval of the terms of the trusteeship agreements and of their alteration or amendment, shall be exercised by the General Assembly.
2.   The Trusteeship Council, operating under the authority of the General Assembly shall assist the General Assembly in carrying out these functions.

CHAPTER XIII. THE TRUSTEESHIP COUNCIL

COMPOSITION

Article 86
1.   The Trusteeship Council shall consist of the following Members of the United Nations:
(a) those Members administering trust territories;
(b) such of those Members mentioned by name in Article 23 as are not administering trust territories; and
(c) as many other Members elected for three-year terms by the General Assembly as may be necessary to ensure that the total number of members of the Trusteeship Council is equally divided between those Members of the United Nations which administer trust territories and those which do not.
2.   Each member of the Trusteeship Council shall designate one specially qualified person to represent it therein.

FUNCTIONS and POWERS

Article 87
1.   The General Assembly and, under its authority, the Trusteeship Council, in carrying out their functions, may:
(a) consider reports submitted by the administering authority;
(b) accept petitions and examine them in consultation with the administering authority;
(c) provide for periodic visits to the respective trust territories at times agreed upon with the administering authority; and
(d) take these and other actions in conformity with the terms of the trusteeship agreements.

Article 88
The Trusteeship Council shall formulate a questionnaire on the political, economic, social, and educational advancement of the inhabitants of each trust territory, and the administering authority for each trust territory within the competence of the General Assembly shall make an annual report to the General Assembly upon the basis of such questionnaire.

VOTING

Article 89
1.   Each member of the Trusteeship Council shall have one vote.
2.   Decisions of the Trusteeship Council shall be made by a majority of the members present and voting.

PROCEDURE

Article 90
1.   The Trusteeship Council shall adopt its own rules of procedure, including the method of selecting its President.
2.   The Trusteeship Council shall meet as required in accordance with its rules, which shall include provision for the convening of meetings on the request of a majority of its members.

Article 91
The Trusteeship Council shall, when appropriate, avail itself of the assistance of the Economic and Social Council and of the specialized agencies in regard to matters with which they are respectively concerned.

CHAPTER XIV. THE INTERNATIONAL COURT OF JUSTICE

Article 92
The International Court of Justice shall be the principal judicial organ of the United Nations. It shall function in accordance with the annexed Statute, which is based upon the Statute of the Permanent Court of International Justice and forms an integral part of the present Charter.

Article 93
1.   All Members of the United Nations are *ipso facto* parties to the Statute of the International Court of Justice.
2.   A state which is not a Member of the United Nations may become a party to the Statute of the International Court of Justice on conditions to be determined in each case by the General Assembly upon the recommendation of the Security Council.

Article 94
1.   Each Member of the United Nations undertakes to comply with the decision of the International Court of Justice in any case to which it is a party.
2.   If any party to a case fails to perform the obligations incumbent upon it under a judgment rendered by the Court, the other party may have recourse to the Security Council, which may, if it deems necessary, make recommendations or decide upon measures to be taken to give effect to the judgment.

Article 95

Nothing in the present Charter shall prevent Members of the United Nations from entrusting the solution of their differences to other tribunals by virtue of agreements already in existence or which may be concluded in the future.

Article 96

1.   The General Assembly or the Security Council may request the International Court of Justice to give an advisory opinion on any legal question.

2.   Other organs of the United Nations and specialized agencies, which may at any time be so authorized by the General Assembly, may also request advisory opinions of the Court on legal questions arising within the scope of their activities.

CHAPTER XV. THE SECRETARIAT

Article 97

The Secretariat shall comprise a Secretary-General and such staff as the Organization may require. The Secretary-General shall be appointed by the General Assembly upon the recommendation of the Security Council. He shall be the chief administrative officer of the Organization.

Article 98

The Secretary-General shall act in that capacity in all meetings of the General Assembly, of the Security Council, of the Economic and Social Council, and of the Trusteeship Council, and shall perform such other functions as are entrusted to him by these organs. The Secretary-General shall make an annual report to the General Assembly on the work of the Organization.

Article 99

The Secretary-General may bring to the attention of the Security Council any matter which in his opinion may threaten the maintenance of international peace and security.

Article 100

1.   In the performance of their duties the Secretary-General and the staff shall not seek or receive instructions from any government or from any other authority external to the Organization. They shall refrain from any action which might reflect on their position as international officials responsible only to the Organization.

2.   Each Member of the United Nations undertakes to respect the exclusively international character of the responsibilities of the Secretary-General and the staff and not to seek to influence them in the discharge of their responsibilities.

Article 101

1.   The staff shall be appointed by the Secretary-General under regulations established by the General Assembly.

2.   Appropriate staffs shall be permanently assigned to the Economic and Social Council, the Trusteeship Council, and, as required, to other organs of the United Nations. These staffs shall form a part of the Secretariat.

3.   The paramount consideration in the employment of the staff and in the determination of the conditions of service shall be the necessity of securing the highest standards of efficiency, competence, and integrity. Due regard shall be paid to the importance of recruiting the staff on as wide a geographical basis as possible.

CHAPTER XVI. MISCELLANEOUS PROVISIONS

Article 102

1.   Every treaty and every international agreement entered into by any Member of the United Nations after the present Charter comes into force shall as soon as possible be registered with the Secretariat and published by it.

2.   No party to any such treaty or international agreement which has not been registered in accordance with the provisions of paragraph 1 of this Article may invoke that treaty or agreement before any organ of the United Nations.

Article 103

In the event of a conflict between the obligations of the Members of the United Nations under the present Charter and their obligations under any other international agreement, their obligations under the present Charter shall prevail.

Article 104

The Organization shall enjoy in the territory of each of its Members such legal capacity as may be necessary for the exercise of its functions and the fulfilment of its purposes.

Article 105

1.   The Organization shall enjoy in the territory of each of its Members such privileges and immunities as are necessary for the fulfilment of its purposes.

2.   Representatives of the Members of the United Nations and officials of the Organization shall similarly enjoy such privileges and immunities as are necessary for the independent exercise of their functions in connexion with the Organization.

3.   The General Assembly may make recommendations with a view to determining the details of the application of paragraphs 1 and 2 of this Article or may propose conventions to the Members of the United Nations for this purpose.

CHAPTER XVII. TRANSITIONAL SECURITY ARRANGEMENTS

Article 106

Pending the coming into force of such special agreements referred to in Article 43 as in the opinion of the Security Council enable it to begin the exercise of its responsibilities under Article 42, the parties to the Four-Nation Declaration, signed at Moscow, 30 October 1943, and France, shall, in accordance with the provisions of paragraph 5 of that Declaration, consult with one another and as occasion requires with other Members of the United Nations with a view to such joint action on behalf of the Organization as may be necessary for the purpose of maintaining international peace and security.

Article 107
Nothing in the present Charter shall invalidate or preclude action, in relation to any state which during the Second World War has been an enemy of any signatory to the present Charter, taken or authorized as a result of that war by the Governments having responsibility for such action.

CHAPTER XVIII. AMENDMENTS

Article 108
Amendments to the present Charter shall come into force for all Members of the United Nations when they have been adopted by a vote of two thirds of the members of the General Assembly and ratified in accordance with their respective constitutional processes by two thirds of the Members of the United Nations, including all the permanent members of the Security Council.

Article 109
1.   A General Conference of the Members of the United Nations for the purpose of reviewing the present Charter may be held at a date and place to be fixed by a two-thirds vote of the members of the General Assembly and by a vote of any nine members of the Security Council. Each Member of the United Nations shall have one vote in the conference.
2.   Any alteration of the present Charter recommended by a two-thirds vote of the conference shall take effect when ratified in accordance with their respective constitutional processes by two thirds of the Members of the United Nations including all the permanent members of the Security Council.
3.   If such a conference has not been held before the tenth annual session of the General Assembly following the coming into force of the present Charter, the proposal to call such a conference shall be placed on the agenda of that session of the General Assembly, and the conference shall be held if so decided by a majority vote of the members of the General Assembly and by a vote of any seven members of the Security Council.

CHAPTER XIX. RATIFICATION AND SIGNATURE

Article 110
1.   The present Charter shall be ratified by the signatory states in accordance with their respective constitutional processes.

2. The ratifications shall be deposited with the Government of the United States of America, which shall notify all the signatory states of each deposit as well as the Secretary-General of the Organization when he has been appointed.

3. The present Charter shall come into force upon the deposit of ratifications by the Republic of China, France, the Union of Soviet Socialist Republics, the United Kingdom of Great Britain and Northern Ireland, and the United States of America, and by a majority of the other signatory states. A protocol of the ratifications deposited shall thereupon be drawn up by the Government of the United States of America which shall communicate copies thereof to all the signatory states.

4. The states signatory to the present Charter which ratify it after it has come into force will become original Members of the United Nations on the date of the deposit of their respective ratifications.

Article 111
The present Charter, of which the Chinese, French, Russian, English, and Spanish texts are equally authentic, shall remain deposited in the archives of the Government of the United States of America. Duly certified copies thereof shall be transmitted by that Government to the Governments of the other signatory states.

IN FAITH WHEREOF the representatives of the Governments of the United Nations have signed the present Charter.
DONE at the city of San Francisco the twenty-sixth day of June, one thousand nine hundred and forty-five.

Appendix 2

Selected Resolutions Concerning Afghanistan and/or International Terrorism

Appendix 2A
United Nations Security Council Resolution 1267[*]

The Security Council,

Reaffirming its previous resolutions, in particular resolutions 1189 (1998) of 13 August 1998, 1193 (1998) of 28 August 1998 and 1214 (1998) of 8 December 1998, and the statements of its President on the situation in Afghanistan,

Reaffirming its strong commitment to the sovereignty, independence, territorial integrity and national unity of Afghanistan, and its respect for Afghanistan's cultural and historical heritage, Reiterating its deep concern over the continuing violations of international humanitarian law and of human rights, particularly discrimination against women and girls, and over the significant rise in the illicit production of opium, and stressing that the capture by the Taliban of the Consulate-General of the Islamic Republic of Iran and the murder of Iranian diplomats and a journalist in Mazar-e-Sharif constituted flagrant violations of established international law, Recalling the relevant international counter-terrorism conventions and in particular the obligations of parties to those conventions to extradite or prosecute terrorists,

Strongly condemning the continuing use of Afghan territory, especially areas controlled by the Taliban, for the sheltering and training of terrorists and planning of terrorist acts, and reaffirming its conviction that the suppression of international terrorism is essential for the maintenance of international peace and security,

Deploring the fact that the Taliban continues to provide safe haven to Usama bin Laden and to allow him and others associated with him to operate a network of terrorist training camps from Taliban-controlled territory and to use Afghanistan as a base from which to sponsor international terrorist operations,

Noting the indictment of Usama bin Laden and his associates by the United States of America for, inter alia, the 7 August 1998 bombings of the United States embassies in Nairobi, Kenya, and Dar es Salaam, Tanzania, and for conspiring to kill American nationals outside the United States, and noting

---

[*] S/RES/1267 (1999), adopted by the Security Council at its 4051st meeting on 15 October 1999.

also the request of the United States of America to the Taliban to surrender them for trial (S/1999/1021),

Determining that the failure of the Taliban authorities to respond to the demands in paragraph 13 of resolution 1214 (1998) constitutes a threat to international peace and security,

Stressing its determination to ensure respect for its resolutions,

Acting under Chapter VII of the Charter of the United Nations,

1. *Insists* that the Afghan faction known as the Taliban, which also calls itself the Islamic Emirate of Afghanistan, comply promptly with its previous resolutions and in particular cease the provision of sanctuary and training for international terrorists and their organizations, take appropriate effective measures to ensure that the territory under its control is not used for terrorist installations and camps, or for the preparation or organization of terrorist acts against other States or their citizens, and cooperate with efforts to bring indicted terrorists to justice;

2. *Demands* that the Taliban turn over Usama bin Laden without further delay to appropriate authorities in a country where he has been indicted, or to appropriate authorities in a country where he will be returned to such a country, or to appropriate authorities in a country where he will be arrested and effectively brought to justice;

3. *Decides* that on 14 November 1999 all States shall impose the measures set out in paragraph 4 below, unless the Council has previously decided, on the basis of a report of the Secretary-General, that the Taliban has fully complied with the obligation set out in paragraph 2 above;

4. *Decides* further that, in order to enforce paragraph 2 above, all States shall:
(a) Deny permission for any aircraft to take off from or land in their territory if it is owned, leased or operated by or on behalf of the Taliban as designated by the Committee established by paragraph 6 below, unless the particular flight has been approved in advance by the Committee on the grounds of humanitarian need, including religious obligation such as the performance of the Hajj;
(b) Freeze funds and other financial resources, including funds derived or generated from property owned or controlled directly or indirectly by the Taliban, or by any undertaking owned or controlled by the Taliban, as designated by the Committee established by paragraph 6 below, and ensure that neither they nor any other funds or financial resources so designated are made available, by their nationals or by any persons within their territory, to or for the benefit of the Taliban or any undertaking owned or controlled, directly

or indirectly, by the Taliban, except as may be authorized by the Committee on a case-by-case basis on the grounds of humanitarian need;

5.   *Urges* all States to cooperate with efforts to fulfil the demand in paragraph 2 above, and to consider further measures against Usama bin Laden and his associates;

6.   *Decides* to establish, in accordance with rule 28 of its provisional rules of procedure, a Committee of the Security Council consisting of all the members of the Council to undertake the following tasks and to report on its work to the Council with its observations and recommendations:

(a) To seek from all States further information regarding the action taken by them with a view to effectively implementing the measures imposed by paragraph 4 above;

(b) To consider information brought to its attention by States concerning violations of the measures imposed by paragraph 4 above and to recommend appropriate measures in response thereto;

(c) To make periodic reports to the Council on the impact, including the humanitarian implications, of the measures imposed by paragraph 4 above;

(d) To make periodic reports to the Council on information submitted to it regarding alleged violations of the measures imposed by paragraph 4 above, identifying where possible persons or entities reported to be engaged in such violations;

(e) To designate the aircraft and funds or other financial resources referred to in paragraph 4 above in order to facilitate the implementation of the measures imposed by that paragraph;

(f) To consider requests for exemptions from the measures imposed by paragraph 4 above as provided in that paragraph, and to decide on the granting of an exemption to these measures in respect of the payment by the International Air Transport Association (IATA) to the aeronautical authority of Afghanistan on behalf of international airlines for air traffic control services;

(g) To examine the reports submitted pursuant to paragraph 9 below;

7.   *Calls upon* all States to act strictly in accordance with the provisions of this resolution, notwithstanding the existence of any rights or obligations conferred or imposed by any international agreement or any contract entered into or any licence or permit granted prior to the date of coming into force of the measures imposed by paragraph 4 above;

8.   *Calls upon* States to bring proceedings against persons and entities within their jurisdiction that violate the measures imposed by paragraph 4 above and to impose appropriate penalties;

9. *Calls upon* all States to cooperate fully with the Committee established by paragraph 6 above in the fulfilment of its tasks, including supplying such information as may be required by the Committee in pursuance of this resolution;

10. *Requests* all States to report to the Committee established by paragraph 6 above within 30 days of the coming into force of the measures imposed by paragraph 4 above on the steps they have taken with a view to effectively implementing paragraph 4 above;

11. *Requests* the Secretary-General to provide all necessary assistance to the Committee established by paragraph 6 above and to make the necessary arrangements in the Secretariat for this purpose;

12. *Requests* the Committee established by paragraph 6 above to determine appropriate arrangements, on the basis of recommendations of the Secretariat, with competent international organizations, neighbouring and other States, and parties concerned with a view to improving the monitoring of the implementation of the measures imposed by paragraph 4 above;

13. *Requests* the Secretariat to submit for consideration by the Committee established by paragraph 6 above information received from Governments and public sources on possible violations of the measures imposed by paragraph 4 above;

14. *Decides* to terminate the measures imposed by paragraph 4 above once the Secretary-General reports to the Security Council that the Taliban has fulfilled the obligation set out in paragraph 2 above;

15. *Expresses* its readiness to consider the imposition of further measures, in accordance with its responsibility under the Charter of the United Nations, with the aim of achieving the full implementation of this resolution;

16. *Decides* to remain actively seized of the matter.

Appendix 2B
United Nations Security Council Resolution 1269[*]

The Security Council,

Deeply concerned by the increase in acts of international terrorism which endangers the lives and well-being of individuals worldwide as well as the peace and security of all States,

Condemning all acts of terrorism, irrespective of motive, wherever and by whomever committed,

Mindful of all relevant resolutions of the General Assembly, including resolution 49/60 of 9 December 1994, by which it adopted the Declaration on Measures to Eliminate International Terrorism,

Emphasizing the necessity to intensify the fight against terrorism at the national level and to strengthen, under the auspices of the United Nations, effective international cooperation in this field on the basis of the principles of the Charter of the United Nations and norms of international law, including respect for international humanitarian law and human rights,

Supporting the efforts to promote universal participation in and implementation of the existing international anti-terrorist conventions, as well as to develop new international instruments to counter the terrorist threat,

Commending the work done by the General Assembly, relevant United Nations organs and specialized agencies and regional and other organizations to combat international terrorism,

Determined to contribute, in accordance with the Charter of the United Nations, to the efforts to combat terrorism in all its forms,

Reaffirming that the suppression of acts of international terrorism, including those in which States are involved, is an essential contribution to the maintenance of international peace and security,

---

[*] S/RES/1269 (1999), adopted by the Security Council at its 4053rd meeting on 19 October 1999.

1.   *Unequivocally condemns* all acts, methods and practices of terrorism as criminal and unjustifiable, regardless of their motivation, in all their forms and manifestations, wherever and by whomever committed, in particular those which could threaten international peace and security;

2.   *Calls upon* all States to implement fully the international anti-terrorist conventions to which they are parties, encourages all States to consider as a matter of priority adhering to those to which they are not parties, and encourages also the speedy adoption of the pending conventions;

3.   *Stresses* the vital role of the United Nations in strengthening international cooperation in combating terrorism and emphasizes the importance of enhanced coordination among States, international and regional organizations;

4.   *Calls upon* all States to take, inter alia, in the context of such cooperation and coordination, appropriate steps to:

  – cooperate with each other, particularly through bilateral and multilateral agreements and arrangements, to prevent and suppress terrorist acts, protect their nationals and other persons against terrorist attacks and bring to justice the perpetrators of such acts;
  – prevent and suppress in their territories through all lawful means the preparation and financing of any acts of terrorism;
  – deny those who plan, finance or commit terrorist acts safe havens by ensuring their apprehension and prosecution or extradition;
  – take appropriate measures in conformity with the relevant provisions of national and international law, including international standards of human rights, before granting refugee status, for the purpose of ensuring that the asylum-seeker has not participated in terrorist acts;
  – exchange information in accordance with international and domestic law, and cooperate on administrative and judicial matters in order to prevent the commission of terrorist acts;

5.   *Requests* the Secretary-General, in his reports to the General Assembly, in particular submitted in accordance with its resolution 50/53 on measures to eliminate international terrorism, to pay special attention to the need to prevent and fight the threat to international peace and security as a result of terrorist activities;

6.   *Expresses* its readiness to consider relevant provisions of the reports mentioned in paragraph 5 above and to take necessary steps in accordance with its responsibilities under the Charter of the United Nations in order to counter terrorist threats to international peace and security;

7.   *Decides* to remain seized of this matter.

Appendix 2C
United Nations Security Council Resolution 1368[*]

The Security Council,

Reaffirming the principles and purposes of the Charter of the United Nations,

Determined to combat by all means threats to international peace and security caused by terrorist acts,

Recognizing the inherent right of individual or collective self-defence in accordance with the Charter,

1. *Unequivocally condemns* in the strongest terms the horrifying terrorist attacks which took place on 11 September 2001 in New York, Washington, D.C. and Pennsylvania and *regards* such acts, like any act of international terrorism, as a threat to international peace and security;

2. *Expresses* its deepest sympathy and condolences to the victims and their families and to the people and Government of the United States of America;

3. *Calls* on all States to work together urgently to bring to justice the perpetrators, organizers and sponsors of these terrorist attacks and *stresses* that those responsible for aiding, supporting or harbouring the perpetrators, organizers and sponsors of these acts will be held accountable;

4. *Calls also* on the international community to redouble their efforts to prevent and suppress terrorist acts including by increased cooperation and full implementation of the relevant international anti-terrorist conventions and Security Council resolutions, in particular resolution 1269 (1999) of 19 October 1999;

5. *Expresses* its readiness to take all necessary steps to respond to the terrorist attacks of 11 September 2001, and to combat all forms of terrorism, in accordance with its responsibilities under the Charter of the United Nations;

6. *Decides* to remain seized of the matter.

---

[*] S/RES/1368 (2001), adopted by the Security Council at its 4370th meeting on 12 September 2001.

Appendix 2D
United Nations Security Council Resolution 1373[*]

The Security Council,

Reaffirming its resolutions 1269 (1999) of 19 October 1999 and 1368 (2001) of 12 September 2001,

Reaffirming also its unequivocal condemnation of the terrorist attacks which took place in New York, Washington, D.C. and Pennsylvania on 11 September 2001, and expressing its determination to prevent all such acts,

Reaffirming further that such acts, like any act of international terrorism, constitute a threat to international peace and security,

Reaffirming the inherent right of individual or collective self-defence as recognized by the Charter of the United Nations as reiterated in resolution 1368 (2001),

Reaffirming the need to combat by all means, in accordance with the Charter of the United Nations, threats to international peace and security caused by terrorist acts,

Deeply concerned by the increase, in various regions of the world, of acts of terrorism motivated by intolerance or extremism,

Calling on States to work together urgently to prevent and suppress terrorist acts, including through increased cooperation and full implementation of the relevant international conventions relating to terrorism,

Recognizing the need for States to complement international cooperation by taking additional measures to prevent and suppress, in their territories through all lawful means, the financing and preparation of any acts of terrorism,

Reaffirming the principle established by the General Assembly in its declaration of October 1970 (resolution 2625 (XXV)) and reiterated by the Security Council in its resolution 1189 (1998) of 13 August 1998, namely that every State has the duty to refrain from organizing, instigating, assisting or

---

[*] S/RES/1373 (2001), adopted by the Security Council at its 4385th meeting on 28 September 2001.

participating in terrorist acts in another State or acquiescing in organized activities within its territory directed towards the commission of such acts,

Acting under Chapter VII of the Charter of the United Nations,

1. *Decides* that all States shall:
(a) Prevent and suppress the financing of terrorist acts;
(b) Criminalize the wilful provision or collection, by any means, directly or indirectly, of funds by their nationals or in their territories with the intention that the funds should be used, or in the knowledge that they are to be used, in order to carry out terrorist acts;
(c) Freeze without delay funds and other financial assets or economic resources of persons who commit, or attempt to commit, terrorist acts or participate in or facilitate the commission of terrorist acts; of entities owned or controlled directly or indirectly by such persons; and of persons and entities acting on behalf of, or at the direction of such persons and entities, including funds derived or generated from property owned or controlled directly or indirectly by such persons and associated persons and entities;
(d) Prohibit their nationals or any persons and entities within their territories from making any funds, financial assets or economic resources or financial or other related services available, directly or indirectly, for the benefit of persons who commit or attempt to commit or facilitate or participate in the commission of terrorist acts, of entities owned or controlled, directly or indirectly, by such persons and of persons and entities acting on behalf of or at the direction of such persons;

2. *Decides also* that all States shall:
(a) Refrain from providing any form of support, active or passive, to entities or persons involved in terrorist acts, including by suppressing recruitment of members of terrorist groups and eliminating the supply of weapons to terrorists;
(b) Take the necessary steps to prevent the commission of terrorist acts, including by provision of early warning to other States by exchange of information;
(c) Deny safe haven to those who finance, plan, support, or commit terrorist acts, or provide safe havens;
(d) Prevent those who finance, plan, facilitate or commit terrorist acts from using their respective territories for those purposes against other States or their citizens;
(e) Ensure that any person who participates in the financing, planning, preparation or perpetration of terrorist acts or in supporting terrorist acts is brought to justice and ensure that, in addition to any other measures against them, such terrorist acts are established as serious criminal offences in domestic laws and regulations and that the punishment duly reflects the seriousness of such terrorist acts;

(f) Afford one another the greatest measure of assistance in connection with criminal investigations or criminal proceedings relating to the financing or support of terrorist acts, including assistance in obtaining evidence in their possession necessary for the proceedings;

(g) Prevent the movement of terrorists or terrorist groups by effective border controls and controls on issuance of identity papers and travel documents, and through measures for preventing counterfeiting, forgery or fraudulent use of identity papers and travel documents;

3. *Calls* upon all States to:

(a) Find ways of intensifying and accelerating the exchange of operational information, especially regarding actions or movements of terrorist persons or networks; forged or falsified travel documents; traffic in arms, explosives or sensitive materials; use of communications technologies by terrorist groups; and the threat posed by the possession of weapons of mass destruction by terrorist groups;

(b) Exchange information in accordance with international and domestic law and cooperate on administrative and judicial matters to prevent the commission of terrorist acts;

(c) Cooperate, particularly through bilateral and multilateral arrangements and agreements, to prevent and suppress terrorist attacks and take action against perpetrators of such acts;

(d) Become parties as soon as possible to the relevant international conventions and protocols relating to terrorism, including the International Convention for the Suppression of the Financing of Terrorism of 9 December 1999;

(e) Increase cooperation and fully implement the relevant international conventions and protocols relating to terrorism and Security Council resolutions 1269 (1999) and 1368 (2001);

(f) Take appropriate measures in conformity with the relevant provisions of national and international law, including international standards of human rights, before granting refugee status, for the purpose of ensuring that the asylum-seeker has not planned, facilitated or participated in the commission of terrorist acts;

(g) Ensure, in conformity with international law, that refugee status is not abused by the perpetrators, organizers or facilitators of terrorist acts, and that claims of political motivation are not recognized as grounds for refusing requests for the extradition of alleged terrorists;

4. *Notes* with concern the close connection between international terrorism and transnational organized crime, illicit drugs, money-laundering, illegal arms trafficking, and illegal movement of nuclear, chemical, biological and other potentially deadly materials, and in this regard *emphasizes* the need to enhance coordination of efforts on national, subregional, regional and international levels in order to strengthen a global response to this serious challenge and threat to international security;

5.   *Declares* that acts, methods, and practices of terrorism are contrary to the purposes and principles of the United Nations and that knowingly financing, planning and inciting terrorist acts are also contrary to the purposes and principles of the United Nations;

6.   *Decides* to establish, in accordance with rule 28 of its provisional rules of procedure, a Committee of the Security Council, consisting of all the members of the Council, to monitor implementation of this resolution, with the assistance of appropriate expertise, and *calls upon* all States to report to the Committee, no later than 90 days from the date of adoption of this resolution and thereafter according to a timetable to be proposed by the Committee, on the steps they have taken to implement this resolution;

7.   *Directs* the Committee to delineate its tasks, submit a work programme within 30 days of the adoption of this resolution, and to consider the support it requires, in consultation with the Secretary-General;

8.   *Expresses* its determination to take all necessary steps in order to ensure the full implementation of this resolution, in accordance with its responsibilities under the Charter;

9.   *Decides* to remain seized of this matter.

Appendix 2E
United Nations Security Council Resolution 1401[*]

The Security Council,

Reaffirming its previous resolutions on Afghanistan, in particular its resolutions 1378 (2001) of 14 November 2001, 1383 (2001) of 6 December 2001, and 1386 (2001) of 20 December 2001,

Recalling all relevant General Assembly resolutions, in particular resolution 56/220 (2001) of 21 December 2001,

Stressing the inalienable right of the Afghan people themselves freely to determine their own political future,

Reaffirming its strong commitment to the sovereignty, independence, territorial integrity and national unity of Afghanistan,

Reiterating its endorsement of the Agreement on provisional arrangements in Afghanistan pending the re-establishment of permanent government institutions, signed in Bonn on 5 December 2001 (S/2001/1154) (the Bonn Agreement), in particular its annex 2 regarding the role of the United Nations during the interim period,

Welcoming the establishment on 22 December 2001 of the Afghan interim authority and looking forward to the evolution of the process set out in the Bonn Agreement,

Stressing the vital importance of combating the cultivation and trafficking of illicit drugs and of eliminating the threat of landmines, as well as of curbing the illicit flow of small arms,

Having considered the report of the Secretary-General of 18 March 2002 (S/2002/278),

Encouraging donor countries that pledged financial aid at the Tokyo Conference on reconstruction assistance to Afghanistan to fulfill their commitments as soon as possible,

---

[*] S/RES/1401 (2002), adopted by the Security Council at its 4501st meeting on 28 March 2002.

Commending the United Nations Special Mission in Afghanistan (UNSMA) for the determination shown in the implementation of its mandate in particularly difficult circumstances,

1. *Endorses* the establishment, for an initial period of 12 months from the date of adoption of this resolution, of a United Nations Assistance Mission in Afghanistan (UNAMA), with the mandate and structure laid out in the report of the Secretary-General of 18 March 2002 (S/2002/278);

2. *Reaffirms* its strong support for the Special Representative of the Secretary-General and *endorses* his full authority, in accordance with its relevant resolutions, over the planning and conduct of all United Nations activities in Afghanistan;

3. *Stresses* that the provision of focussed recovery and reconstruction assistance can greatly assist in the implementation of the Bonn Agreement and, to this end, *urges* bilateral and multilateral donors, in particular through the Afghanistan Support Group and the Implementation Group, to coordinate very closely with the Special Representative of the Secretary-General, the Afghan Interim Administration and its successors;

4. *Stresses also*, in the context of paragraph 3 above, that while humanitarian assistance should be provided wherever there is a need, recovery or reconstruction assistance ought to be provided, through the Afghan Interim Administration and its successors, and implemented effectively, where local authorities contribute to the maintenance of a secure environment and demonstrate respect for human rights;

5. *Calls upon* all Afghan parties to cooperate with UNAMA in the implementation of its mandate and to ensure the security and freedom of movement of its staff throughout the country;

6. *Requests* the International Security Assistance Force, in implementing its mandate in accordance with resolution 1386 (2001), to continue to work in close consultation with the Secretary-General and his Special Representative;

7. *Requests* the Secretary-General to report to the Council every four months on the implementation of this resolution;

8. *Decides* to remain actively seized of the matter.

Appendix 2F
United Nations Security Council Resolution 1419[*]

The Security Council,

Reaffirming its previous resolutions on Afghanistan, in particular its resolution 1383 (2001) of 6 December 2001,

Reaffirming also its strong commitment to the sovereignty, independence, territorial integrity and national unity of Afghanistan,

Reaffirming also its strong commitment to help the people of Afghanistan to bring to an end the tragic conflicts in Afghanistan and promote lasting peace, stability, and respect for human rights,

Reaffirming also its strong support for international efforts to root out terrorism, in keeping with the Charter of the United Nations, and reaffirming also its resolutions 1368 (2001) of 12 September 2001 and 1373 (2001) of 28 September 2001,

Reiterating its endorsement of the Agreement on Provisional Arrangements in Afghanistan Pending the Re-establishment of Permanent Government Institutions, signed in Bonn on 5 December 2001 (S/2001/1154) (the Bonn Agreement), and *welcoming* initial steps for its implementation, including the establishment of the Human Rights and Judicial Commissions,

1. *Welcomes* the successful and peaceful holding, from 11 June to 19 June, of the Emergency Loya Jirga opened by former King Mohammed Zaher, the "Father of the Nation", and *notes* with particular satisfaction the large participation of women, as well as the representation of all ethnic and religious communities;

2. *Commends* the Afghan people for the success of the Emergency Loya Jirga and encourages them to continue to exercise their inalienable right to determine freely their own political future;

3. *Welcomes* the election, by the Emergency Loya Jirga, of the Head of State, President Hamid Karzai, and the establishment of the Transitional Authority;

---

[*] S/RES/1419 (2002), adopted by the Security Council at its 4560th meeting on 26 June 2002.

4. *Reiterates* its strong support for the Transitional Authority in the full implementation of the Bonn Agreement, including the establishment of a Constitutional Commission, and in strengthening the central government, building a national army and police force, implementing demobilization/reintegration activities and improving the security situation throughout Afghanistan, combating illicit drug trafficking, ensuring respect for human rights, implementing judicial sector reform, establishing the basis for a sound economy and reconstructing productive capacity and infrastructure;

5. *Calls on* all Afghan groups, in this regard, to cooperate fully with the Transitional Authority in order to complete the process according to the Bonn Agreement and to implement the decisions of the Emergency Loya Jirga;

6. *Urges* the Transitional Authority to build on efforts of the Interim Administration to eradicate the annual poppy crop;

7. *Urges also* the Transitional Authority to build further on efforts of the Interim Administration to promote the welfare and interests of Afghan women and children and to provide education to boys and girls;

8. *Commends* the role of the United Nations system in support of efforts by the Afghans, *reiterates* its strong support for the Special Representative of the Secretary-General, Mr. Lakhdar Brahimi, and the staff of the United Nations Assistance Mission in Afghanistan (UNAMA), and *reaffirms* its endorsement of the full authority of the Special Representative of the Secretary-General, in accordance with its relevant resolutions, over the planning and conduct of all United Nations activities in Afghanistan;

9. *Commends also* the contribution of the International Security Assistance Force (ISAF) in providing a secure environment for the Emergency Loya Jirga;

10. *Stresses* once again the importance of continued international support to complete the process according to the Bonn Agreement, *calls upon* donor countries that pledged financial aid at the Tokyo conference to fulfil their commitments promptly and *calls upon* all Member States to support the Transitional Authority and to provide long-term assistance, as well as current budget support, for the current expenses of the Transitional Authority, and for the social and economic reconstruction and rehabilitation of Afghanistan as a whole;

11. *Calls for* significantly greater and more rapid international assistance to the vast number of Afghan refugees and internally displaced persons to facilitate their orderly return and effective reintegration into society in order to contribute to the stability of the entire country;

12. *Calls upon* all Afghan groups to support full and unimpeded access by humanitarian organizations to people in need and to ensure the safety and security of humanitarian workers;

13. *Decides* to remain actively seized of the matter.

Appendix 2G
United Nations Security Council Resolution 1453[*]

The Security Council,

Reaffirming its previous resolutions on Afghanistan,

Reaffirming also its strong commitment to the sovereignty, independence, territorial integrity and national unity of Afghanistan, and to peace and stability throughout the region,

Recognizing the Transitional Administration as the sole legitimate Government of Afghanistan, pending democratic elections in 2004, and reiterating its strong support for the full implementation of the Agreement on Provisional Arrangements in Afghanistan Pending the Re-establishment of Permanent Government Institutions (the Bonn Agreement),

Reaffirming its strong commitment to assist the Transitional Administration in its efforts to ensure security, prosperity, tolerance and respect for human rights for all people of Afghanistan, and to combat terrorism, extremism and narco-trafficking,

1. *Welcomes and endorses* the Kabul Declaration on Good-Neighbourly Relations signed by the Transitional Administration of Afghanistan and the Governments of China, Iran, Pakistan, Tajikistan, Turkmenistan and Uzbekistan, the States neighbouring Afghanistan, in Kabul on 22 December 2002 (S/2002/1416);

2. *Calls on* all States to respect the Declaration and to support the implementation of its provisions;

3. *Requests* the Secretary-General to report to the Council as appropriate on the implementation of the Declaration, in the context of his regular reporting on Afghanistan, including information provided by the signatories;

4. *Decides* to remain seized of the matter.

---

[*] S/RES/1453 (2002), adopted by the Security Council at its 4682nd meeting on 24 December 2002.

Appendix 2H
United Nations Security Council Resolution 1456[*]

The Security Council,

Decides to adopt the attached declaration on the issue of combating terrorism.

Annex

The Security Council,

Meeting at the level of Ministers for Foreign Affairs on 20 January 2003 reaffirms that:

– terrorism in all its forms and manifestations constitutes one of the most serious threats to peace and security;
– any acts of terrorism are criminal and unjustifiable, regardless of their motivation, whenever and by whomsoever committed and are to be unequivocally condemned, especially when they indiscriminately target or injure civilians;
– there is a serious and growing danger of terrorist access to and use of nuclear, chemical, biological and other potentially deadly materials, and therefore a need to strengthen controls on these materials;
– it has become easier, in an increasingly globalized world, for terrorists to exploit sophisticated technology, communications and resources for their criminal objectives;
– measures to detect and stem the flow of finance and funds for terrorist purposes must be urgently strengthened;
– terrorists must also be prevented from making use of other criminal activities such as transnational organized crime, illicit drugs and drug trafficking, money-laundering and illicit arms trafficking;
– since terrorists and their supporters exploit instability and intolerance to justify their criminal acts the Security Council is determined to counter this by contributing to peaceful resolution of disputes and by working to create a climate of mutual tolerance and respect;
– terrorism can only be defeated, in accordance with the Charter of the United Nations and international law, by a sustained comprehensive approach involving

---

[*] S/RES/1456 (2003), adopted by the Security Council at its 4688th meeting on 20 January 2003.

the active participation and collaboration of all States, international and regional organizations, and by redoubled efforts at the national level.

* * *

The Security Council therefore calls for the following steps to be taken:

1.   All States must take urgent action to prevent and suppress all active and passive support to terrorism, and in particular comply fully with all relevant resolutions of the Security Council, in particular resolutions 1373 (2001), 1390 (2002) and 1455 (2003);

2. The Security Council calls upon States to:
(a)   become a party, as a matter of urgency, to all relevant international conventions and protocols relating to terrorism, in particular the 1999 international convention for the suppression of the financing of terrorism and to support all international initiatives taken to that aim, and to make full use of the sources of assistance and guidance which are now becoming available;
(b)   assist each other, to the maximum extent possible, in the prevention, investigation, prosecution and punishment of acts of terrorism, wherever they occur;
(c)   cooperate closely to implement fully the sanctions against terrorists and their associates, in particular Al-Qaeda and the Taliban and their associates, as reflected in resolutions 1267 (1999), 1390 (2002) and 1455 (2003), to take urgent actions to deny them access to the financial resources they need to carry out their actions, and to cooperate fully with the Monitoring Group established pursuant to resolution 1363 (2001);

3.   States must bring to justice those who finance, plan, support or commit terrorist acts or provide safe havens, in accordance with international law, in particular on the basis of the principle to extradite or prosecute;

4.   The Counter-Terrorism Committee must intensify its efforts to promote the implementation by Member States of all aspects of resolution 1373 (2001), in particular through reviewing States' reports and facilitating international assistance and cooperation, and through continuing to operate in a transparent and effective manner, and in that regard the Council;
(i)   stresses the obligation on States to report to the CTC, according to the timetable set by the CTC, calls on the 13 States who have not yet submitted a first report and on the 56 States who are late in submitting further reports to do so by 31 March, and requests the CTC to report regularly on progress;
(ii)   calls on States to respond promptly and fully to the CTC's requests for information, comments and questions in full and on time, and instructs the CTC to inform the Council of progress, including any difficulties it encounters;

(iii) requests the CTC in monitoring the implementation of resolution 1373 (2001) to bear in mind all international best practices, codes and standards which are relevant to the implementation of resolution 1373 (2001), and underlines its support for the CTC's approach in constructing a dialogue with each State on further action required to fully implement resolution 1373 (2001);

5.   States should assist each other to improve their capacity to prevent and fight terrorism, and notes that such cooperation will help facilitate the full and timely implementation of resolution 1373 (2001), and invites the CTC to step up its efforts to facilitate the provision of technical and other assistance by developing targets and priorities for global action;

6.   States must ensure that any measure taken to combat terrorism comply with all their obligations under international law, and should adopt such measures in accordance with international law, in particular international human rights, refugee, and humanitarian law;

7.   International organizations should evaluate ways in which they can enhance the effectiveness of their action against terrorism, including by establishing dialogue and exchanges of information with each other and with other relevant international actors, and directs this appeal in particular to those technical agencies and organizations whose activities relate to the control of the use of or access to nuclear, chemical, biological and other deadly materials; in this context the importance of fully complying with existing legal obligations in the field of disarmament, arms limitation and non-proliferation and, where necessary, strengthening international instruments in this field should be underlined;

8.   Regional and subregional organizations should work with the CTC and other international organizations to facilitate sharing of best practice in the fight against terrorism, and to assist their members in fulfilling their obligation to combat terrorism;

9.   Those participating in the Special Meeting of the Counter-Terrorism Committee with international regional and subregional organizations on 7 March 2003 should use that opportunity to make urgent progress on the matters referred to in this declaration which involve the work of such organizations;

* * *

The Security Council also:

10. Emphasizes that continuing international efforts to enhance dialogue and broaden the understanding among civilizations, in an effort to prevent the indiscriminate targeting of different religions and cultures, to further strengthen the campaign against terrorism, and to address unresolved regional conflicts and

the full range of global issues, including development issues, will contribute to international cooperation and collaboration, which by themselves are necessary to sustain the broadest possible fight against terrorism;

11. Reaffirms its strong determination to intensify its fight against terrorism in accordance with its responsibilities under the Charter of the United Nations, and takes note of the contributions made during its meeting on 20 January 2003 with a view to enhancing the role of the United Nations in this regard, and invites Member States to make further contributions to this end;

12. Invites the Secretary General to present a report within 28 days summarizing any proposals made during its ministerial meeting and any commentary or response to these proposals by any Security Council member;

13. Encourages Member States of the United Nations to cooperate in resolving all outstanding issues with a view to the adoption, by consensus, of the draft comprehensive convention on international terrorism and the draft international convention for the suppression of acts of nuclear terrorism;

14. Decides to review actions taken towards the realization of this declaration at further meetings of the Security Council.

Appendix 2I
United Nations General Assembly Resolution 49/60[*]
Measures to Eliminate International Terrorism

The General Assembly,

Recalling its resolution 46/51 of 9 December 1991 and its decision 48/411 of 9 December 1993,

Taking note of the report of the Secretary-General,

Having considered in depth the question of measures to eliminate international terrorism,

Convinced that the adoption of the declaration on measures to eliminate international terrorism should contribute to the enhancement of the struggle against international terrorism,

1. Approves the Declaration on Measures to Eliminate International Terrorism, the text of which is annexed to the present resolution;

2. Invites the Secretary-General to inform all States, the Security Council, the International Court of Justice and the relevant specialized agencies, organizations and organisms of the adoption of the Declaration;

3. Urges that every effort be made in order that the Declaration becomes generally known and is observed and implemented in full;

4. Urges States, in accordance with the provisions of the Declaration, to take all appropriate measures at the national and international levels to eliminate terrorism;

5. Invites the Secretary-General to follow up closely the implementation of the present resolution and the Declaration, and to submit to the General Assembly at its fiftieth session a report thereon, relating, in particular, to the modalities of implementation of paragraph 10 of the Declaration;

6. Decides to include in the provisional agenda of its fiftieth session the item entitled "Measures to eliminate international terrorism", in order to examine the

---

[*] A/RES/49/60, adopted by the General Assembly at its 84th plenary meeting on 9 December 1994.

report of the Secretary-General requested in paragraph 5 above, without prejudice to the annual or biennial consideration of the item.

ANNEX

Declaration on Measures to Eliminate International Terrorism

The General Assembly,

Guided by the purposes and principles of the Charter of the United Nations,

Recalling the Declaration on Principles of International Law concerning Friendly Relations and Cooperation among States in accordance with the Charter of the United Nations, the Declaration on the Strengthening of International Security, the Definition of Aggression, the Declaration on the Enhancement of the Effectiveness of the Principle of Refraining from the Threat or Use of Force in International Relations, the Vienna Declaration and Programme of Action, adopted by the World Conference on Human Rights, the International Covenant on Economic, Social and Cultural Rights and the International Covenant on Civil and Political Rights,

Deeply disturbed by the world-wide persistence of acts of international terrorism in all its forms and manifestations, including those in which States are directly or indirectly involved, which endanger or take innocent lives, have a deleterious effect on international relations and may jeopardize the security of States,

Deeply concerned by the increase, in many regions of the world, of acts of terrorism based on intolerance or extremism,

Concerned at the growing and dangerous links between terrorist groups and drug traffickers and their paramilitary gangs, which have resorted to all types of violence, thus endangering the constitutional order of States and violating basic human rights,

Convinced of the desirability for closer coordination and cooperation among States in combating crimes closely connected with terrorism, including drug trafficking, unlawful arms trade, money laundering and smuggling of nuclear and other potentially deadly materials, and bearing in mind the role that could be played by both the United Nations and regional organizations in this respect,

Firmly determined to eliminate international terrorism in all its forms and manifestations,

Convinced also that the suppression of acts of international terrorism, including those in which States are directly or indirectly involved, is an essential element for the maintenance of international peace and security,

Convinced further that those responsible for acts of international terrorism must be brought to justice,

Stressing the imperative need to further strengthen international cooperation between States in order to take and adopt practical and effective measures to prevent, combat and eliminate all forms of terrorism that affect the international community as a whole,

Conscious of the important role that might be played by the United Nations, the relevant specialized agencies and States in fostering widespread cooperation in preventing and combating international terrorism, inter alia, by increasing public awareness of the problem,

Recalling the existing international treaties relating to various aspects of the problem of international terrorism, inter alia, the Convention on Offences and Certain Other Acts Committed on Board Aircraft, signed at Tokyo on 14 September 1963, the Convention for the Suppression of Unlawful Seizure of Aircraft, signed at The Hague on 16 December 1970, the Convention for the Suppression of Unlawful Acts against the Safety of Civil Aviation, concluded at Montreal on 23 September 1971, the Convention on the Prevention and Punishment of Crimes against Internationally Protected Persons, including Diplomatic Agents, adopted in New York on 14 December 1973, the International Convention against the Taking of Hostages, adopted in New York on 17 December 1979, the Convention on thePhysical Protection of Nuclear Material, adopted at Vienna on 3 March 1980, the Protocol for the Suppression of Unlawful Acts of Violence at Airports Serving International Civil Aviation, supplementary to the Convention for the Suppression of Unlawful Acts against the Safety of Civil Aviation, signed at Montreal on 24 February 1988, the Convention for the Suppression of Unlawful Acts against the Safety of Maritime Navigation, done at Rome on 10 March 1988, the Protocol for the Suppression of Unlawful Acts against the Safety of Fixed Platforms located on the Continental Shelf, done at Rome on 10 March 1988, and the Convention on the Marking of Plastic Explosives for the Purpose of Detection, done at Montreal on 1 March 1991,

Welcoming the conclusion of regional agreements and mutually agreed declarations to combat and eliminate terrorism in all its forms and manifestations,

Convinced of the desirability of keeping under review the scope of existing international legal provisions to combat terrorism in all its forms and manifestations, with the aim of ensuring a comprehensive legal framework for the prevention and elimination of terrorism,

Solemnly declares the following:

I

1. The States Members of the United Nations solemnly reaffirm their unequivocal condemnation of all acts, methods and practices of terrorism, as criminal and unjustifiable, wherever and by whomever committed, including those which jeopardize the friendly relations among States and peoples and threaten the territorial integrity and security of States;

2. Acts, methods and practices of terrorism constitute a grave violation of the purposes and principles of the United Nations, which may pose a threat to international peace and security, jeopardize friendly relations among States, hinder international cooperation and aim at the destruction of human rights, fundamental freedoms and the democratic bases of society;

3. Criminal acts intended or calculated to provoke a state of terror in the general public, a group of persons or particular persons for political purposes are in any circumstance unjustifiable, whatever the considerations of a political, philosophical, ideological, racial, ethnic, religious or any other nature that may be invoked to justify them;

II

4. States, guided by the purposes and principles of the Charter of the United Nations and other relevant rules of international law, must refrain from organizing, instigating, assisting or participating in terrorist acts in territories of other States, or from acquiescing in or encouraging activities within their territories directed towards the commission of such acts;

5. States must also fulfil their obligations under the Charter of the United Nations and other provisions of international law with respect to combating international terrorism and are urged to take effective and resolute measures in accordance with the relevant provisions of international law and international standards of human rights for the speedy and final elimination of international terrorism, in particular:

(a) To refrain from organizing, instigating, facilitating, financing, encouraging or tolerating terrorist activities and to take appropriate practical measures to ensure that their respective territories are not used for terrorist installations or training camps, or for the preparation or organization of terrorist acts intended to be committed against other States or their citizens;

(b) To ensure the apprehension and prosecution or extradition of perpetrators of terrorist acts, in accordance with the relevant provisions of their national law;

(c) To endeavour to conclude special agreements to that effect on a bilateral, regional and multilateral basis, and to prepare, to that effect, model agreements on cooperation;

(d) To cooperate with one another in exchanging relevant information concerning the prevention and combating of terrorism;

(e) To take promptly all steps necessary to implement the existing international conventions on this subject to which they are parties, including the harmonization of their domestic legislation with those conventions;

(f) To take appropriate measures, before granting asylum, for the purpose of ensuring that the asylum seeker has not engaged in terrorist activities and, after granting asylum, for the purpose of ensuring that the refugee status is not used in a manner contrary to the provisions set out in subparagraph (a) above;

6.   In order to combat effectively the increase in, and the growing international character and effects of, acts of terrorism, States should enhance their cooperation in this area through, in particular, systematizing the exchange of information concerning the prevention and combating of terrorism, as well as by effective implementation of the relevant international conventions and conclusion of mutual judicial assistance and extradition agreements on a bilateral, regional and multilateral basis;

7.   In this context, States are encouraged to review urgently the scope of the existing international legal provisions on the prevention, repression and elimination of terrorism in all its forms and manifestations, with the aim of ensuring that there is a comprehensive legal framework covering all aspects of the matter;

8.   Furthermore States that have not yet done so are urged to consider, as a matter of priority, becoming parties to the international conventions and protocols relating to various aspects of international terrorism referred to in the preamble to the present Declaration;

III

9.   The United Nations, the relevant specialized agencies and intergovernmental organizations and other relevant bodies must make every effort with a view to promoting measures to combat and eliminate acts of terrorism and to strengthening their role in this field;

10. The Secretary-General should assist in the implementation of the present Declaration by taking, within existing resources, the following practical measures to enhance international cooperation:

(a) A collection of data on the status and implementation of existing multilateral, regional and bilateral agreements relating to international terrorism, including information on incidents caused by international terrorism and criminal prosecutions and sentencing, based on information received from the depositaries of those agreements and from Member States;

(b) A compendium of national laws and regulations regarding the prevention and suppression of international terrorism in all its forms and manifestations, based on information received from Member States;

(c) An analytical review of existing international legal instruments relating to international terrorism, in order to assist States in identifying aspects of this matter that have not been covered by such instruments and could be addressed to develop further a comprehensive legal framework of conventions dealing with international terrorism;

(d) A review of existing possibilities within the United Nations system for assisting States in organizing workshops and training courses on combating crimes connected with international terrorism;

IV

11. All States are urged to promote and implement in good faith and effectively the provisions of the present Declaration in all its aspects;

12. Emphasis is placed on the need to pursue efforts aiming at eliminating definitively all acts of terrorism by the strengthening of international cooperation and progressive development of international law and its codification, as well as by enhancement of coordination between, and increase of the efficiency of, the United Nations and the relevant specialized agencies, organizations and bodies.

Appendix 2J
United Nations General Assembly Resolution 51/210[*]
Measures to Eliminate International Terrorism

The General Assembly,

Recalling its resolution 49/60 of 9 December 1994, by which it adopted the Declaration on Measures to Eliminate International Terrorism, and its resolution 50/53 of 11 December 1995,

Recalling also the Declaration on the Occasion of the Fiftieth Anniversary of the United Nations,

Guided by the purposes and principles of the Charter of the United Nations,

Deeply disturbed by the persistence of terrorist acts, which have taken place worldwide,

Stressing the need further to strengthen international cooperation between States and between international organizations and agencies, regional organizations and arrangements and the United Nations in order to prevent, combat and eliminate terrorism in all its forms and manifestations, wherever and by whomsoever committed,

Mindful of the need to enhance the role of the United Nations and the relevant specialized agencies in combating international terrorism,

Noting, in this context, all regional and international efforts to combat international terrorism, including those of the Organization of African Unity, the Organization of American States, the Organization of the Islamic Conference, the South Asian Association for Regional Cooperation, the European Union, the Council of Europe, the Movement of Non-Aligned Countries and the countries of the group of seven major industrialized countries and the Russian Federation,

Taking note of the report of the Director-General of the United Nations Educational, Scientific and Cultural Organization on educational activities under the project entitled "Towards a culture of peace",

---

[*] A/RES/51/210, adopted by the General Assembly at its 88th plenary meeting on 17 December 1996.

Recalling that in the Declaration on Measures to Eliminate International Terrorism the General Assembly encouraged States to review urgently the scope of the existing international legal provisions on the prevention, repression and elimination of terrorism in all its forms and manifestations, with the aim of ensuring that there was a comprehensive legal framework covering all aspects of the matter,

Bearing in mind the possibility of considering in the future the elaboration of a comprehensive convention on international terrorism,

Noting that terrorist attacks by means of bombs, explosives or other incendiary or lethal devices have become increasingly widespread, and stressing the need to supplement the existing legal instruments in order to address specifically the problem of terrorist attacks carried out by such means,

Recognizing the need to enhance international cooperation to prevent the use of nuclear materials for terrorist purposes and to develop an appropriate legal instrument,

Recognizing also the need to strengthen international cooperation to prevent the use of chemical and biological materials for terrorist purposes,

Convinced of the need to implement effectively and supplement the provisions of the Declaration on Measures to Eliminate International Terrorism,

Having examined the report of the Secretary-General,

I

1.   Strongly condemns all acts, methods and practices of terrorism as criminal and unjustifiable, wherever and by whomsoever committed;

2.   Reiterates that criminal acts intended or calculated to provoke a state of terror in the general public, a group of persons or particular persons for political purposes are in any circumstance unjustifiable, whatever the considerations of a political, philosophical, ideological, racial, ethnic, religious or other nature that may be invoked to justify them;

3.   Calls upon all States to adopt further measures in accordance with the relevant provisions of international law, including international standards of human rights, to prevent terrorism and to strengthen international cooperation in combating terrorism and, to that end, to consider the adoption of measures such as those contained in the official document adopted by the group of seven major industrialized countries and the Russian Federation at the Ministerial Conference on Terrorism, held in Paris on 30 July 1996, and the plan of action adopted by the

Inter-American Specialized Conference on Terrorism, held at Lima from 23 to 26 April 1996 under the auspices of the Organization of American States, and in particular calls upon all States:

(a) To recommend that relevant security officials undertake consultations to improve the capability of Governments to prevent, investigate and respond to terrorist attacks on public facilities, in particular means of public transport, and to cooperate with other Governments in this respect;

(b) To accelerate research and development regarding methods of detection of explosives and other harmful substances that can cause death or injury, undertake consultations on the development of standards for marking explosives in order to identify their origin in post-blast investigations, and promote cooperation and transfer of technology, equipment and related materials, where appropriate;

(c) To note the risk of terrorists using electronic or wire communications systems and networks to carry out criminal acts and the need to find means, consistent with national law, to prevent such criminality and to promote cooperation where appropriate;

(d) To investigate, when sufficient justification exists according to national laws, and acting within their jurisdiction and through appropriate channels of international cooperation, the abuse of organizations, groups or associations, including those with charitable, social or cultural goals, by terrorists who use them as a cover for their own activities;

(e) To develop, if necessary, especially by entering into bilateral and multilateral agreements and arrangements, mutual legal assistance procedures aimed at facilitating and speeding investigations and collecting evidence, as well as cooperation between law enforcement agencies in order to detect and prevent terrorist acts;

(f) To take steps to prevent and counteract, through appropriate domestic measures, the financing of terrorists and terrorist organizations, whether such financing is direct or indirect through organizations which also have or claim to have charitable, social or cultural goals or which are also engaged in unlawful activities such as illicit arms trafficking, drug dealing and racketeering, including the exploitation of persons for purposes of funding terrorist activities, and in particular to consider, where appropriate, adopting regulatory measures to prevent and counteract movements of funds suspected to be intended for terrorist purposes without impeding in any way the freedom of legitimate capital movements and to intensify the exchange of information concerning international movements of such funds;

4. Also calls upon all States, with the aim of enhancing the efficient implementation of relevant legal instruments, to intensify, as and where appropriate, the exchange of information on facts related to terrorism and, in so doing, to avoid the dissemination of inaccurate or unverified information;

5. Reiterates its call upon States to refrain from financing, encouraging, providing training for or otherwise supporting terrorist activities;

6. Urges all States that have not yet done so to consider, as a matter of priority, becoming parties to the Convention on Offences and Certain Other Acts Committed on Board Aircraft, signed at Tokyo on 14 September 1963, the Convention for the Suppression of Unlawful Seizure of Aircraft, signed at The Hague on 16 December 1970, the Convention for the Suppression of Unlawful Acts against the Safety of Civil Aviation, concluded at Montreal on 23 September 1971, the Convention on the Prevention and Punishment of Crimes against Internationally Protected Persons, including Diplomatic Agents, adopted in New York on 14 December 1973, the International Convention against the Taking of Hostages, adopted in New York on 17 December 1979, the Convention on the Physical Protection of Nuclear Material, signed at Vienna on 3 March 1980, the Protocol for the Suppression of Unlawful Acts of Violence at Airports Serving International Civil Aviation, supplementary to the Convention for the Suppression of Unlawful Acts against the Safety of Civil Aviation, signed at Montreal on 24 February 1988, the Convention for the Suppression of Unlawful Acts against the Safety of Maritime Navigation, done at Rome on 10 March 1988, the Protocol for the Suppression of Unlawful Acts against the Safety of Fixed Platforms located on the Continental Shelf, done at Rome on 10 March 1988, and the Convention on the Marking of Plastic Explosives for the Purpose of Detection, done at Montreal on 1 March 1991, and calls upon all States to enact, as appropriate, domestic legislation necessary to implement the provisions of those Conventions and Protocols, to ensure that the jurisdiction of their courts enables them to bring to trial the perpetrators of terrorist acts and to provide support and assistance to other Governments for those purposes;

II

7. Reaffirms the Declaration on Measures to Eliminate International Terrorism contained in the annex to resolution 49/60;

8. Approves the Declaration to Supplement the 1994 Declaration on Measures to Eliminate International Terrorism, the text of which is annexed to the present resolution;

III

9. Decides to establish an Ad Hoc Committee, open to all States Members of the United Nations or members of specialized agencies or of the International Atomic Energy Agency, to elaborate an international convention for the suppression of terrorist bombings and, subsequently, an international convention for the suppression of acts of nuclear terrorism, to supplement related existing international instruments, and thereafter to address means of further developing a

comprehensive legal framework of conventions dealing with international terrorism;

10. Decides also that the Ad Hoc Committee will meet from 24 February to 7 March 1997 to prepare the text of a draft international convention for the suppression of terrorist bombings, and recommends that work continue during the fifty-second session of the General Assembly from 22 September to 3 October 1997 in the framework of a working group of the Sixth Committee;

11. Requests the Secretary-General to provide the Ad Hoc Committee with the necessary facilities for the performance of its work;

12. Requests the Ad Hoc Committee to report to the General Assembly at its fifty-second session on progress made towards the elaboration of the draft convention;

13. Recommends that the Ad Hoc Committee be convened in 1998 to continue its work as referred to in paragraph 9 above;

IV

14. Decides to include in the provisional agenda of its fifty-second session the item entitled "Measures to eliminate international terrorism".

ANNEX

Declaration to Supplement the 1994 Declaration on Measures
to Eliminate International Terrorism

The General Assembly,

Guided by the purposes and principles of the Charter of the United Nations,

Recalling the Declaration on Measures to Eliminate International Terrorism adopted by the General Assembly by its resolution 49/60 of 9 December 1994,

Recalling also the Declaration on the Occasion of the Fiftieth Anniversary of the United Nations,

Deeply disturbed by the worldwide persistence of acts of international terrorism in all its forms and manifestations, including those in which States are directly or indirectly involved, which endanger or take innocent lives, have a deleterious effect on international relations and may jeopardize the security of States,

Underlining the importance of States developing extradition agreements or arrangements as necessary in order to ensure that those responsible for terrorist acts are brought to justice,

Noting that the Convention relating to the Status of Refugees, done at Geneva on 28 July 1951, does not provide a basis for the protection of perpetrators of terrorist acts, noting also in this context articles 1, 2, 32 and 33 of the Convention, and emphasizing in this regard the need for States parties to ensure the proper application of the Convention,

Stressing the importance of full compliance by States with their obligations under the provisions of the 1951 Convention and the 1967 Protocol relating to the Status of Refugees, including the principle of non-refoulement of refugees to places where their life or freedom would be threatened on account of their race, religion, nationality, membership in a particular social group or political opinion, and affirming that the present Declaration does not affect the protection afforded under the terms of the Convention and Protocol and other provisions of international law,

Recalling article 4 of the Declaration on Territorial Asylum adopted by the General Assembly by its resolution 2312 (XXII) of 14 December 1967,

Stressing the need further to strengthen international cooperation between States in order to prevent, combat and eliminate terrorism in all its forms and manifestations,

Solemnly declares the following:

1.   The States Members of the United Nations solemnly reaffirm their unequivocal condemnation of all acts, methods and practices of terrorism as criminal and unjustifiable, wherever and by whomsoever committed, including those which jeopardize friendly relations among States and peoples and threaten the territorial integrity and security of States;

2.   The States Members of the United Nations reaffirm that acts, methods and practices of terrorism are contrary to the purposes and principles of the United Nations; they declare that knowingly financing, planning and inciting terrorist acts are also contrary to the purposes and principles of the United Nations;

3.   The States Members of the United Nations reaffirm that States should take appropriate measures in conformity with the relevant provisions of national and international law, including international standards of human rights, before granting refugee status, for the purpose of ensuring that the asylum-seeker has not participated in terrorist acts, considering in this regard relevant information as to whether the asylum-seeker is subject to investigation for or is charged with or has

been convicted of offences connected with terrorism and, after granting refugee status, for the purpose of ensuring that that status is not used for the purpose of preparing or organizing terrorist acts intended to be committed against other States or their citizens;

4.   The States Members of the United Nations emphasize that asylum-seekers who are awaiting the processing of their asylum applications may not thereby avoid prosecution for terrorist acts;

5.   The States Members of the United Nations reaffirm the importance of ensuring effective cooperation between Member States so that those who have participated in terrorist acts, including their financing, planning or incitement, are brought to justice; they stress their commitment, in conformity with the relevant provisions of international law, including international standards of human rights, to work together to prevent, combat and eliminate terrorism and to take all appropriate steps under their domestic laws either to extradite terrorists or to submit the cases to their competent authorities for the purpose of prosecution;

6.   In this context, and while recognizing the sovereign rights of States in extradition matters, States are encouraged, when concluding or applying extradition agreements, not to regard as political offences excluded from the scope of those agreements offences connected with terrorism which endanger or represent a physical threat to the safety and security of persons, whatever the motives which may be invoked to justify them;

7.   States are also encouraged, even in the absence of a treaty, to consider facilitating the extradition of persons suspected of having committed terrorist acts, insofar as their national laws permit;

8.   The States Members of the United Nations emphasize the importance of taking steps to share expertise and information about terrorists, their movements, their support and their weapons and to share information regarding the investigation and prosecution of terrorist acts.

Appendix 2K
United Nations General Assembly Resolution 54/164[*]
Human Rights and Terrorism

The General Assembly,

Guided by the Charter of the United Nations, the Universal Declaration of Human Rights, the Declaration on Principles of International Law concerning Friendly Relations and Cooperation among States in accordance with the Charter of the United Nations and the International Covenants on Human Rights,

Recalling the Declaration on the Occasion of the Fiftieth Anniversary of the United Nations,

Recalling also the Vienna Declaration and Programme of Action adopted by the World Conference on Human Rights on 25 June 1993, in which the Conference reaffirmed that terrorism is indeed aimed at the destruction of human rights, fundamental freedoms and democracy,

Recalling further its resolutions 48/122 of 20 December 1993, 49/185 of 23 December 1994, 50/186 of 22 December 1995 and 52/133 of 12 December 1997,

Recalling in particular its resolution 52/133, in which it requested the Secretary-General to seek the views of Member States on the implications of terrorism, in all its forms and manifestations, for the full enjoyment of human rights and fundamental freedoms,

Recalling previous resolutions of the Commission on Human Rights, and taking note, in particular, of resolution 1999/27 of 26 April 1999, as well as the relevant resolutions of the Subcommission on the Promotion and Protection of Human Rights,

Alarmed that acts of terrorism in all its forms and manifestations aimed at the destruction of human rights have continued despite national and international efforts,

---

[*] A/RES/54/164, adopted by the General Assembly at its 54th plenary meeting on 24 February 2000.

Bearing in mind that the essential and most basic human right is the right to life,

Bearing in mind also that terrorism creates an environment that destroys the right of people to live in freedom from fear,

Reiterating that all States have an obligation to promote and protect all human rights and fundamental freedoms and that every individual should strive to secure their universal and effective recognition and observance,

Seriously concerned about the gross violations of human rights perpetrated by terrorist groups,

Profoundly deploring the increasing number of innocent persons, including women, children and the elderly, killed, massacred and maimed by terrorists in indiscriminate and random acts of violence and terror, which cannot be justified under any circumstances,

Noting with great concern the growing connection between the terrorist groups and other criminal organizations engaged in the illegal traffic in arms and drugs at the national and international levels, as well as the consequent commission of serious crimes such as murder, extortion, kidnapping, assault, the taking of hostages and robbery,

Emphasizing the importance of Member States taking appropriate steps to deny safe haven to those who plan, finance or commit terrorist acts, by ensuring their apprehension and prosecution or extradition,

Mindful of the need to protect the human rights of and guarantees for the individual in accordance with the relevant human rights principles and instruments, in particular the right to life,

Reaffirming that all measures to counter terrorism must be in strict conformity with the relevant provisions of international law including international human rights standards,

1. *Expresses its solidarity* with the victims of terrorism;

2. *Condemns* the violations of the right to live free from fear and of the right to life, liberty and security;

3. *Reiterates its unequivocal condemnation* of the acts, methods and practices of terrorism, in all its forms and manifestations, as activities aimed at the destruction of human rights, fundamental freedoms and democracy, threatening the territorial integrity and security of States, destabilizing legitimately constituted Governments,

undermining pluralistic civil society and having adverse consequences for the economic and social development of States;

4.　*Calls upon* States to take all necessary and effective measures in accordance with relevant provisions of international law, including international human rights standards, to prevent, combat and eliminate terrorism in all its forms and manifestations, wherever and by whomever committed;

5.　*Urges* the international community to enhance cooperation at the regional and international levels in the fight against terrorism, in accordance with relevant international instruments, including those relating to human rights, with the aim of its eradication;

6.　*Condemns* the incitement of ethnic hatred, violence and terrorism;

7.　*Commends* those Governments that have communicated their views on the implications of terrorism in response to the note verbale by the Secretary-General dated 16 August 1999;

8.　*Welcomes* the report of the Secretary-General, and requests him to continue to seek the views of Member States on the implications of terrorism, in all its forms and manifestations, for the full enjoyment of all human rights and fundamental freedoms, with a view to incorporating them in his report;

9.　*Decides* to consider this question at its fifty-sixth session, under the item entitled "Human rights questions".

Appendix 2L
United Nations Commission on Human Rights
Resolution 1999/27[*]
Human Rights and Terrorism

The Commission on Human Rights,

Guided by the Charter of the United Nations, the Universal Declaration of Human Rights, the Declaration on Principles of International Law concerning Friendly Relations and Cooperation among States in accordance with the Charter of the United Nations and the International Covenants on Human Rights,

Recalling the Declaration on the Occasion of the Fiftieth Anniversary of the United Nations, adopted by the General Assembly in its resolution 50/6 of 24 October 1995,

Recalling also the Vienna Declaration and Programme of Action (A/CONF.157/23), adopted by the World Conference on Human Rights, held at Vienna from 14 to 25 June 1993,

Recalling further General Assembly resolutions 46/51 of 9 December 1991, 49/60 of 9 December 1994, 50/53 of 11 December 1995, 50/186 of 22 December 1995, 51/210 of 17 December 1996 and 52/133 of 12 December 1997, as well as its own resolution 1998/47 of 17 April 1998,

Noting resolution 1998/29 of 26 August 1998 of the Sub-Commission on Prevention of Discrimination and Protection of Minorities, requesting its Special Rapporteur on human rights and terrorism to submit a preliminary report based on her working paper (E/CN.4/Sub.2/1997/28) to the Sub-Commission at its fifty-first session, a progress report at its fifty-second session and a final report at its fifty-third session,

Regretting that the negative impact of terrorism, in all its dimensions, on human rights continues to remain alarming, despite national and international efforts to combat it,

---

[*] E/CN.4/RES/1999/27.

Convinced that terrorism, in all its forms and manifestations, wherever and by whomever committed, can never be justified in any instance, including as a means to promote and protect human rights,

Conscious of the increasing importance of the role played by the United Nations in combating terrorism,

Bearing in mind that the most essential and basic human right is the right to life,

Bearing in mind also that terrorism in many cases poses a severe challenge to democracy, civil society and the rule of law,

Bearing in mind further that terrorism creates an environment that destroys the freedom from fear of the people,

Profoundly deploring the high number of innocent persons, including women, children and the elderly, killed, massacred and maimed by terrorists in indiscriminate and random acts of violence and terror, which cannot be justified under any circumstances,

Noting with great concern that many terrorist groups are connected with other criminal organizations engaged in the illegal traffic in arms and illicit drug trafficking at the national and international levels, as well as the consequent commission of serious crimes such as murder, extortion, kidnapping, assault, taking of hostages, robbery, money laundering and rape,

Mindful of the need to protect the human rights of and guarantees for the individual in accordance with the relevant human rights instruments and standards, particularly the right to life,

Reiterating that all States have an obligation to promote and protect human rights and fundamental freedoms, and that everyone should strive to secure their universal and effective recognition and observance,

Recognizing the need to improve international cooperation on criminal matters and national measures so as to address impunity which can contribute to the continued occurrence of terrorism,

Stressing the need further to strengthen international cooperation between States, international organizations and agencies, regional organizations and arrangements and the United Nations in order to prevent, combat and eliminate terrorism in all its forms and manifestations, wherever and by whomever committed, and inviting interested non-governmental organizations to join States in condemning terrorism,

Reaffirming that all measures to counter terrorism must be in strict conformity with international law, including international human rights standards,

Seriously concerned at the gross violations of human rights perpetrated by terrorist groups,

1. *Reiterates the unequivocal condemnation* of all acts, methods and practices of terrorism, regardless of their motivation, in all their forms and manifestations, wherever and by whomever committed, as acts aimed at the destruction of human rights, fundamental freedoms and democracy, threatening the territorial integrity and security of States, destabilizing legitimately constituted Governments, undermining pluralistic civil society and the rule of law and having adverse consequences for the economic and social development of the State;

2. *Condemns* the violations of the right to live free from fear and of the right to life, liberty and security;

3. *Expresses its solidarity* with the victims of terrorism;

4. *Condemns* incitement of ethnic hatred, violence and terrorism;

5. *Calls upon* States to take all necessary and effective measures, in strict conformity with international law, including international human rights standards, to prevent, combat and eliminate terrorism in all its forms and manifestations, wherever and by whomever committed;

6. *Urges* the international community to enhance cooperation at the regional and international levels in the fight against terrorism in all its forms and manifestations, in accordance with relevant international instruments, including those relating to human rights, with the aim of its eradication;

7. *Calls upon* States, in particular within their respective national frameworks and in conformity with their international commitments in the field of human rights, to enhance their cooperation with a view to bringing terrorists to justice;

8. *Requests*, in this context, the Special Rapporteur of the Sub-Commission on Prevention of Discrimination and Protection of Minorities, in her forthcoming preliminary report on human rights and terrorism, to give attention to the question of impunity;

9. *Urges* all relevant human rights mechanisms and procedures, as appropriate, to address the consequences of the acts, methods and practices of terrorist groups in their forthcoming reports to the Commission;

10. *Requests* the Secretary-General to continue to collect information, including a compilation of studies and publications, on the implications of terrorism, as well as on the effects of the fight against terrorism, on the full enjoyment of human rights from all relevant sources, including Governments, specialized agencies, intergovernmental organizations, non-governmental organizations and academic institutions, and to make it available to the concerned special rapporteurs and working groups of the Commission on Human Rights for their consideration;

11. *Decides* to continue consideration of the question at its fifty-sixth session as a matter of priority.

Appendix 3

Agreement on Provisional Arrangements in Afghanistan Pending the Re-Establishment of Permanent Government Institutions[*]

The participants in the UN Talks on Afghanistan,

In the presence of the Special Representative of the Secretary-General for Afghanistan,

Determined to end the tragic conflict in Afghanistan and promote national reconciliation, lasting peace, stability and respect for human rights in the country,

Reaffirming the independence, national sovereignty and territorial integrity of Afghanistan,

Acknowledging the right of the people of Afghanistan to freely determine their own political future in accordance with the principles of Islam, democracy, pluralism and social justice,

Expressing their appreciation to the Afghan mujahidin who, over the years, have defended the independence, territorial integrity and national unity of the country and have played a major role in the struggle against terrorism and oppression, and whose sacrifice has now made them both heroes of jihad and champions of peace, stability and reconstruction of their beloved homeland, Afghanistan,

Aware that the unstable situation in Afghanistan requires the implementation of emergency interim arrangements and expressing their deep appreciation to His Excellency Professor Burhanuddin Rabbani for his readiness to transfer power to an interim authority which is to be established pursuant to this agreement,

Recognizing the need to ensure broad representation in these interim arrangements of all segments of the Afghan population, including groups that have not been adequately represented at the UN Talks on Afghanistan,

Noting that these interim arrangements are intended as a first step toward the establishment of a broad-based, gender-sensitive, multi-ethnic and fully

---

[*] The "Bonn Agreement", signed at Bonn on 5 January 2001.

representative government, and are not intended to remain in place beyond the specified period of time,

Recognizing that some time may be required for a new Afghan security force to be fully constituted and functional and that therefore other security provisions detailed in Annex I to this agreement must meanwhile be put in place,

Considering that the United Nations, as the internationally recognized impartial institution, has a particularly important role to play, detailed in Annex II to this agreement, in the period prior to the establishment of permanent institutions in Afghanistan,

Have agreed as follows:

THE INTERIM AUTHORITY

I. General provisions

1) An Interim Authority shall be established upon the official transfer of power on 22 December 2001.

2) The Interim Authority shall consist of an Interim Administration presided over by a Chairman, a Special Independent Commission for the Convening of the Emergency Loya Jirga, and a Supreme Court of Afghanistan, as well as such other courts as may be established by the Interim Administration. The composition, functions and governing procedures for the Interim Administration and the Special Independent Commission are set forth in this agreement.

3) Upon the official transfer of power, the Interim Authority shall be the repository of Afghan sovereignty, with immediate effect. As such, it shall, throughout the interim period, represent Afghanistan in its external relations and shall occupy the seat of Afghanistan at the United Nations and in its specialized agencies, as well as in other international institutions and conferences.

4) An Emergency Loya Jirga shall be convened within six months of the establishment of the Interim Authority. The Emergency Loya Jirga will be opened by His Majesty Mohammed Zaher, the former King of Afghanistan. The Emergency Loya Jirga shall decide on a Transitional Authority, including a broad-based transitional administration, to lead Afghanistan until such time as a fully representative government can be elected through free and fair elections to be held no later than two years from the date of the convening of the Emergency Loya Jirga.

5) The Interim Authority shall cease to exist once the Transitional Authority has been established by the Emergency Loya Jirga.

6) A Constitutional Loya Jirga shall be convened within eighteen months of the establishment of the Transitional Authority, in order to adopt a new constitution for Afghanistan. In order to assist the Constitutional Loya Jirga prepare the proposed Constitution, the Transitional Administration shall, within two months of its commencement and with the assistance of the United Nations, establish a Constitutional Commission.

II. Legal framework and judicial system

1) The following legal framework shall be applicable on an interim basis until the adoption of the new Constitution referred to above:
i) The Constitution of 1964, (a) to the extent that its provisions are not inconsistent with those contained in this agreement, and (b) with the exception of those provisions relating to the monarchy and to the executive and legislative bodies provided in the Constitution; and
ii) existing laws and regulations, to the extent that they are not inconsistent with this agreement or with international legal obligations to which Afghanistan is a party, or with those applicable provisions contained in the Constitution of 1964, provided that the Interim Authority shall have the power to repeal or amend those laws and regulations.

2) The judicial power of Afghanistan shall be independent and shall be vested in a Supreme Court of Afghanistan, and such other courts as may be established by the Interim Administration. The Interim Administration shall establish, with the assistance of the United Nations, a Judicial Commission to rebuild the domestic justice system in accordance with Islamic principles, international standards, the rule of law and Afghan legal traditions.

III. Interim Administration

A. *Composition*

1) The Interim Administration shall be composed of a Chairman, five Vice Chairmen and 24 other members. Each member, except the Chairman, may head a department of the Interim Administration.

2) The participants in the UN Talks on Afghanistan have invited His Majesty Mohammed Zaher, the former King of Afghanistan, to chair the Interim Administration. His Majesty has indicated that he would prefer that a suitable candidate acceptable to the participants be selected as the Chair of the Interim Administration.

3) The Chairman, the Vice Chairmen and other members of the Interim Administration have been selected by the participants in the UN Talks on Afghanistan, as listed in Annex IV to this agreement. The selection has been made

on the basis of professional competence and personal integrity from lists submitted by the participants in the UN Talks, with due regard to the ethnic, geographic and religious composition of Afghanistan and to the importance of the participation of women.

4) No person serving as a member of the Interim Administration may simultaneously hold membership of the Special Independent Commission for the Convening of the Emergency Loya Jirga.

B. *Procedures*

1) The Chairman of the Interim Administration, or in his/her absence one of the Vice Chairmen, shall call and chair meetings and propose the agenda for these meetings.

2) The Interim Administration shall endeavour to reach its decisions by consensus. In order for any decision to be taken, at least 22 members must be in attendance. If a vote becomes necessary, decisions shall be taken by a majority of the members present and voting, unless otherwise stipulated in this agreement. The Chairman shall cast the deciding vote in the event that the members are divided equally.

C. *Functions*

1) The Interim Administration shall be entrusted with the day-to-day conduct of the affairs of state, and shall have the right to issue decrees for the peace, order and good government of Afghanistan.

2) The Chairman of the Interim Administration or, in his/her absence, one of the Vice Chairmen, shall represent the Interim Administration as appropriate.

3) Those members responsible for the administration of individual departments shall also be responsible for implementing the policies of the Interim Administration within their areas of responsibility.

4) Upon the official transfer of power, the Interim Administration shall have full jurisdiction over the printing and delivery of the national currency and special drawing rights from international financial institutions. The Interim Administration shall establish, with the assistance of the United Nations, a Central Bank of Afghanistan that will regulate the money supply of the country through transparent and accountable procedures.

5) The Interim Administration shall establish, with the assistance of the United Nations, an independent Civil Service Commission to provide the Interim Authority and the future Transitional Authority with shortlists of candidates for

key posts in the administrative departments, as well as those of governors and uluswals,* in order to ensure their competence and integrity.

6) The Interim Administration shall, with the assistance of the United Nations, establish an independent Human Rights Commission, whose responsibilities will include human rights monitoring, investigation of violations of human rights, and development of domestic human rights institutions. The Interim Administration may, with the assistance of the United Nations, also establish any other commissions to review matters not covered in this agreement.

7) The members of the Interim Administration shall abide by a Code of Conduct elaborated in accordance with international standards.

8) Failure by a member of the Interim Administration to abide by the provisions of the Code of Conduct shall lead to his/her suspension from that body. The decision to suspend a member shall be taken by a two-thirds majority of the membership of the Interim Administration on the proposal of its Chairman or any of its Vice Chairmen.

9) The functions and powers of members of the Interim Administration will be further elaborated, as appropriate, with the assistance of the United Nations.

IV. The Special Independent Commission for the Convening of the Emergency Loya Jirga

1) The Special Independent Commission for the Convening of the Emergency Loya Jirga shall be established within one month of the establishment of the Interim Authority. The Special Independent Commission will consist of twenty-one members, a number of whom should have expertise in constitutional or customary law. The members will be selected from lists of candidates submitted by participants in the UN Talks on Afghanistan as well as Afghan professional and civil society groups. The United Nations will assist with the establishment and functioning of the commission and of a substantial secretariat.

2) The Special Independent Commission will have the final authority for determining the procedures for and the number of people who will participate in the Emergency Loya Jirga. The Special Independent Commission will draft rules and procedures specifying (i) criteria for allocation of seats to the settled and nomadic population residing in the country; (ii) criteria for allocation of seats to the Afghan refugees living in Iran, Pakistan, and elsewhere, and Afghans from the diaspora; (iii) criteria for inclusion of civil society organizations and prominent individuals, including Islamic scholars, intellectuals, and traders, both within the country and in the diaspora. The Special Independent Commission will ensure that due attention is paid to the representation in the Emergency Loya Jirga of a

---

* Translated to mean "district administrators".

significant number of women as well as all other segments of the Afghan population.

3) The Special Independent Commission will publish and disseminate the rules and procedures for the convening of the Emergency Loya Jirga at least ten weeks before the Emergency Loya Jirga convenes, together with the date for its commencement and its suggested location and duration.

4) The Special Independent Commission will adopt and implement procedures for monitoring the process of nomination of individuals to the Emergency Loya Jirga to ensure that the process of indirect election or selection is transparent and fair. To pre-empt conflict over nominations, the Special Independent Commission will specify mechanisms for filing of grievances and rules for arbitration of disputes.

5) The Emergency Loya Jirga will elect a Head of the State for the Transitional Administration and will approve proposals for the structure and key personnel of the Transitional Administration.

V. Final provisions

1) Upon the official transfer of power, all mujahidin, Afghan armed forces and armed groups in the country shall come under the command and control of the Interim Authority, and be reorganized according to the requirements of the new Afghan security and armed forces.

2) The Interim Authority and the Emergency Loya Jirga shall act in accordance with basic principles and provisions contained in international instruments on human rights and international humanitarian law to which Afghanistan is a party.

3) The Interim Authority shall cooperate with the international community in the fight against terrorism, drugs and organized crime. It shall commit itself to respect international law and maintain peaceful and friendly relations with neighbouring countries and the rest of the international community.

4) The Interim Authority and the Special Independent Commission for the Convening of the Emergency Loya Jirga will ensure the participation of women as well as the equitable representation of all ethnic and religious communities in the Interim Administration and the Emergency Loya Jirga.

5) All actions taken by the Interim Authority shall be consistent with Security Council resolution 1378 (14 November 2001) and other relevant Security Council resolutions relating to Afghanistan.

6) Rules of procedure for the organs established under the Interim Authority will be elaborated as appropriate with the assistance of the United Nations.

This agreement, of which the annexes constitute an integral part, done in Bonn on this 5th day of December 2001 in the English language, shall be the authentic text, in a single copy which shall remain deposited in the archives of the United Nations. Official texts shall be provided in Dari and Pashto, and such other languages as the Special Representative of the Secretary-General may designate. The Special Representative of the Secretary-General shall send certified copies in English, Dari and Pashto to each of the participants.

For the participants in the UN Talks on Afghanistan:

Ms. Amena Afzali
Mr. S. Hussain Anwari
Mr. Hedayat Amin Arsala
Mr. Sayed Hamed Gailani
Mr. Rahmatullah Musa Ghazi
Eng. Abdul Hakim
Mr. Houmayoun Jareer
Mr. Abbas Karimi
Mr. Mustafa Kazimi
Dr. Azizullah Ludin
Mr. Ahmad Wali Massoud
Mr. Hafizullah Asif Mohseni
Prof. Mohammad Ishaq Nadiri
Mr. Mohammad Natiqi
Mr. Yunus Qanooni
Dr. Zalmai Rassoul
Mr. H. Mirwais Sadeq
Dr. Mohammad Jalil Shams
Prof. Abdul Sattar Sirat
Mr. Humayun Tandar
Mrs. Sima Wali
General Abdul Rahim Wardak
Mr. Pacha Khan Zadran

Witnessed for the United Nations by:

Mr. Lakhdar Brahimi
Special Representative of the Secretary-General for Afghanistan

ANNEX I
INTERNATIONAL SECURITY FORCE

1. The participants in the UN Talks on Afghanistan recognize that the responsibility for providing security and law and order throughout the country resides with the Afghans themselves. To this end, they pledge their commitment to do all within their means and influence to ensure such security, including for all United Nations and other personnel of international governmental and non-governmental organizations deployed in Afghanistan.

2. With this objective in mind, the participants request the assistance of the international community in helping the new Afghan authorities in the establishment and training of new Afghan security and armed forces.

3. Conscious that some time may be required for the new Afghan security and armed forces to be fully constituted and functioning, the participants in the UN Talks on Afghanistan request the United Nations Security Council to consider authorizing the early deployment to Afghanistan of a United Nations mandated force. This force will assist in the maintenance of security for Kabul and its surrounding areas. Such a force could, as appropriate, be progressively expanded to other urban centres and other areas.

4. The participants in the UN Talks on Afghanistan pledge to withdraw all military units from Kabul and other urban centres or other areas in which the UN mandated force is deployed. It would also be desirable if such a force were to assist in the rehabilitation of Afghanistan's infrastructure.

ANNEX II
ROLE OF THE UNITED NATIONS DURING THE INTERIM PERIOD

1. The Special Representative of the Secretary-General will be responsible for all aspects of the United Nations' work in Afghanistan.

2. The Special Representative shall monitor and assist in the implementation of all aspects of this agreement.

3. The United Nations shall advise the Interim Authority in establishing a politically neutral environment conducive to the holding of the Emergency Loya Jirga in free and fair conditions. The United Nations shall pay special attention to the conduct of those bodies and administrative departments which could directly influence the convening and outcome of the Emergency Loya Jirga.

4. The Special Representative of the Secretary-General or his/her delegate may be invited to attend the meetings of the Interim Administration and the Special Independent Commission on the Convening of the Emergency Loya Jirga.

5. If for whatever reason the Interim Administration or the Special Independent Commission were actively prevented from meeting or unable to reach a decision on a matter related to the convening of the Emergency Loya Jirga, the Special Representative of the Secretary-General shall, taking into account the views expressed in the Interim Administration or in the Special Independent Commission, use his/her good offices with a view to facilitating a resolution to the impasse or a decision.

6. The United Nations shall have the right to investigate human rights violations and, where necessary, recommend corrective action. It will also be responsible for the development and implementation of a programme of human rights education to promote respect for and understanding of human rights.

ANNEX III
REQUEST TO THE UNITED NATIONS BY THE PARTICIPANTS AT THE UN TALKS ON AFGHANISTAN

The participants in the UN Talks on Afghanistan hereby

1. Request that the United Nations and the international community take the necessary measures to guarantee the national sovereignty, territorial integrity and unity of Afghanistan as well as the non-interference by foreign countries in Afghanistan's internal affairs;

2. Urge the United Nations, the international community, particularly donor countries and multilateral institutions, to reaffirm, strengthen and implement their commitment to assist with the rehabilitation, recovery and reconstruction of Afghanistan, in coordination with the Interim Authority;

3. Request the United Nations to conduct as soon as possible (i) a registration of voters in advance of the general elections that will be held upon the adoption of the new constitution by the constitutional Loya Jirga and (ii) a census of the population of Afghanistan.

4. Urge the United Nations and the international community, in recognition of the heroic role played by the mujahidin in protecting the independence of Afghanistan and the dignity of its people, to take the necessary measures, in coordination with the Interim Authority, to assist in the reintegration of the mujahidin into the new Afghan security and armed forces;

5. Invite the United Nations and the international community to create a fund to assist the families and other dependents of martyrs and victims of the war, as well as the war disabled;

6. Strongly urge that the United Nations, the international community and regional organizations cooperate with the Interim Authority to combat international terrorism, cultivation and trafficking of illicit drugs and provide Afghan farmers with financial, material and technical resources for alternative crop production.

ANNEX IV
COMPOSITION OF THE INTERIM ADMINISTRATION

Chairman   Hamid Karzai

Vice Chairmen

Vice-Chair & Women's Affairs: Dr. Sima Samar

Vice-Chair & Defence: Muhammad Qassem Fahim

Vice-Chair & Planning: Haji Muhammad Mohaqqeq

Vice-Chair & Water and Electricity: Shaker Kargar

Vice-Chair & Finance: Hedayat Amin Arsala

Members

Department of Foreign Affairs: Dr. Abdullah Abdullah

Department of the Interior: Muhammad Yunus Qanooni

Department of Commerce: Seyyed Mustafa Kazemi*

Department of Mines & Industries: Muhammad Alem Razm

Department of Small Industries: Aref Noorzai

Department of Information & Culture: Dr. Raheen Makhdoom

Department of Communication: Ing. Abdul Rahim

Department of Labour & Social Affairs: Mir Wais Sadeq*

Department of Hajj & Auqaf: Mohammad Hanif Hanif Balkhi

Department of Martyrs & Disabled: Abdullah Wardak*

Department of Education: Abdul Rassoul Amin

Department of Higher Education: Dr. Sharif Faez

Department of Public Health: Dr. Suhaila Seddiqi

Department of Public Works: Abdul Khaliq Fazal

Department of Rural Development:	Abdul Malik Anwar
Department of Urban Development:	Haji Abdul Qadir
Department of Reconstruction:	Amin Farhang
Department of Transport:	Sultan Hamid Sultan
Department for the Return of Refugees:	Enayatullah Nazeri
Department of Agriculture:	Seyyed Hussein Anwari*
Department of Irrigation:	Haji Mangal Hussein
Department of Justice:	Abdul Rahim Karimi
Department of Air Transport & Tourism:	Abdul Rahman
Department of Border Affairs:	Amanullah Zadran

---

* A variation of the spelling of each of these names appears on p265.

Appendix 4

Letter dated 2 October 2003 from the Secretary-General of the North Atlantic Treaty Organization addressed to the Secretary-General of the United Nations[*]

As you are aware, on 11 August 2003, the North Atlantic Treaty Organization (NATO) assumed strategic command, control and coordination of the International Security Assistance Force (ISAF). On 1 October, the North Atlantic Council agreed upon a longer-term strategy for NATO in its ISAF role in Afghanistan. In a spirit of transparency and coordination, I would like to share with you this strategy (see enclosure).

NATO is committed to the success of its mission in Afghanistan and is convinced that the Afghan authorities, with the assistance of the international community, will be able to bring about a self-sustaining, stable and democratic Afghanistan.

I will keep you informed about further developments in the North Atlantic Council's deliberations.

(Signed) Lord Robertson of Port Ellen

---

[*] Set out as an Annex to the letter dated 7 October 2003 from the United Nations Secretary-General to the President of the United Nations Security Council, S/2003/970.

Enclosure
Longer-term strategy for the North Atlantic Treaty Organization in its International Security Assistance Force role in Afghanistan

The North Atlantic Treaty Organization (NATO) is in Afghanistan in its International Security Assistance Force (ISAF) role in order to support the international community's efforts towards implementation of the Bonn Agreement, as mandated by United Nations Security Council resolution 1386 (2001). The aim is to assist in the emergence of a united and sovereign Afghanistan, with, inter alia, a broad-based, multi-ethnic representative government, integrated into the international community and cooperating with its neighbours. NATO's long-term strategy in this context includes the following elements:

Alliance Political Objective

Support for implementation of the Bonn process, as mandated by Security Council resolution 1386 (2001), in cooperation and coordination with key international organizations, in particular the United Nations and the European Union, by assisting the Afghan Transitional Authority (ATA) to meet its responsibility to provide security and order. Additional factors to consider in developing further the Alliance's over-arching political objective include:

1. An expanded ISAF mandate will require a specific United Nations Security Council resolution; other critical factors include resolution of the existing shortfalls in the Combined Joint Statement of Requirement (CJSOR) and a willingness to deploy additional resources;

2. The need for enhanced coordination and cooperation between ISAF, the United Nations Assistance Mission in Afghanistan (UNAMA), Afghan authorities, Operation Enduring Freedom (OEF) and non-governmental organizations (NGOs);

3. The need for a coherent public diplomacy and information campaign;

4. Continued analysis of the political dynamics that would affect the activities of foreign peace support forces in Afghanistan.

Desired ISAF End-State

A self-sustaining, moderate and democratic Afghan government, in line with the relevant United Nations Security Council resolutions, able to exercise its authority and to operate throughout Afghanistan, without the need for ISAF to help provide security. Key components of this end-state would include:

1. Satisfactory progress towards completion of the disarmament, demobilization and reintegration (DDR) programme, under United Nations auspices;

2. Satisfactory progress, supported by bilateral training, towards the build-up of the Afghan National Army (ANA) as an operationally effective, multi-ethnic military force able to provide security for the Afghan population, United Nations agencies, other international organizations and NGOs;

3. Satisfactory progress towards strengthening the central government and internal security related institutions, in particular the establishment of a functioning Afghan national police force and judiciary;

4. Satisfactory progress in the development and implementation of effective counter-narcotics activities;

5. The successful implementation of the constitutional Loya Jirga and approval of a new constitution endorsed and widely accepted by Afghanistan's various ethnic groups, in accordance with the Bonn Agreement;

6. Election of a representative government to succeed the Afghan Transitional Authority (ATA) through free and fair elections, in accordance with the Bonn Agreement;

7. Removal or modification of the behaviour of the warlords, bringing them into broad-based and ethnically balanced central government institutions and bringing relations between the central government and provincial governments into conformity with constitutional provisions;

8. The satisfactory evolution of Afghanistan's relations with neighbouring countries in a peaceful manner;

9. Progress towards the resolution of the terrorist threat from the Taliban, al-Qa'ida and other extremist groups.

Benchmarks for an Alliance Hand-Over Strategy

Progress in achieving the components listed above should be measured in periodic reviews of ISAF.

Appendix 5

Kabul Declaration on Good-Neighbourly Relations[*]

The Transitional Administration of Afghanistan and the governments of the People's Republic of China, Islamic Republic of Iran, Islamic Republic of Pakistan, Republic of Tajikistan, Republic of Turkmenistan and Republic of Uzbekistan, the states neighbouring Afghanistan;

Determined that the people of Afghanistan should enjoy security, stability, prosperity, territorial integrity, democracy and human rights after so many years of conflict, suffering and deprivation;

United in their desire for peace and stability in the region;

Sharing a determination to defeat terrorism, extremism, and narco-trafficking;

Celebrating the first anniversary of the formation of the new Afghan Administration as a result of the Bonn Talks and the progress made in implementing the Bonn Agreement, and recognising that significant challenges lie ahead in creating prosperity and stability;

Solemnly reaffirm their commitment to constructive and supportive bilateral relationships based on the principles of territorial integrity, mutual respect, friendly relations, co-operation and non-interference in each other's internal affairs;

Welcome the combined efforts of the wider international community to provide the support required for rebuilding Afghanistan as it continues to take its rightful place in the community of nations, and express their commitment to participate in this process;

And, furthermore, decide to bring this declaration to the attention of the United Nations Security Council and gain the support of other states for it.

---

[*] The "Kabul Declaration", signed at Kabul on 22 December 2002.

Appendix 6

Selected Resolutions Concerning Iraq

Appendix 6A
United Nations Security Council Resolution 660*

The Security Council,

Alarmed by the invasion of Kuwait on 2 August 1990 by the military forces of Iraq,

Determining that there exists a breach of international peace and security as regards the Iraqi invasion of Kuwait,

Acting under Articles 39 and 40 of the Charter of the United Nations,

1.   *Condemns* the Iraqi invasion of Kuwait;

2.   *Demands* that Iraq withdraw immediately and unconditionally all its forces to the positions in which they were located on 1 August 1990;

3.   *Calls upon* Iraq and Kuwait to begin immediately intensive negotiations for the resolution of their differences and supports all efforts in this regard, and especially those of the League of Arab States;

4.   *Decides* to meet again as necessary to consider further steps to ensure compliance with the present resolution.

---

* S/RES/660 (1990), adopted by the Security Council at its 2932nd meeting on 2 August 1990.

Appendix 6B
United Nations Security Council Resolution 661[*]

The Security Council,

Reaffirming its resolution 660 (190) of 2 August 1990,

Deeply concerned that that resolution has not been implemented and that the invasion by Iraq of Kuwait continues, with further loss of human life and material destruction,

Determined to bring the invasion and occupation of Kuwait by Iraq to an end and to restore the sovereignty, independence and territorial integrity of Kuwait,

Noting that the legitimate Government of Kuwait has expressed its readiness to comply with resolution 660 (1990),

Mindful of its responsibilities under the Charter of the United Nations for the maintenance of international peace and security,

Affirming the inherent right of individual or collective self-defence, in response to the armed attack by Iraq against Kuwait, in accordance with Article 51 of the Charter,

Acting under Chapter VII of the Charter,

1. *Determines* that Iraq so far has failed to comply with paragraph 2 of resolution 660 (1990) and has usurped the authority of the legitimate Government of Kuwait;

2. *Decides,* as a consequence, to take the following measures to secure compliance of Iraq with paragraph 2 of resolution 660 (1990) and to restore the authority of the legitimate Government of Kuwait;

3. *Decides* that all States shall prevent:
(a) The import into their territories of all commodities and products originating in Iraq or Kuwait exported therefrom after the date of the present resolution;

---

[*] S/RES/661 (1990), adopted by the Security Council at its 2933rd meeting on 6 August 1990.

(b) Any activities by their nationals or in their territories which would promote or are calculated to promote the export or trans-shipment of any commodities or products from Iraq or Kuwait; and any dealings by their nationals or their flag vessels or in their territories in any commodities or products originating in Iraq or Kuwait and exported therefrom after the date of the present resolution, including in particular any transfer of funds to Iraq or Kwait for the purposes of such activities or dealings;

(c) The sale or supply by their nationals or from their territories or using their flag vessels of any commodities or products, including weapons or any other military equipment, whether or not originating in their territories but not including supplies intended strictly for medical purposes, and, in humanitarian circumstances, foodstuffs, to any person or body in Iraq or Kuwait or to any person or body for the purposes of any business carried on in or operated from Iraq or Kuwait, and any activities by their nationals or in their territories which promote or are calculated to promote such sale or supply of commodities or products;

4. *Decides* that all States shall not make available to the Government of Iraq, or to any commercial, industrial or public utility undertaking in Iraq or Kuwait, any funds or any other financial or economic resources and shall prevent their nationals and any persons within their territories from removing from their territories or otherwise making available to that Government or to any such undertaking any such funds or resources and from remitting any other funds to persons or bodies within Iraq or Kuwait, except payments exclusively for strictly medical or humanitarian purposes and, in humanitarian circumstances, foodstuffs;

5. *Calls upon* all States, including States non-members of the United Nations, to act strictly in accordance with the provisions of the present resolution notwithstanding any contract entered into or licence granted before the date of the present resolution;

6. *Decides* to establish, in accordance with rule 28 of the provisional rules of procedure, a Committee of the Security Council consisting of all the members of the Council, to undertake the following tasks and to report on its work to the Council with its observations and recommendations:

(a) To examine the reports on the progress of the implementation of the present resolution which will be submitted by the Secretary-General;

(b) To seek from all States further information regarding the action taken by them concerning the effective implementation of the provisions laid down in the present resolution;

7. *Calls upon* all States to co-operate fully with the Committee in the fulfillment of its tasks, including supplying such information as may be sought by the Committee in pursuance of the present resolution;

8. *Requests* the Secretary-General to provide all necessary assistance to the Committee and to make the necessary arrangements in the Secretariat for that purpose;

9. *Decides* that, notwithstanding paragraphs 4 to 8 above, nothing in the present resolution shall prohibit assistance to the legitimate Government of Kuwait, and calls upon all States:
(a) To take appropriate measures to protect assets of the legitimate Government of Kuwait and its agencies;
(b) Not to recognize any regime set up by the occupying Power;

10. *Requests* the Secretary-General to report to the Security Council on the progress made in the implementation of the present resolution, the first report to be submitted within thirty days;

11. *Decides* to keep this item on its agenda and to continue its efforts to put an early end to the invasion by Iraq.

Appendix 6C
United Nations Security Council Resolution 678[*]

The Security Council,

Recalling its resolutions 660 (1990) of 2 August 1990, 661 (1990) of 6 August 1990, 662 (1990) of 9 August 1990, 664 (1990) of 18 August 1990, 665 (1990) of 25 August 1990, 666 (1990) of 13 September 1990, 667 (1990) of 16 September 1990, 669 (1990) of 24 September 1990, 670 (1990) of 25 September 1990, 674 (1990) of 29 October 1990, and 677 (1990) of 28 November 1990,

Noting that, despite all efforts by the United Nations, Iraq refuses to comply with its obligations to implement resolution 660 (1990) and the above-mentioned subsequent resolutions, in flagrant contempt of the Security Council,

Mindful of its duties and responsibilities under the Charter of the United Nations for the maintenance and preservation of international peace and security,

Determined to secure full compliance with its decisions.

Acting under Chapter VII of the Charter,

1.   *Demands* that Iraq comply fully with resolution 660 (1990) and all subsequent relevant resolutions, and decides, while maintaining all its decisions, to allow Iraq one final opportunity, as a pause of goodwill, to do so;

2.   *Authorizes* Member States co-operating with the Government of Kuwait, unless Iraq on or before 15 January 1991 fully implements, as set forth in paragraph 1 above, the above-mentioned resolutions, to use all necessary means to uphold and implement resolution 660 (1990) and all subsequent relevant resolutions and to restore international peace and security in the area;

3.   *Requests* all States to provide appropriate support for the actions undertaken in pursuance of paragraph 2 above;

---

[*] S/RES/678 (1990), adopted by the Security Council at its 2963rd meeting on 29 November 1990.

4.   *Requests* the States concerned to keep the Security Council regularly informed on the progress of actions undertaken pursuant to paragraphs 2 and 3 above;

5.   *Decides* to remain actively seized of the matter.

Appendix 6D
United Nations Security Council Resolution 687[*]

The Security Council,

Recalling its resolutions 660 (1990) of 2 August 1990, 661 (1990) of 6 August 1990, 662 (1990) of 9 August 1990, 664 (1990) of 18 August 1990, 665 (1990) of 25 August 1990, 666 (1990) of 13 September 1990, 667 (1990) of 16 September 1990, 669 (1990) of 24 September 1990, 670 (1990) of 25 September 1990, 674 (1990) of 29 October 1990, 677 (1990) of 28 November 1990, 678 (1990) of 29 November 1990 and 686 (1991) of 2 March 1991,

Welcoming the restoration to Kuwait of its sovereignty, independence and territorial integrity and the return of its legitimate Government,

Affirming the commitment of all Member States to the sovereignty, territorial integrity and political independence of Kuwait and Iraq, and noting the intention expressed by the Member States cooperating with Kuwait under paragraph 2 of resolution 678 (1990) to bring their military presence in Iraq to an end as soon as possible consistent with paragraph 8 of resolution 686 (1991),

Reaffirming the need to be assured of Iraq's peaceful intentions in the light of its unlawful invasion and occupation of Kuwait,

Taking note of the letter dated 27 February 1991 from the Deputy Prime Minister and Minister for Foreign Affairs of Iraq addressed to the President of the Security Council and of his letters of the same date addressed to the President of the Council and to the Secretary-General, and those letters dated 3 March and 5 March he addressed to them, pursuant to resolution 686 (1991),

Noting that Iraq and Kuwait, as independent sovereign States, signed at Baghdad on 4 October 1963 "Agreed Minutes between the State of Kuwait and the Republic of Iraq regarding the restoration of friendly relations, recognition and related matters", thereby formally recognizing the boundary between Iraq and Kuwait and the allocation of islands, which Agreed Minutes were registered with the United Nations in accordance with Article 102 of the Charter of the United Nations and in which Iraq recognized the independence

---

[*] S/RES/687 (1991), adopted by the Security Council at its 2983rd meeting on 9 April 1991.

and complete sovereignty of the State of Kuwait with its boundaries as specified in the letter of the Prime Minister of Iraq dated 21 July 1932 and as accepted by the ruler of Kuwait in his letter dated 10 August 1932,

Conscious of the need for demarcation of the said boundary,

Conscious also of the statements by Iraq threatening to use weapons in violation of its obligations under the Protocol for the Prohibition of the Use in War of Asphyxiating, Poisonous or Other Gases, and of Bacteriological Methods of Warfare, signed at Geneva on 17 June 1925, and of its prior use of chemical weapons and affirming that grave consequences would follow any further use by Iraq of such weapons,

Recalling that Iraq has subscribed to the Final Declaration adopted by all States participating in the Conference of States Parties to the 1925 Geneva Protocol and Other International States, held in Paris from 7 to 11 January 1989, establishing the objective of universal elimination of chemical and biological weapons,

Recalling also that Iraq has signed the Convention on the Prohibition of the Development, Production and Stockpiling of Bacteriological (Biological) and Toxin Weapons and on Their Destruction, of 10 April 1972,

Noting the importance of Iraq ratifying the Convention,

Noting also the importance of all States adhering to the Convention and encouraging its forthcoming review conference to reinforce the authority, efficiency and universal scope of the Convention,

Stressing the importance of an early conclusion by the Conference on Disarmament of its work on a convention on the universal prohibition of chemical weapons and of universal adherence thereto,

Aware of the use by Iraq of ballistic missiles in unprovoked attacks and therefore of the need to take specific measures in regard to such missiles located in Iraq,

Concerned by the reports in the hands of Member States that Iraq has attempted to acquire materials for a nuclear-weapons programme contrary to its obligations under the Treaty on the Non-Proliferation of Nuclear Weapons of 1 July 1968,

Recalling the objective of the establishment of a nuclear-weapon-free zone in the region of the Middle East,

Conscious of the threat that all weapons of mass destruction pose to peace and security in the area and of the need to work towards the establishment of the Middle East of a zone free of such weapons,

Conscious also of the objective of achieving balanced and comprehensive control of armaments in the region,

Conscious further of the importance of achieving the objectives noted above using all available means, including a dialogue among the States of the region,

Noting that resolution 686 (1991) marked the lifting of the measures imposed by resolution 661 (1990) in so far as they applied to Kuwait,

Noting also that despite the progress being made in fulfilling the obligations of resolution 686 (1991), many Kuwaiti and third-State nationals are still not accounted for and property remains unreturned,

Recalling the International Convention against the Taking of Hostages opened for signature in New York on 18 December 1979, which categorizes all acts of taking hostages as manifestations of international terrorism,

Deploring threats made by Iraq during the recent conflict to make use of terrorism against targets outside Iraq and the taking of hostages by Iraq,

Taking note with grave concern of the reports transmitted by the Secretary-General on 20 March and 28 March 1991, and conscious of the necessity to meet urgently the humanitarian needs in Kuwait and Iraq,

Bearing in mind its objective of restoring international peace and security in the area as set out in its recent resolutions,

Conscious of the need to take the following measures acting under Chapter VII of the Charter,

1.   *Affirms* all thirteen resolutions noted above, except as expressly changed below to achieve the goals of the present resolution, including a formal cease-fire;

A

2.   *Demands* that Iraq and Kuwait respect the inviolability of the international boundary and the allocation of islands set out in the "Agreed Minutes between the State of Kuwait and the Republic of Iraq regarding the restoration of friendly relations, recognition and the related matters", signed by them in the exercise of their sovereignty at Baghdad on 4 October 1963 and registered with the United Nations;

3.   *Calls upon* the Secretary-General to lend his assistance to make arrangements with Iraq and Kuwait to demarcate the boundary between Iraq and Kuwait, drawing on appropriate material including the maps transmitted with the letter dated 28 March 1991 addressed to him by the Permanent Representative of the United Kingdom of Great Britain and Northern Ireland to the United Nations, and to report back to the Council within one month;

4.   *Decides* to guarantee the inviolability of the abovementioned international boundary and to take, as appropriate, all necessary measures to that end in accordance with the Charter of the United Nations;

B

5.   *Requests* the Secretary-General, after consulting with Iraq and Kuwait, to submit within three days to the Council for its approval a plan for the immediate deployment of a United Nations observer unit to monitor the Khawr 'Abd Allah and a demilitarized zone, which is hereby established, extending ten kilometres into Iraq and five kilometres into Kuwait from the boundary referred to in the "Agreed Minutes between the State of Kuwait and the Republic of Iraq regarding the restoration of friendly relations, recognition and related matters"; to deter violations of the boundary through its presence in and surveillance of the demilitarized zone and to observe any hostile or potentially hostile action mounted from the territory of one State against the other, and also requests the Secretary-General to report regularly to the Council on the operations of the unit and to do so immediately if there are serious violations of the zone or potential threats to peace;

6.   *Notes* that as soon as the Secretary-General notifies the Council of the completion of the deployment of the United Nations observer unit, the conditions will be established for the Member States cooperating with Kuwait in accordance with resolution 678 (1990) to bring their military presence in Iraq to an end consistent with resolution 686 (1991);

C

7.   *Invites* Iraq to reaffirm unconditionally its obligations under the Protocol for the Prohibition of the Use in War of Asphyxiating, Poisonous or Other Gases, and of Bacteriological Methods of Warfare, signed at Geneva on 17 June 1925, and to ratify the Convention on the Prohibition of the Development, Production and Stockpiling of Bacteriological (Biological) and Toxin Weapons and on Their Destruction, of 10 April 1972;

8.   *Decides* that Iraq shall unconditionally accept the destruction, removal, or

rendering harmless, under international supervision of:

(a) All chemical and biological weapons and all stocks of agents and all related subsystems and components and all research, development, support and manufacturing facilities related thereto;

(b) All ballistic missiles with a range grater than one hundred and fifty kilometres, and related major parts and repair and production facilities;

9. *Decides also*, for the implementation of paragraph 8, the following:

(a) Iraq shall submit to the Secretary-General, within fifteen days of the adoption of the present resolution, a declaration on the locations, amounts and types of all items specified in paragraph 8 and agree to urgent, on-site inspection as specified below;

(b) The Secretary-General, in consultation with the appropriate Governments and, where appropriate, with the Director-General of the World Health Organization, within forty-five days of the adoption of the present resolution shall develop and submit to the Council for approval a plan calling for the completion of the following acts within forty-five days of such approval:

  (i) The forming of a special commission which shall carry out immediate on-site inspection of Iraq's biological, chemical and missile capabilities, based on Iraq's declarations and the designation of any additional locations by the special commission itself;

  (ii) The yielding by Iraq of possession to the Special Commission for destruction, removal or rendering harmless, taking into account the requirements of public safety, of all items specified under paragraph 8 (a) including items at the additional locations designated by the Special Commission under paragraph (i) and the destruction by Iraq, under the supervision of the Special Commission, of all its missile capabilities, including launchers, as specified under paragraph 8 (b);

  (iii) The provision by the Special Commission to the Director General of the International Atomic Energy Agency of the assistance and cooperation required in paragraphs 12 and 13;

10. *Decides further* that Iraq shall unconditionally undertake not to use, develop, construct or acquire any of the items specified in paragraphs 8 and 9, and requests the Secretary-General, in consultation with the Special Commission, to develop a plan for the future ongoing monitoring and verification of Iraq's compliance with the present paragraph, to be submitted to the Council for the approval within one hundred and twenty days of the passage of the present resolution;

11. *Invites* Iraq to reaffirm unconditionally its obligations under the Treaty on the Non-Proliferation of Nuclear Weapons, of 1 July 1968;

12. *Decides* that Iraq shall unconditionally agree not to acquire or develop nuclear weapons or nuclear-weapon-usable material or any subsystems or components or any research, development, support or manufacturing facilities related to the above;

to submit to the Secretary-General and the Director General of the International Atomic Energy Agency within fifteen days of the adoption of the present resolution a declaration of the locations, amounts and types of all items specified above; to place all of its nuclear-weapon-usable materials under the exclusive control, for custody and removal, of the Agency, with the assistance and cooperation of the Special Commission as provided for in the plan of the Secretary-General discussed in paragraph 9 (b); to accept, in accordance with the arrangements provided for in paragraph 13, urgent on-site inspection and the destruction, removal or rendering harmless as appropriate of all items specified above; and to accept the plan discussed in paragraph 13 for the future ongoing monitoring and verification of its compliance with these undertakings;

13. *Requests* the Director General of the International Atomic Energy Agency, through the Secretary-General and with the assistance and cooperation of the Special Commission as provided for in the plan of the Secretary-General referred to in paragraph 9 (b), to carry out immediate on-site inspection of Iraq's nuclear capabilities based on Iraq's declarations and the designation of any additional locations by the Special Commission; to develop a plan for submission to the Council within forty-five days calling for the destruction, removal or rendering harmless as appropriate of all items listed in paragraph 12; to carry out the plan within forty-five days following approval by the Council and to develop a plan, taking into account the rights and obligations of Iraq under the Treaty on the Non-Proliferation of Nuclear Weapons, for the future ongoing monitoring and verification of Iraq's compliance with paragraph 12, including an inventory of all nuclear material in Iraq subject to the Agency's verification and inspection to confirm that Agency safeguards cover all relevant nuclear activities in Iraq, to be submitted to the Council for approval within one hundred and twenty days of the adoption of the present resolution;

14. *Notes* that the actions to be taken by Iraq in paragraphs 8 to 13 represent steps towards the goal of establishing in the Middle East a zone free from weapons of mass destruction and all missiles for their delivery and the objective of a global ban on chemical weapons;

D

15. *Requests* the Secretary-General to report to the Council on the steps taken to facilitate the return of all Kuwaiti property seized by Iraq, including a list of any property that Kuwait claims has not been returned or which has not been returned intact;

E

16. *Reaffirms* that Iraq, without prejudice to its debts and obligations arising prior to 2 August 1990, which will be addressed through the normal mechanisms, is

liable under international law for any direct loss, damage – including environmental damage and the depletion of natural resources – or injury to foreign Governments, nationals and corporations as a result of its unlawful invasion and occupation of Kuwait;

17. *Decides* that all Iraqi statements made since 2 August 1990 repudiating its foreign debt are null and void, and demands that Iraq adhere scrupulously to all its obligations concerning servicing and repayment of its foreign debt;

18. *Decides also* to create a fund to pay compensation for claims that fall within paragraph 16 and to establish a commission that will administer the fund;

19. *Directs* the Secretary-General to develop and present to the Council for decision, no later than thirty days following the adoption of the present resolution, recommendations for the Fund to be established in accordance with paragraph 18 and for a programme to implement the decisions in paragraphs 16 to 18, including the following: administration of the Fund; mechanisms for determining the appropriate level of Iraq's contribution to the Fund, based on a percentage of the value of its exports of petroleum and petroleum products, not to exceed a figure to be suggested to the Council by the Secretary-General, taking into account the requirements of the people of Iraq, Iraq's payment capacity as assessed in conjunction with the international financial institutions taking into consideration external debt service, and the needs of the Iraqi economy; arrangements for ensuring that payments are made to the Fund; the process by which funds will be allocated and claims paid; appropriate procedures for evaluating losses, listing claims and verifying their validity, and resolving disputed claims in respect of Iraq's liability as specified in paragraph 16; and the composition of the Commission designated above;

F

20. *Decides*, effective immediately, that the prohibitions against the sale or supply to Iraq of commodities or products other than medicine and health supplies, and prohibitions against financial transactions related thereto contained in resolution 661 (1990), shall not apply to foodstuffs notified to the Security Council Committee established by resolution 661 (1990) concerning the situation between Iraq and Kuwait or, with the approval of that Committee, under the simplified and accelerated "no-objection" procedure, to materials and supplies for essential civilian needs as identified in the report to the Secretary-General dated 20 March 1991, and in any further findings of humanitarian need by the Committee.

21. *Decides* to review the provisions of paragraph 20 every sixty days in the light of the policies and practices of the Government of Iraq, including the implementation of all relevant resolutions of the Council, for the purpose of determining whether to reduce or lift the prohibitions referred to therein;

22. *Decides also* that upon the approval by the Council of the programme called for in paragraph 19 and upon Council agreement that Iraq has completed all actions contemplated in paragraphs 8 to 13, the prohibitions against the import of commodities and products originating in Iraq and the prohibitions against financial transactions related thereto contained in resolution 661 (1990) shall have no further force or effect;

23. *Decides further* that, pending action by the Council under paragraph 22, the Security Council Committee established by resolution 661 (1990) concerning the situation between Iraq and Kuwait shall be empowered to approve, when required to assure adequate financial resources on the part of Iraq to carry out the activities under paragraph 20, exceptions to the prohibition against the import of commodities and products originating in Iraq;

24. *Decides* that, in accordance with resolution 661 (1990) and subsequent related resolutions and until it takes a further decision, all States shall continue to prevent the sale or supply to Iraq, or the promotion or facilitation of such sale or supply by their nationals or from their territories or using their flag vessels or aircraft, of:
(a) Arms and related *material* of all types, specifically including the sale or transfer through other means of all forms of conventional military equipment, including for paramilitary forces, and spare parts and components and their means of production for such equipment;
(b) Items specified and defined in paragraphs 8 and 12 not otherwise covered above;
(c) Technology under licensing or other transfer arrangements used in the production, utilization or stockpiling of items specified in paragraphs (a) and (b);
(d) Personnel or materials for training or technical support services relating to the design, development, manufacture, use, maintenance or support of items specified in paragraphs (a) and (b);

25. *Calls upon* all States and international organizations to act strictly in accordance with paragraph 24, notwithstanding the existence of any contracts, agreements, licences or any other arrangements;

26. *Requests* the Secretary-General, in consultation with appropriate Governments, to develop within sixty days, for the approval of the Council, guidelines to facilitate full international implementation of paragraphs 24, 25 and 27, and to make them available to all States and to establish a procedure for updating these guidelines periodically;

27. *Calls upon* all States to maintain such national controls and procedures and to take such other actions consistent with the guidelines to be established by the Council under paragraph 26 as may be necessary to ensure compliance with the

terms of paragraph 24, and calls upon international organizations to take all appropriate steps to assist in ensuring such full compliance;

28. *Agrees* to review its decisions in paragraphs 22 to 25, except for the items specified and defined in paragraphs 8 and 12, on a regular basis and in any case one hundred and twenty days following the adoption of the present resolution, taking into account Iraq's compliance with the resolution and general progress towards the control of armaments in the region;

29. *Decides* that all States, including Iraq, shall take the necessary measures to ensure that no claim shall lie at the instance of the government of Iraq, or of any person or body in Iraq, or of any person claiming through or for the benefit of any such person or body, in connection with any contract or other transaction where its performance was affected by reason of the measures taken by the Council in resolution 661 (1990) and related resolutions;

G

30. *Decides* that, in furtherance of its commitment to facilitate the repatriation of all Kuwait and third-State nationals, Iraq shall extend all necessary cooperation to the International Committee of the Red Cross by providing lists of such person, facilitating the access of the International Committee to all such persons wherever located or detained and facilitating the search by the International Committee for those Kuwaiti and third-State nationals still unaccounted for;

31. *Invites* the International Committee of the Red Cross to keep the Secretary-General apprised, as appropriate, of all activities undertaken in connection with facilitating the repatriation or return of all Kuwaiti and third-State nationals or their remains present in Iraq on or after 2 August 1990;

32. *Requires* Iraq to inform the Council that it will not commit or support any act of international terrorism or allow any organization directed towards commission of such acts to operate within its territory and to condemn unequivocally and renounce all acts, methods and practices of terrorism.

33. *Declares* that, upon official notification by Iraq to the Secretary-General and to the Security Council of its acceptance of the above provisions, a formal cease-fire is effective between Iraq and Kuwait and the Member States cooperating with Kuwait in accordance with resolution 678 (1990);

34. *Decides* to remain seized of the matter and to take such further steps as may be required for the implementation of the present resolution and to secure peace and security in the region.

Appendix 6E
United Nations Security Council Resolution 707*

The Security Council,

Recalling its resolution 687 (1991) of 3 April 1991 and its other resolutions on this matter,

Recalling also the letter of 11 April 1991 from the President of the Security Council to the Permanent Representative of Iraq to the United Nations, in which he noted that on the basis of Iraq's written agreement to implement fully resolution 687 (1991), the preconditions for a cease-fire established in paragraph 33 of that resolution had been met,

Taking note with grave concern of the letters dated 26 and 28 June and 4 July 1991 from the Secretary-General to the President of the Security Council, conveying information received from the Executive Chairman of the Special Commission and from the high-level mission to Iraq which establishes Iraq's failure to comply with its obligations under resolution 687 (1991),

Recalling further the statement issued by the President of the Security Council on 28 June 1991 requesting that a high-level mission consisting of the Executive Chairman of the Special Commission, the Director General of the International Atomic Energy Agency and the Under-Secretary-General for Disarmament Affairs be dispatched to meet with officials at the highest levels of the Government of Iraq at the earliest opportunity to obtain written assurance that Iraq will fully and immediately cooperate in the inspection of the locations identified by the Special Commission and present for immediate inspection any of those items that may have been transported from those locations,

Having taken note with dismay of the report of the high-level mission to the Secretary-General on the results of its meetings with the highest levels of the Iraqi Government,

Gravely concerned by the information provided to the Council by the International Atomic Energy Agency on 15 and 25 July 1991 regarding the

---

* S/RES/707 (1991), adopted by the Security Council at its 3004th meeting on 15 August 1991.

actions of the Government of Iraq in flagrant violation of resolution 687 (1991),

Gravely concerned also by the letter of 7 July 1991 from the Minister of Foreign Affairs of Iraq addressed to the Secretary-General and subsequent statements and findings that Iraq's notifications of 18 and 28 April were incomplete and that certain related activities had been concealed, facts both of which constitute material breaches of its obligations under resolution 687 (1991),

Noting, having been informed by letters dated 26 and 28 June and 4 July 1991 from the Secretary-General, that Iraq has not fully complied with all of its undertakings relating to the privileges, immunities and facilities to be accorded to the Special Commission and the Agency inspection teams mandated under resolution 687 (1991),

Affirming that in order for the Special Commission to carry out its mandate under paragraphs 9(b)(i-iii) of resolution 687 (1991) to inspect Iraq's chemical and biological weapons and ballistic missile capabilities and to take possession of the elements referred to in that resolution for destruction, removal or rendering harmless, full disclosure on the part of Iraq as required in paragraph 9(a) of resolution 687 (1991) is essential,

Affirming also that in order for the International Atomic Energy Agency, with the assistance and cooperation of the Special Commission, to determine what nuclear-weapon-usable material or any subsystems or components or any research, development, support or manufacturing facilities related to them need, in accordance with paragraph 13 of resolution 687 (1991), to be destroyed, removed or rendered harmless, Iraq is required to make a declaration of all its nuclear programmes, including any which it claims are for purposes not related to nuclear-weapons-usable material,

Affirming further that the aforementioned failures of Iraq to act in strict conformity with its obligations under resolution 687 (1991) constitute a material breach of its acceptance of the relevant provisions of that resolution which established a cease-fire and provided the conditions essential to the restoration of peace and security in the region,

Affirming, moreover, that Iraq's failure to comply with the safeguards agreement it concluded with the International Atomic Energy Agency pursuant to the Treaty on the Non-Proliferation of Nuclear Weapons of 1 July 1968, as established by the Board of Governors of the Agency in its resolution of 18 July 1991, constitutes a breach of its international obligations,

Determined to ensure full compliance with resolution 687 (1991), and in particular its section C,

Acting under Chapter VII of the Charter of the United Nations,

1. *Condemns* Iraq's serious violation of a number of its obligations under section C of resolution 687 (1991) and of its undertakings to cooperate with the Special Commission and the International Atomic Energy Agency, which constitutes a material breach of the relevant provisions of that resolution which established a cease-fire and provided the conditions essential to the restoration of peace and security in the region;

2. *Also condemns* non-compliance by the Government of Iraq with its obligations under its safeguards agreement with the International Atomic Energy Agency, as established by the Board of Governors of the Agency in its resolution of 18 July 1991, which constitutes a violation of its commitments as a party to the Treaty on the Non-Proliferation of Nuclear Weapons of 1 July 1968;

3. *Demands* that Iraq:
(a) Provide without further delay full, final and complete disclosure, as required by resolution 687 (1991), of all aspects of its programmes to develop weapons of mass destruction and ballistic missiles with a range greater than one hundred and fifty kilometres and of all holdings of such weapons, their components and production facilities and locations, as well as all other nuclear programmes, including any which it claims are for purposes not related to nuclear-weapon-usable material;
(b) Allow the Special Commission, the International Atomic Energy Agency and their inspection teams immediate, unconditional and unrestricted access to any and all areas, facilities, equipment, records and means of transportation which they wish to inspect;
(c) Cease immediately any attempt to conceal, move or destroy any material equipment relating to its nuclear, chemical or biological weapons or ballistic missile programmes, or material or equipment relating to its other nuclear activities, without notification to and prior consent of the Special Commission;
(d) Make available immediately to the Special Commission, the Agency and their inspection teams any items to which they were previously denied access;
(e) Allow the Special Commission, the Agency and their inspection teams to conduct both fixed-wing and helicopter flights throughout Iraq for all relevant purposes, including inspection, surveillance, aerial surveys, transportation and logistics, without interference of any kind and upon such terms and conditions as may be determined by the Special Commission, and to make full use of their own aircraft and such airfields in Iraq as they may determine are most appropriate for the work of the Commission;
(f) Halt all nuclear activities of any kind, except for use of isotopes for medical, agricultural or industrial purposes, until the Council determines that Iraq is in

full compliance with the present resolution and with paragraphs 12 and 13 of resolution 687 (1991) and the Agency determines that Iraq is in full compliance with its safeguards agreement with the Agency;

(g) Ensure complete enjoyment, in accordance with its previous undertakings, of the privileges, immunities and facilities accorded to the representatives of the Special Commission and the Agency and guarantee their complete safety and freedom of movement;

(h) Immediately provide or facilitate the provision of any transportation and medical or logistical support requested by the Special Commission, the Agency or their inspection teams;

(i) Respond fully, completely and promptly to any questions or requests from the Special Commission, the Agency and their inspection teams;

4. *Determines* that Iraq retains no ownership interest in items to be destroyed, removed or rendered harmless pursuant to paragraph 12 of resolution 687 (1991);

5. *Requires* the Government of Iraq forthwith to comply fully and without delay with all its international obligations, including those set out in the present resolution, in resolution 687 (1991), in the Treaty on the Non-Proliferation of Nuclear Weapons and in its safeguards agreement with the International Atomic Energy Agency;

6. *Decides* to remain seized of this matter.

Appendix 6F
United Nations Security Council Resolution 715[*]

The Security Council,

Recalling its resolutions 687 (1991) of 3 April 1991 and 707 (1991) of 15 August 1991 and its other resolutions on this matter,

Recalling in particular that under resolution 687 (1991) the Secretary-General and the Director General of the International Atomic Energy Agency were requested to develop plans for future ongoing monitoring and verification and to submit them to the Security Council for approval,

Taking note of the report and note of the Secretary-General, transmitting the plans submitted by the Secretary-General and Director General of the Agency,

Acting under Chapter VII of the Charter of the United Nations,

1. *Approves*, in accordance with the provisions of resolutions 687 (1991), 707 (1991) and the present resolution, the plans submitted by the Secretary-General and the Director General of the International Atomic Energy Agency;

2. *Decides* that the Special Commission shall carry out the plan submitted by the Secretary-General, as well as continuing to discharge its other responsibilities under resolutions 687 (1991), 699 (1991) of 17 June 1991 and 707 (1991) and performing such other functions as are conferred upon it under the present resolution;

3. *Requests* the Director General of the Agency to carry out, with the assistance and cooperation of the Special Commission, the plan submitted by him and to continue to discharge his other responsibilities under resolutions 687 (1991), 699 (1991) and 707 (1991);

4. *Decides* that the Special Commission, in the exercise of its responsibilities as a subsidiary organ of the Security Council, shall:
(a) Continue to have the responsibility of designating additional locations for inspections and overflights;

---

[*] S/RES/715 (1991), adopted by the Security Council at its 3012th meeting on 11 October 1991.

(b) Continue to render assistance and cooperation to the Director General of the Agency by providing him, by mutual agreement, with the necessary special expertise and logistical, informational and other operational support for the carrying out of the plan submitted by him;

(c) Perform such other functions, in cooperation in the nuclear field with the Director General of the Agency, as may be necessary to coordinate activities under the plans approved by the present resolution, including making use of commonly available services and information to the fullest extent possible, in order to achieve maximum efficiency and optimum use of resources;

5.   *Demands* that Iraq meet unconditionally all its obligations under the plans approved by the present resolution and cooperate fully with the Special Commission and the Director General of the Agency in carrying out the plans;

6.   *Decides* to encourage the maximum assistance, in cash and in kind, from all Member States to support the Special Commission and the Director General of the Agency in carrying out their activities under the plans approved by the present resolution, without prejudice to Iraq's liability for the full costs of such activities;

7.   *Requests* the Security Council Committee established under resolution 661 (1990) concerning the situation between Iraq and Kuwait, the Special Commission and the Director General of the Agency to develop in cooperation a mechanism for monitoring any future sales or supplies by other countries to Iraq of items relevant to the implementation of section C of resolution 687 (1991) and other relevant resolutions, including the present resolution and the plans approved hereunder;

8.   *Requests* the Secretary-General and the Director General of the Agency to submit to the Security Council reports on the implementation of the plans approved by the present resolution, when requested by the Security Council and in any event at least every six months after the adoption of this resolution;

9.   *Decides* to remain seized of the matter.

Appendix 6G
United Nations Security Council Resolution 1154[*]

The Security Council,

Recalling all its previous relevant resolutions, which constitute the governing standard of Iraqi compliance,

Determined to ensure immediate and full compliance by Iraq without conditions or restrictions with its obligations under resolution 687 (1991) and the other relevant resolutions,

Reaffirming the commitment of all Member States to the sovereignty, territorial integrity and political independence of Iraq, Kuwait and the neighbouring States,

Acting under Chapter VII of the Charter of the United Nations,

1. *Commends* the initiative by the Secretary-General to secure commitments from the Government of Iraq on compliance with its obligations under the relevant resolutions, and in this regard endorses the memorandum of understanding signed by the Deputy Prime Minister of Iraq and the Secretary-General on 23 February 1998 (S/1998/166) and looks forward to its early and full implementation;

2. *Requests* the Secretary-General to report to the Council as soon as possible with regard to the finalization of procedures for Presidential sites in consultation with the Executive Chairman of the United Nations Special Commission and the Director General of the International Atomic Energy Agency (IAEA);

3. *Stresses* that compliance by the Government of Iraq with its obligations, repeated again in the memorandum of understanding, to accord immediate, unconditional and unrestricted access to the Special Commission and the IAEA in conformity with the relevant resolutions is necessary for the implementation of resolution 687 (1991), but that any violation would have severest consequences for Iraq;

---

[*] S/RES/1154 (1998), adopted by the Security Council at its 3858th meeting on 2 March 1998.

4.   *Reaffirms* its intention to act in accordance with the relevant provisions of resolution 687 (1991) on the duration of the prohibitions referred to in that resolution and notes that by its failure so far to comply with its relevant obligations Iraq has delayed the moment when the Council can do so;

5.   *Decides*, in accordance with its responsibility under the Charter, to remain actively seized of the matter, in order to ensure implementation of this resolution, and to secure peace and security in the area.

Appendix 6H
United Nations Security Council Resolution 1441[*]

The Security Council,

Recalling all its previous relevant resolutions, in particular its resolutions 661 (1990) of 6 August 1990, 678 (1990) of 29 November 1990, 686 (1991) of 2 March 1991, 687 (1991) of 3 April 1991, 688 (1991) of 5 April 1991, 707 (1991) of 15 August 1991, 715 (1991) of 11 October 1991, 986 (1995) of 14 April 1995, and 1284 (1999) of 17 December 1999, and all the relevant statements of its President,

Recalling also its resolution 1382 (2001) of 29 November 2001 and its intention to implement it fully,

Recognizing the threat Iraq's non-compliance with Council resolutions and proliferation of weapons of mass destruction and long-range missiles poses to international peace and security,

Recalling that its resolution 678 (1990) authorized Member States to use all necessary means to uphold and implement its resolution 660 (1990) of 2 August 1990 and all relevant resolutions subsequent to resolution 660 (1990) and to restore international peace and security in the area,

Further recalling that its resolution 687 (1991) imposed obligations on Iraq as a necessary step for achievement of its stated objective of restoring international peace and security in the area,

Deploring the fact that Iraq has not provided an accurate, full, final, and complete disclosure, as required by resolution 687 (1991), of all aspects of its programmes to develop weapons of mass destruction and ballistic missiles with a range greater than one hundred and fifty kilometres, and of all holdings of such weapons, their components and production facilities and locations, as well as all other nuclear programmes, including any which it claims are for purposes not related to nuclear-weapons-usable material,

---

[*] S/RES/1441 (2002), adopted by the Security Council at its 4644th meeting on 8 November 2002. The Annex to Resolution 1441 as not been reproduced herein.

Deploring further that Iraq repeatedly obstructed immediate, unconditional, and unrestricted access to sites designated by the United Nations Special Commission (UNSCOM) and the International Atomic Energy Agency (IAEA), failed to cooperate fully and unconditionally with UNSCOM and IAEA weapons inspectors, as required by resolution 687 (1991), and ultimately ceased all cooperation with UNSCOM and the IAEA in 1998,

Deploring the absence, since December 1998, in Iraq of international monitoring, inspection, and verification, as required by relevant resolutions, of weapons of mass destruction and ballistic missiles, in spite of the Council's repeated demands that Iraq provide immediate, unconditional, and unrestricted access to the United Nations Monitoring, Verification and Inspection Commission (UNMOVIC), established in resolution 1284 (1999) as the successor organization to UNSCOM, and the IAEA, and regretting the consequent prolonging of the crisis in the region and the suffering of the Iraqi people,

Deploring also that the Government of Iraq has failed to comply with its commitments pursuant to resolution 687 (1991) with regard to terrorism, pursuant to resolution 688 (1991) to end repression of its civilian population and to provide access by international humanitarian organizations to all those in need of assistance in Iraq, and pursuant to resolutions 686 (1991), 687 (1991), and 1284 (1999) to return or cooperate in accounting for Kuwaiti and third country nationals wrongfully detained by Iraq, or to return Kuwaiti property wrongfully seized by Iraq,

Recalling that in its resolution 687 (1991) the Council declared that a ceasefire would be based on acceptance by Iraq of the provisions of that resolution, including the obligations on Iraq contained therein,

Determined to ensure full and immediate compliance by Iraq without conditions or restrictions with its obligations under resolution 687 (1991) and other relevant resolutions and recalling that the resolutions of the Council constitute the governing standard of Iraqi compliance,

Recalling that the effective operation of UNMOVIC, as the successor organization to the Special Commission, and the IAEA is essential for the implementation of resolution 687 (1991) and other relevant resolutions,

Noting that the letter dated 16 September 2002 from the Minister for Foreign Affairs of Iraq addressed to the Secretary-General is a necessary first step toward rectifying Iraq's continued failure to comply with relevant Council resolutions,

Noting further the letter dated 8 October 2002 from the Executive Chairman of UNMOVIC and the Director-General of the IAEA to General Al-Saadi of the Government of Iraq laying out the practical arrangements, as a follow-up to their meeting in Vienna, that are prerequisites for the resumption of inspections in Iraq by UNMOVIC and the IAEA, and expressing the gravest concern at the continued failure by the Government of Iraq to provide confirmation of the arrangements as laid out in that letter,

Reaffirming the commitment of all Member States to the sovereignty and territorial integrity of Iraq, Kuwait, and the neighbouring States,

Commending the Secretary-General and members of the League of Arab States and its Secretary-General for their efforts in this regard,

Determined to secure full compliance with its decisions,

Acting under Chapter VII of the Charter of the United Nations,

1.   *Decides* that Iraq has been and remains in material breach of its obligations under relevant resolutions, including resolution 687 (1991), in particular through Iraq's failure to cooperate with United Nations inspectors and the IAEA, and to complete the actions required under paragraphs 8 to 13 of resolution 687 (1991);

2.   *Decides*, while acknowledging paragraph 1 above, to afford Iraq, by this resolution, a final opportunity to comply with its disarmament obligations under relevant resolutions of the Council; and accordingly decides to set up an enhanced inspection regime with the aim of bringing to full and verified completion the disarmament process established by resolution 687 (1991) and subsequent resolutions of the Council;

3.   *Decides* that, in order to begin to comply with its disarmament obligations, in addition to submitting the required biannual declarations, the Government of Iraq shall provide to UNMOVIC, the IAEA, and the Council, not later than 30 days from the date of this resolution, a currently accurate, full, and complete declaration of all aspects of its programmes to develop chemical, biological, and nuclear weapons, ballistic missiles, and other delivery systems such as unmanned aerial vehicles and dispersal systems designed for use on aircraft, including any holdings and precise locations of such weapons, components, subcomponents, stocks of agents, and related material and equipment, the locations and work of its research, development and production facilities, as well as all other chemical, biological, and nuclear programmes, including any which it claims are for purposes not related to weapon production or material;

4.   *Decides* that false statements or omissions in the declarations submitted by Iraq pursuant to this resolution and failure by Iraq at any time to comply with, and

cooperate fully in the implementation of, this resolution shall constitute a further material breach of Iraq's obligations and will be reported to the Council for assessment in accordance with paragraphs 11 and 12 below;

5. *Decides* that Iraq shall provide UNMOVIC and the IAEA immediate, unimpeded, unconditional, and unrestricted access to any and all, including underground, areas, facilities, buildings, equipment, records, and means of transport which they wish to inspect, as well as immediate, unimpeded, unrestricted, and private access to all officials and other persons whom UNMOVIC or the IAEA wish to interview in the mode or location of UNMOVIC's or the IAEA's choice pursuant to any aspect of their mandates; further decides that UNMOVIC and the IAEA may at their discretion conduct interviews inside or outside of Iraq, may facilitate the travel of those interviewed and family members outside of Iraq, and that, at the sole discretion of UNMOVIC and the IAEA, such interviews may occur without the presence of observers from the Iraqi Government; and instructs UNMOVIC and requests the IAEA to resume inspections no later than 45 days following adoption of this resolution and to update the Council 60 days thereafter;

6. *Endorses* the 8 October 2002 letter from the Executive Chairman of UNMOVIC and the Director-General of the IAEA to General Al-Saadi of the Government of Iraq, which is annexed hereto, and decides that the contents of the letter shall be binding upon Iraq;

7. *Decides* further that, in view of the prolonged interruption by Iraq of the presence of UNMOVIC and the IAEA and in order for them to accomplish the tasks set forth in this resolution and all previous relevant resolutions and notwithstanding prior understandings, the Council hereby establishes the following revised or additional authorities, which shall be binding upon Iraq, to facilitate their work in Iraq:

– UNMOVIC and the IAEA shall determine the composition of their inspection teams and ensure that these teams are composed of the most qualified and experienced experts available;
– All UNMOVIC and IAEA personnel shall enjoy the privileges and immunities, corresponding to those of experts on mission, provided in the Convention on Privileges and Immunities of the United Nations and the Agreement on the Privileges and Immunities of the IAEA;
– UNMOVIC and the IAEA shall have unrestricted rights of entry into and out of Iraq, the right to free, unrestricted, and immediate movement to and from inspection sites, and the right to inspect any sites and buildings, including immediate, unimpeded, unconditional, and unrestricted access to Presidential Sites equal to that at other sites, notwithstanding the provisions of resolution 1154 (1998) of 2 March 1998;

– UNMOVIC and the IAEA shall have the right to be provided by Iraq the names of all personnel currently and formerly associated with Iraq's chemical, biological, nuclear, and ballistic missile programmes and the associated research, development, and production facilities;

– Security of UNMOVIC and IAEA facilities shall be ensured by sufficient United Nations security guards;

– UNMOVIC and the IAEA shall have the right to declare, for the purposes of freezing a site to be inspected, exclusion zones, including surrounding areas and transit corridors, in which Iraq will suspend ground and aerial movement so that nothing is changed in or taken out of a site being inspected;

– UNMOVIC and the IAEA shall have the free and unrestricted use and landing of fixed- and rotary-winged aircraft, including manned and unmanned reconnaissance vehicles;

– UNMOVIC and the IAEA shall have the right at their sole discretion verifiably to remove, destroy, or render harmless all prohibited weapons, subsystems, components, records, materials, and other related items, and the right to impound or close any facilities or equipment for the production thereof; and

– UNMOVIC and the IAEA shall have the right to free import and use of equipment or materials for inspections and to seize and export any equipment, materials, or documents taken during inspections, without search of UNMOVIC or IAEA personnel or official or personal baggage;

8. *Decides* further that Iraq shall not take or threaten hostile acts directed against any representative or personnel of the United Nations or the IAEA or of any Member State taking action to uphold any Council resolution;

9. *Requests* the Secretary-General immediately to notify Iraq of this resolution, which is binding on Iraq; demands that Iraq confirm within seven days of that notification its intention to comply fully with this resolution; and demands further that Iraq cooperate immediately, unconditionally, and actively with UNMOVIC and the IAEA;

10. *Requests* all Member States to give full support to UNMOVIC and the IAEA in the discharge of their mandates, including by providing any information related to prohibited programmes or other aspects of their mandates, including on Iraqi attempts since 1998 to acquire prohibited items, and by recommending sites to be inspected, persons to be interviewed, conditions of such interviews, and data to be collected, the results of which shall be reported to the Council by UNMOVIC and the IAEA;

11. *Directs* the Executive Chairman of UNMOVIC and the Director-General of the IAEA to report immediately to the Council any interference by Iraq with inspection activities, as well as any failure by Iraq to comply with its disarmament obligations, including its obligations regarding inspections under this resolution;

12. *Decides* to convene immediately upon receipt of a report in accordance with paragraphs 4 or 11 above, in order to consider the situation and the need for full compliance with all of the relevant Council resolutions in order to secure international peace and security;

13. *Recalls*, in that context, that the Council has repeatedly warned Iraq that it will face serious consequences as a result of its continued violations of its obligations;

14. *Decides* to remain seized of the matter.

Appendix 7

Plan Developed by the Director General of the International Atomic Energy Agency (IAEA) for the Destruction, Removal or Rendering Harmless of Nuclear-Weapons-Usable Materials in Iraq[*]

Note by the Secretary-General

The Secretary-General has the honour to submit to the members of the Security Council the attached letter addressed to him under paragraph 13 of Security Council resolution 687 (1991) by the Director General of the International Atomic Energy Agency (IAEA), and its enclosure containing a plan for the destruction, removal and rendering harmless of items specified in paragraph 12 of that resolution.

Annex
Letter dated 16 May 1991 from the Director General of the International Atomic Energy Agency (IAEA) addressed to the Secretary-General

Under paragraph 13 of Security Council resolution 687 (1991), the Director General of the IAEA is requested, through the Secretary-General of the United Nations, to develop within forty-five days of the adoption of the resolution a plan for the destruction, removal and rendering harmless of the items specified in paragraph 12 of the resolution.

May I accordingly kindly ask you to submit the attached plan to the Security Council.

(Signed) Hans BLIX

---

[*] S/22615, 17 May 1991.

Enclosure
Plan for the destruction, removal and rendering harmless of the items
specified in paragraph 12 of Security Council resolution 687 (1991)

Introduction

1. Paragraph 13 of Security Council resolution 687 (1991) *inter alia* requests the Director General of IAEA through the Secretary-General, with the assistance and cooperation of the Special Commission ... to develop a plan for submission to the Security Council within 45 days calling for the destruction, removing or rendering harmless of all items listed in paragraph 12 of the resolution.

2. In order to implement the actions required of the Agency pursuant to paragraphs 12 and 13 of the resolution, the Director General of IAEA established on 15 April 1991 an action team placed under the direction of an Agency Deputy Director General and composed of a Deputy Director for Administration and Management and a Deputy Director for Operations.

3. The Agency established contact with the Special Commission set up by the Secretary-General following the approval by the Security Council on 19 April 1991 of the Secretary-General's report submitted to it in document S/22508. Assistance and cooperation is being rendered by the Special Commission and certain modalities for this cooperation have been agreed upon.

Immediate on-site inspection

4. On 18 April 1991, the Government of Iraq submitted to the Director General of IAEA a declaration required by paragraph 12 of resolution 687 (1991). Further information was provided on 27 April 1991.

5. The first on-site inspection, based on the Iraqi declaration to IAEA and additional designations by the Special Commission, started on 15 May 1991. The inspection team on this occasion was headed by a Chief Inspector appointed by IAEA and consisted of 34 persons, including Agency officials and experts as well as representatives and other personnel of the Special Commission. The team's expertise covers all areas of nuclear technology as well as supporting specialties such as radiation protection, explosive ordnance disposal, communications and field security.

The plan

Nuclear-weapons-usable material

6. Nuclear-weapons-usable material or, as it is referred to in Agency practice, "direct-use material"[*1] cannot be destroyed or rendered harmless in Iraq. The Agency will have to take exclusive control of this material for custody and removal from Iraq pursuant to paragraph 12. This is considered to be the foremost task to be undertaken. Known amounts of direct-use material, located in the Tuwaitha area and listed in the Iraqi statement of 27 April 1991, are contained in fresh or irradiated fuel assemblies. Part of this material appears to be stored in accessible conditions. The on-site inspection, which is now under way, is verifying declared quantities and conditions of this material. Further direct-use material, according to the Iraqi declaration, consisting of irradiated fuel assemblies for the IRT-5000 nuclear research reactor is buried under the rubble of the reactor building. In all probability, a complex and costly decommissioning operation will be needed to render this material accessible for removal and disposal.

7. Following the preliminary on-site verification now under way of the existence of irradiated direct-use material in the damaged reactor building, it is intended to begin the early removal of easily accessible direct-use material, the decommissioning of the building and the removal of the irradiated fuel assemblies, once their accessibility is achieved.

8. In the event that any additional sites are designated by the Special Commission under paragraphs 9 (b) (ii) and 13 of resolution 687 (1991) further inspections will be carried out.

9. The Agency will take custody, through the application of Agency verification, containment and surveillance methods, of the direct-use material in Iraq. Agency safeguards will be applied to all direct-use material removed from Iraq.

10. Negotiations with countries possessing the technology for the transportation and storage of direct-use material to ascertain their willingness to receive this material are under way. Consideration is being given to various options for the long-term disposal or rendering harmless of this material.

Other items subject to paragraph 12 of resolution 687 (1991)

11. The declaration of Iraq listed only direct-use material and a yellow-cake production unit. Inspection of sites for other items subject to paragraph 12 of resolution 687 (1991) that may be designated by the Special Commission will aim

to determine if such items exist and, if so, to remove, destroy or render them harmless.

12. Identification of research, development, support or manufacturing facilities and materials relevant or connected to reprocessing of irradiated fuel and isotopic enrichment of uranium will be given priority as they are capable of producing additional direct-use material.

Endnotes:
*1 - Direct-use material is nuclear material that can be converted into nuclear explosives components without transmutation or further enrichment, as for instance plutonium containing less than 80 per cent plutonium-238, high-enriched uranium (HEU) (uranium enriched to 20 per cent uranium-235 or more) and uranium-233.

Appendix 8

Advice of the Attorney General to the United Kingdom on the Legal Basis for the Use of Force Against Iraq[*]

Question: To ask HMG what is the Attorney General's view of the legal basis for the use of force against Iraq

Answer: The Attorney General (Lord Goldsmith):

Authority to use force against Iraq exists from the combined effect of resolutions 678, 687 and 1441. All of these resolutions were adopted under Chapter VII of the UN Charter which allows the use of force for the express purpose of restoring international peace and security:

1. In resolution 678 the Security Council authorised force against Iraq, to eject it from Kuwait and to restore peace and security in the area.

2. In resolution 687, which set out the ceasefire conditions after Operation Desert Storm, the Security Council imposed continuing obligations on Iraq to eliminate its weapons of mass destruction in order to restore international peace and security in the area. Resolution 678 suspended but did not terminate the authority to use force under resolution 678.

3. A material breach of resolution 687 revives the authority to use force under resolution 678.

4. In resolution 1441 the Security Council determined that Iraq has been and remains in material breach of resolution 687, because it has not fully complied with its obligations to disarm under that resolution.

5. The Security Council in resolution 1441 gave Iraq "a final opportunity to comply with its disarmament obligations" and warned of "serious consequences" if it did not.

---

[*] Contained within the Report of a Committee of Privy Counsellors, *Review of Intelligence on Weapons of Mass Destruction*, ordered by the United Kingdom House of Commons to be printed 14 July 2004, Annex D.

6. The Security Council also decided in resolution 1441 that, if Iraq failed at any time to comply with and cooperate fully in the implementation of resolution 1441, that would constitute a further material breach.

7. It is plain that Iraq has failed to so comply and therefore Iraq was at the time of resolution 1441 and continues to be in material breach.

8. Thus, the authority to use force under resolution 678 has revived and so continues today.

9. Resolution 1441 would in terms have provided that a further decision of the Security Council to sanction force was required if that had been intended. Thus, all that resolution 1441 requires is reporting to and discussion by the Security Council of Iraq's failures, but not an express further decision to authorise force.

I have lodged a copy of this answer, together with resolutions 678, 687 and 1441, in the Library of both Houses.

17 March 2003

Index